The Cat

History, Biology, and Behavior

MURIEL BEADLE

Drawings by E. John Pfiffner

SIMON AND SCHUSTER
NEW YORK

DESIGNED BY IRVING PERKINS
MANUFACTURED IN THE UNITED STATES OF AMERICA

3 4 5 6 7 8 9 10

LIBRARY OF CONGRESS CATALOGING IN PUBLICATION DATA

Beadle, Muriel.
The cat : history, biology, and behavior.

Bibliography: p.
Includes index.
1.   Cats.   I.   Title.
SF442.B4   636.8   76-53770
Figure 10 is taken from "How Does a Cat Fall on Its Feet?" by Donald McDonald. This material first appeared in *New Scientist* London, the weekly review of science and technology.
"Calling the Cat" in Chapter 17 is reprinted by permission of Coward, McCann & Geoghegan, Inc. It is from *Compass Rose* by Elizabeth Coatsworth. Copyright 1929 by Coward-McCann, Inc.; renewed.
ISBN 0-671-22451-4

For Cathleen Jordan

Contents

9

CHAPTER 6 *Ups and Downs* 75

MULTILINGUAL TERMS FOR "CAT." PAGAN RESIDUE IN CHRISTIAN ATTITUDES TOWARD CATS. EARLY VALUE AS MOUSERS. LEGENDS, FABLES, NURSERY RHYMES. IDENTIFICATION WITH WITCHES. THE CAT OF LALANDE. VICTORIAN SENTIMENTALITY. CATS IN ASIA.

CHAPTER 7 *Earning Their Keep* 89

MINOR IMPORTANCE AS COMMODITIES. UNGOVERNABILITY AS CHATTELS. EIGHTEENTH- AND NINETEENTH-CENTURY DETRACTORS. BRITAIN'S POST OFFICE CATS. OTHERS EMPLOYED BY GOVERNMENT AND BUSINESS. DECLINING MODERN USE IN RODENT CONTROL. LIMITATIONS AS RATTERS. MODERN ROLE AS COMPANIONS.

CHAPTER 8 *How Sociable?* 100

DIFFERING WILD HERITAGE OF CATS AND DOGS. FELINE RESPONSES TO LIVING IN GROUPS. TERRITORIAL DEFENSE. MUTUAL USE OF HOME RANGES. ROLE OF SIGHT AND SMELL IN RECOGNITION OF OTHER CATS. CAPACITY FOR FRIENDSHIP.

CHAPTER 9 *Sex and Reproduction* 112

REPRODUCTIVE CYCLES OF FEMALES. ONSET OF PUBERTY. COURTSHIP. COITUS. FREQUENCY OF MATING AND SELECTIVENESS IN CHOICE OF PARTNER. ABERRANT SEXUAL BEHAVIOR. BIRTH CONTROL METHODS. PREGNANCY. BIRTH.

CHAPTER 10 *The Young Family* 123

KITTENS' NURSING BEHAVIOR. KEEPING THE LITTER TOGETHER. RATE OF GROWTH. ADOPTION OF OTHER YOUNG. FELINE AUNTS AND UNCLES. FATHERING. DEVELOPMENT OF PAW PREFERENCES. DEPTH PERCEPTION. TOILET TRAINING. FEMALE AGGRESSIVENESS IN DEFENSE OF KITTENS.

CHAPTER 11 *The Older Family* 134

INDIVIDUATION OF KITTENS. IMPORTANCE OF PLAY. DEVELOPMENT OF PLAY PATTERNS. WEANING. LEARNING TO HUNT AND KILL PREY. ROLE OF EXPERIENCE. FRIENDSHIPS AMONG PREY AND PREDATOR.

CHAPTER 12 *The Genetics of Breed* 146

THE CAT FANCY. SHOW BREEDS. GENETIC PRINCIPLES OF BREEDING. FORMATION OF PIGMENT AND ACTION OF GENES UPON IT. FUR LENGTH AND TEXTURE. TAILLESSNESS. POLYDACTYLISM. THE SEX-LINKED COLOR GENE. RELATIONSHIP OF WHITE FUR TO BLUE EYES AND DEAFNESS.

The Cat

To the Reader

THIS STARTED OUT to be a book with a single purpose: to provide more detailed information about cats' biology and behavior than has previously been available outside of textbooks and scholarly journals. My intention was to answer—for myself and other cat owners—questions of the sort that have occurred to me from time to time in connection with my own cats. M'zelle, for example, often asserts her authority as the household's top cat by driving the other two away from their food dishes. Yet she never tries to displace Cleo, the newcomer, when she sneaks into M'zelle's sleeping box. Mary K, the middle cat, refuses to curl up in a human lap but sits instead with her paws on one's knee and her rump up. Cleo is not interested in catnip mice, hardly ever chases anything, and invites a caress by throwing herself onto her side at one's feet. Are those actions unique to our cats or are they common to most, and are there reasons for such behavior?

Cats being as idiosyncratic as they are, I have certainly not found the explanation for every peculiarity of every cat, but I have answered my own questions and acquired more general information about cats than is contained in most cat books. Material has been drawn from the work of zoologists, geneticists, anatomists, ethologists and other animal behaviorists, neurophysiologists, ophthalmologists, virologists, and veterinarians. The following pages contain precise and thorough descriptions of cats' physical structure and sensory systems and their functioning, cats' social and sexual behavior, the rearing of kittens, health patterns, longevity, and breed and personality differences. I have also gathered as much material as I could find on the controversial topic of cats' homing powers. I hope you will agree that the original purpose of the book has been satisfactorily served.

While I was learning about feline physiology and psychology, however, I discovered that cats are more interesting as a species than as individuals. They are the product of two kinds of evolutionary pressures: those exerted by natural selection in the wild and those imposed by the cultural milieu which they share with human beings. The same can be said of dogs, but because both dogs and people naturally live in groups, there is more drama in the cat's decision to swap solitary life in the wild for the company of men. So this book has become a social history too—partly from the feline viewpoint, partly from ours. It reviews the history of the cat as a domesticated animal, notes the origins and traces the development of human attitudes toward it, records the uses we have made of it, considers its status in modern society. That material was drawn from literature, the social sciences, and the law.

There is a bibliography at the end of the book which lists my sources alphabetically by author. There are two omissions: Edward Topsell's *Historie of Foure-footed Beasts*, which was published in England in 1607, and the Count de Buffon's *Histoire Naturelle*, a multivolume work which was published in France during the second half of the eighteenth century and was translated into English by William Smellie. I had access to the University of Chicago library and was therefore able to use original copies of these books. They are not available at the average public library but can be found in other university libraries or rare-book collections. I have quoted extensively from Topsell and Buffon and also from nineteenth-century and early twentieth-century authors—partly because I find the language charming and partly because their approach to writing about animals differs markedly from current fashion and helps to document changing attitudes toward cats.

Of the modern books, Fernand Méry's *The Life, History and Magic of the Cat* is the best pictorial record you are likely to find. Although it is rich with photographs, its greater value lies in its reproduction of paintings, sculpture, drawings, prints, and other forms of the graphic arts which together represent 4,000 years of art history. Among the textbooks, I recommend R. F. Ewer's *Ethology of Mammals* (especially to anyone who isn't quite sure what "ethology" is) and *The Carnivores*. Cats are only one of many species described by Ewer, but they are the sole topic of Paul Leyhausen's major work, *Verhaltensstudien an Katzen*. Cat fanciers who understand German should read Leyhausen in the original. His book, which has not been translated into English, was read to me by a University of Chicago graduate student, Eileen Fitzsimmons (whose scholarly specialty is German folk literature, so we both learned a lot). Leyhausen is much quoted in textbooks, but his work has not been as fully reported in a book for general readership as it is in this one.

Although there is a chapter on health and nutrition, this is not a cat-care manual. It will supplement the book of that type which may already be—and certainly should be—in any cat owner's library. My own early cats were reared and doctored according to the advice in a book first published in 1946 and since revised a couple of times. Although I still turn to it occasionally, as to an old friend, I would suggest that any new cat owner buy a manual whose first publication occurred no more than five years ago and whose author is a veterinarian. Otherwise, you may not be getting the benefit of important new research findings about feline nutrition and control of disease.

I have been touched by the willingness of many scholars to answer questions or hunt down hard-to-locate material for me. Paul Leyhausen, for one, has been a most generous correspondent and mentor. Neil B. Todd is another; he not only responded to particular queries but also provided auxiliary material and introduced me to scientists whose work I should otherwise have missed. Special thanks are also due to Mme. G. Feuillebois, librarian of the Paris Observatory, for digging out the story of "the cat of Lalande"; and to Mrs. F. X. de Clifford, who searched her World War II diaries for entries about London's wartime cats. I also appreciate the courtesy of several other distant correspondents: Philip Dreux, who did a cat census in Antarctica; Anne Innis Dagg, who has been pursuing studies of animal locomotion in Australia; Ian Porter of the British Home Office; Ian Shine, who sent a history of the Post Office cats; and G. D. Harroway of the British High Commission in Auckland.

The following people also went to extra trouble in my behalf: Bonnie Beaver, James C. Boudreau, James Bruce, Thomas J. Burke, S. Chandrasekhar, Luis de la Torre, Donald De Vogelaere, John J. Fennessy, Mrs. T. H.

Griffey, Lloyd Hawes, Eckhard Hess, Milton Hildebrand, William P. Malm, Barbara Miller, Virginia McDavid, Frank W. Newell, J. Bradley Powers, Colette Rasmussen, J. B. Rhine, Ward Richter, Jay S. Rosenblatt, Sherman Rosenfeld, John Rust, Janet Sauer, U. S. Seal, Mary Silvester, Erwin Small, Roger Sperry, Arthur Thompson, George J. Todaro, Theodore J. Voneida, Laurie Wilkins, John A. Wilson, and Judith Wright.

That John Pfiffner has done his usual painstaking job of anatomical research and elegant execution is apparent in the illustrations. He is a genial and patient collaborator as well as a gifted artist. We are grateful to Paul Leyhausen for providing a photograph of the cat being bitten by a mouse and to Theodore J. Voneida for a photograph of the cat wearing goggles, both of which appear as sketches in Figure 11.

Finally, thanks to the reference librarians at the University of Chicago's Regenstein Library for their frequent and patient assistance, and to Mary Haynes for typing the manuscript. At home, my husband provided professional guidance in matters pertaining to genetics and personal encouragement in general. It was nice to have the cats around in order to verify the observations of the textbook writers, but they were otherwise no help at all, demanding as they do to be fed on their schedule and not at my convenience.

MURIEL BEADLE

Chicago, Illinois
May 1976

CHAPTER I

The Chase

CATS ARE BEAUTIFUL and graceful animals, soft and sleek to the touch, amiable in expression, patient with children who carry them about with hind legs dangling, amusing when they pounce upon a ball of crinkled cellophane or chase the spots of dappled sunlight on a wall. Cats are small and clean and cuddlesome, as millions of lonely people can testify: the purr of a cat on a lap makes solitude endurable.

Nevertheless, as William Salmon said in the seventeenth century, "cats are Beasts of prey, even the tame ones." Many of their most beguiling traits, in fact, stem from their specialization for hunting and killing. That is what they were evolved to do and it is the key to their biology and behavior, whether one is talking about wild cats, farm cats, or cats who spend their lives in city apartments without ever seeing a mouse.

Watch a cat stretch. Dozing, it makes a compact, rounded mass: head pulled in, legs bent and held close to the sides, feet tucked under, tail wrapped around one flank. Awakening, it elevates itself in a single vertical thrust, the legs straight and the feet well under the body, the back arched into a parody of a Halloween cat. Then the geometry changes again. The fore legs, with the paws splayed out, stretch forward, the rear end lifts, the hind legs push backward. The spine seems to ripple, and the animal suddenly looks twice as long as it did a few seconds earlier.

Or watch a cat jump. Perhaps it has arrived at a high wall which it knows to be ideal for sunbathing. Perhaps it has seen something on top of a refrigerator that needs investigating. The cat half crouches, its head lifted toward its objective. It may even briefly rise up on its haunches to raise its line of vision. The eyes shift in tiny movements as they scan the target. (Very deliberate, this; by choice a cat never hurries.) The hindquarters wiggle a bit, but the tail is still. Then the cat launches itself into an apparently effortless jump—five, six, even seven feet. It lands gently, with no wavering of the body or flailing of the limbs, gives its fur a quick lick, and goes about its business.

Let it be said immediately that cats are not ardent athletes. They aren't even very fond of exercise; on outdoor strolls, they punctuate their progress with many pauses for rest and reflection. But when they *have* to move fast, their exceptionally limber backbones endow them with both speed and agility. They have seven cervical, thirteen thoracic, seven lumbar, and three sacral vertebrae, five more than an adult human being has; the extras are located in that part of the spinal column which extends back from the shoulder blades. They are attached to muscles so powerful that the backbone can flex, extend, or twist by as much as 180 degrees.

Alternate flexion and extension of the vertebral column also increase the speed of a cat's run. The University of California zoologist Milton Hildebrand, who has long studied animal locomotion, puts it this way: "The back advances like the body of a measuring worm at the same time the legs are swinging back and forth." This enhances forward motion because cats straighten their backs only when their hind feet are on the ground and arch their backs only when their fore feet are on the ground. Hildebrand says, "Muscles of the legs pressing on the ground prevent the hindquarters from decelerating, so all of the increase in body length is added to the stride length. Similarly, the forelimbs prevent, or at least reduce, deceleration of the forequarters as the back is flexed; therefore shortening of the body is also added to stride length." This kind of spinal motion induces rotation of the bones linking the vertebrae to the limbs, which helps the limbs to "reach out farther, front and back, and strike and leave the ground at more acute angles than they would if the spine were held rigid. Again, this increases stride length."

It is not the flexible spine alone that aids running. Cats and other good runners have practically no collarbone, which in man and many other animals inhibits the degree to which the shoulder can move. Nor are the shoulder blades of running animals positioned as they are in human beings. (See Figure 1.) Our shoulder blades are horizontal braces across the back of the chest. A cat's lie along the side of the chest. Because these bones pivot halfway up their length, the shoulder joints attached to them can rise higher and travel in wider arcs than those in animals with horizontally placed shoulder blades. (One can easily see the swing of these bones in a panther pacing its zoo cage, or in the slow walk of an old and dignified house cat; when cats are actually running, their shoulder movements are a blur.) Hildebrand estimates that the walking stride of the cheetah is increased by about four and a half inches as a result of this skeletal structure. Combining it with backbone flexion and extension enables the cheetah to achieve a running stride as long as that of a horse, despite its smaller size.

Domestic cats cannot run as fast as wild cats, primarily because their legs are shorter. But even domestic cats can outdistance dogs of equal size, so long as the course to be run is not too long. All cats are built for sprints rather than marathons. Their chest cavities are relatively small, and neither lungs nor heart have the capacity to sustain a long run requiring endurance as well as speed.

The feet of cats and other runners are also specialized for swift locomotion. In animals that place the soles of the feet flat on the ground, the five toes are so positioned that the longer three, the middle ones, are nearly uniform in length. This arrangement gives the animal a good broad base of support, but it also opposes a large surface to the resistance of the ground. When the foot moves, the friction generated by those broad soles is enough to make running difficult, which explains in part why animals with this kind of foot do not run well. In good runners, the parts equivalent to the human wrist or heel are elevated. (See Figure 1.) The animal places only the ball of its foot on the ground (unless it has hoofs, in which case it runs on the tips of its toes). In cats, a vestigial first toe remains, high up on the ankle. Of the other four toes, the middle two are the longest. Cats' feet are shorter, narrower in diameter, and have thinner, lighter bones than those of like-sized animals that walk on the soles of their feet.

Over years of evolution for speed the bones have become selectively elongated, the metatarsals in particular being a third again as long as those of a non-running animal. To withstand the shock of impact when such a

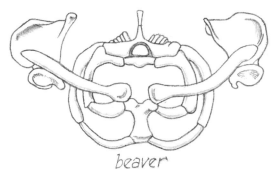

beaver

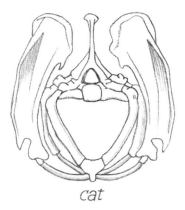

cat

FIGURE 1. *When catching prey, cats keep their bodies low, thrust forward from hind legs securely planted on the ground. Comparisons of shoulder blades (top) and feet (bottom) show why the cat is a better runner than the beaver or the bear.*

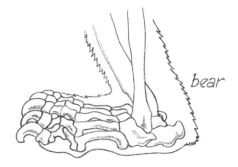

bear

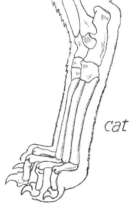

cat

small foot slams obliquely down upon an unyielding surface, the foot bones of running animals have also been simplified, fused, compacted, and otherwise modified for strength. This process comes to a climax in the horse, where the five toes of the ancestral mammal have fused into one thick bone and extremely elastic ligaments have been developed to bend the fetlock joint, both to diminish landing shock and to give the foot a springy upward thrust.

Running, of course, presupposes walking. Nature's basic rule for walking quadrupeds is that no foot shall be lifted until the animal's center of gravity lies over the triangle formed by the three feet on the ground. The usual sequence is one in which the right hind leg, say, is followed by the left fore leg, left hind leg, right fore leg, and so on. The object is to create sufficient stability so the animal can stop at any moment without falling over. At the same time, however, the walking pattern must take account of the fact that the fore legs, which support more weight than the hind legs, exert a retarding force when they hit the ground. The back legs, therefore, must provide the power for propulsion. The movement of the limbs is phased so that each hind leg is at that stage in its movement which provides maximal propulsive force when the diagonally opposite fore leg hits the ground.

The cat's version of this walk varies from that of most other four-legged animals because its fore legs swing inward in such a way that both feet land on almost the same track. The left paw print and the right paw print line up behind each other, as if they were following a chalk line directly below the center of the cat's body. This is why cats are so adept at walking along fence rails, traverse rods, and headboards of beds. The hind legs do not swing inward quite as much as the fore legs, but even they need no more than a two-inch width of surface for support.

When an animal needs to go faster than a walk, it must sacrifice the stable underpinning provided by its having three legs on the ground at any one time. Like most quadrupeds, cats then go into a trot, a gait in which a hind foot is lifted an instant before the diagonally opposite fore foot hits the ground, leaving the animal for a moment with only two feet in contact with the ground.

And if greater speed is necessary? Anne Innis Dagg, a Canadian zoologist who studies animal gaits, says that each gait is distinct; they do not intergrade with each other to any extent. "The walk," she says, "could be considered as the first gear of a car, the trot or pace [both legs on a side moving together] as second gear, and the gallop as third gear."* The gallop is essentially a series of jumps, in the course of which only one limb at a time touches the ground. Between these moments of contact, the animal is suspended in space. Domestic cats *can* gallop, but—in common with weasels, squirrels, and rabbits, all of them good leapers but with fairly short legs—prefer to use what is called a half-bound. A. Brazier Howell, another expert on animal locomotion, describes this gait as one in which "an animal springs from both hind feet at once and lands first on one foot, immediately shifting its weight to the other, which has stepped ahead, as in the gallop. . . . One probable advantage is that during the long leap, the animal has a better opportunity for gathering its hindquarters in position for another impulse than it could at a regular gallop."

To discuss in any detail the kinds of muscles that make movement possible would require an anatomy lesson as a preamble. Suffice it to say that muscle action is described in terms of motor units, each one being composed of a nerve cell within the spinal cord or base of the brain plus a nerve fiber connecting it to a group of skeletal muscle fibers. An impulse generated in a nerve cell travels along the nerve fiber and causes contraction of the muscle fibers, which consequently move a bone. There are two kinds of motor units: fast twitch and slow twitch. Different muscles tend to be linked to one kind only. The cat's body has a very high percentage of fast-twitch muscles, and these add their measure to the animal's speed and agility.

At no time is it more important for an animal to have full control of its body than when stalking prey. That's why, popular belief to the contrary, the average cat does *not* spring off the ground in an arching leap and swoop down on its intended victim. Foxes hunt that way, but cats do so only when forced to hunt in tall grass (often with indifferent success, for an airborne attack is not their style). The fundamental feline rule of the chase is to keep the body low to the ground throughout pursuit and the hind legs *on* the ground during capture.

In 1896, Henri de Toulouse-Lautrec illustrated a dinner menu for a

---

* Dagg is currently analyzing the footfall patterns of dogs by dipping each of the animal's four feet into a different color of tempera paint, then allowing the dog to walk or trot across a sheet of paper. She has not yet attempted to use cats.

friend, choosing as his subject a cat in the process of getting *its* dinner. That much-reproduced sketch (now in the collections of the Art Institute of Chicago) vividly translates into a visual medium both the swiftness and silence characteristic of a stalking cat; Toulouse-Lautrec's mouse is blissfully unaware of its impending demise. Silent progress is assured by paw pads so soft and pliant that they slither over small objects which a hard-surfaced foot might displace. Tufts of fur between the paw pads further muffle sound. The spongy resilience of the pads also provides shock absorbers for the running feet.

Cats chase and sometimes kill birds, insects, reptiles, and fish, but small mammals, especially rodents, are the prey they hunt most successfully; indeed, these are the animals that cats were evolved to hunt. Their skill depends on experience, but the basic repertoire of actions leading to the kill has been bred into them by natural selection. They respond in specific ways to certain stimuli associated with rodents, and the fact that the proper stimulus initiates prey-catching behavior even in the absence of prey attests to the purely instinctive character of the response.

The crinkling of paper into a ball, for instance, alerts any house cat to the possibility of a game of toss and catch. Its responsiveness to that rustling sound, however, had its origin in the noises made by prehistoric mice in burrows under surveillance by prehistoric cats. Similarly, the kitten who amuses its owner by persistently probing with its paw into a box with a hole in the top is responding to the round shape of some primeval burrow's entrance and the unseen but sensed presence of a chamber below.

The German zoologist Paul Leyhausen once did some experiments whose purpose was to discover how many mice a cat would kill at one sitting. (Fifteen, on the average.) Cats and mice were put into big cages and additional mice were introduced until the cats were surfeited and would chase and kill no longer. Two interesting feline behaviors were noted. When a cat had caught a mouse but saw another mouse approaching a man-made burrow in the cage, the cat left the mouse it had already caught and leaped for the mouse that was near the hole. Yet the same cat paid no attention to escaping mice that scrambled through openings in the wire-mesh screen around the cage. The conclusion had to be that it was the three-dimensional aspect of the burrow—the combination of roundness and depth—to which the cat was responding.

Toward the end of the same experiment, when the cats were tired of chasing and killing, they sometimes sat in patient watch beside the mouse-hole in the cage, despite the presence of live mice scurrying around the cage floor behind them. And one of them, when its interest in hunting began to revive, ignored a mouse in the open in favor of flushing out a mouse that was hiding under a ledge.

In the following pages, other examples will be given of cats' responses to "cues" provided by the behavior or physical attributes of their prey. These instinctive actions have been observed and analyzed in great detail by Leyhausen, in both laboratory and field conditions, for more than twenty years. Much of the record is on film. Every textbook on animal behavior draws heavily on Leyhausen's work. In this and the next chapter, it will be both quoted and paraphrased.

When a cat first spots a small mammal in motion, it closes the distance between them by a belly-to-the-ground dash which Leyhausen calls a "slink-run." As soon as it finds a clump of grass or other cover, it pauses and "ambushes," again holding its body as flat as possible: fore legs so far under the body that the elbows protrude sideways, the entire sole of each hind foot on the ground, head stretched forward, ears pointed in the same direction, whiskers spread. (The cat's powerful muscles enable it to freeze in place for very long periods; it uses patience as if it were a weapon.) The eyes follow every movement of the prey, and only a gently twitching tail betrays excitement. The ambush provides information about the intended victim's speed and direction and enables the cat accurately to gauge its own course when it comes into the open.

The attack may begin with yet another cautious sortie. But then the cat's hind legs push back, its tail twitches with greater intensity, its hind feet begin to rise and fall in "treading" movements which accelerate until the whole rump is swinging in rhythm. The final "spring" is not a spring but a thrust, the fore legs being propelled forward by the hind legs, which do not themselves leave the ground. (See Figure 1.) Almost immediately, the cat spreads its hind legs farther apart, both as a braking device and to stabilize it during the coming battle. So deeply ingrained is the feline stay-on-the-ground rule that kittens who have never hunted will pause during a play chase to set their hind feet down before they pounce. And the big wild cats who sometimes conceal themselves in trees as they lie in wait for prey jump to the ground before they attack. Only there do they have the firm footing that is necessary for the next phase of the job: to hold on to and kill a struggling victim.

Should the captured animal be a mouse, not much of a contest lies ahead; but rats have formidable weapons of defense. If a cat does not wholly surprise a rat and make a clean catch, the rat may leap at the cat's head, meanwhile uttering a series of piercing shrieks. Such behavior absolutely terrifies a cat, even one that is bigger than the rat. Leyhausen says it is courage and not size that makes a cat a good ratter, "and even good ratters prefer to hunt small or half-grown rats which don't go on the offense." It is truly remarkable that one of the champion ratters of record (according to Gerald Wood's *Animal Facts and Feats,* an adaptation of the *Guinness Book of World Records*) was a five-month-old kitten named Peter, who lived in an English railway station. Peter killed 400 rats, most of them as large as he was, during a four-week period in the summer of 1938.

Brown rats (the kind that inhabit city sewers) are especially fierce. If a cat continues a fight with a full-grown brown rat, it switches to a technique that is quite unlike its usual killing behavior. The cat pulls in its head, lays back its ears, braces itself on its hind legs, and pummels the rat with its fore paws. The blows are angled sideways from above, the paws being curled in as if the cat were tossing something toward its chest. A rain of such blows can finish off a rat, but only a very few cats will battle with a rat this way.

Cats also run into difficulties when hunting birds. The few who do master the skill tend to become specialists and hunt birds in preference to other prey, but the majority of cats get no further than the chase. One reason is their predilection for the ambush as a hunting technique, behind which lies their expectation that anything which moves on the ground will stay there. Confronted with the erratic hopping pattern that birds display when they are on the ground, most cats continue to stalk and ambush right up to the moment the bird flies away. The expression on the cat's face then shows dumfounded disbelief: *it* was doing everything correctly, so what went wrong? Cats who become bird specialists learn to attack a bird as soon as they spot it. Leyhausen had a cat of this sort and reports that it eliminated the ambush from its mouse-hunting repertoire too.

Absence of contact with the ground during the moment of capture is another reason most cats are mediocre bird catchers. With hind legs supporting it, a cat can change direction or length of thrust to counter evasive movement by the prey, but once in the air all the cat has going for it is momentum. (See Figure 2.) It may catch the bird, but too forceful a leap can turn into a somersault and the cat can lose the bird while trying to regain its own equilibrium. Ground-nesting birds are, of course, at much greater risk.

A number of zoologists and conservationists have checked the validity of assertions that cats are a serious menace to birds. The method used is to examine stomach contents of animals that have been run over on the highways or have been deliberately hunted, trapped, or shot. In Germany, W. Lindemann analyzed the stomach contents of European wild cats who had been bagged by hunters and found that rodents made up 77 percent of the contents; birds, 14 percent. In the United States, similar studies of feral cats (domestic cats gone wild) have produced these results:

Investigator	Place	Mammals	Birds
N. N. Nilsson (1940)	Oregon	61.8%	18.9%
F. B. McMurry and C. G. Sperry (1941)	Oklahoma	55.0%	4.0%
E. L. Hubbs (1951)	California	64.0%	25.0%

A less analytical record was kept by a Michigan farmer, one of whose cats brought its catch to the house. During an eighteen-month period, that mighty hunter carried in 1,623 small mammals (1,600 of them mice) and 62 small birds.

The Hubbs study, done in cooperation with the California Division of Fish and Game, was undertaken to discover the effect of feral cats on the wild animal population in the Sacramento Valley. The 219 cat stomachs examined showed a shifting seasonal diet, birds being more frequently caught in the spring and summer and rodents in the fall and winter. Just over half the birds were game birds—mallard, pheasant, quail, and coot—and many of them were thought to have been nesting hens. Hubbs characterized as "extravagant" the claims made by bird lovers that cats "eat three-fourths of the songbirds hatched" but said that cats might be a sufficient menace to game birds to warrant cat-control programs in areas where pheasants or ducks breed. At the same time, he considered them "of real benefit to farmers because they take such great numbers of rodents."

The study by McMurry and Sperry included both residential and rural areas in Oklahoma, among them a wildlife refuge. In the wildlife refuge, the cats caught a great many lizards and insects but neither songbirds nor game birds. Their small catch of birds was made in residential areas. A far larger proportion of their stomach contents—26.5 percent—was garbage, campground or household refuse such as potato skins, corn husks, bits of cooked meat and vegetables, egg shells, even cellophane. This kind of "food" is probably the basic diet of stray cats in cities today, enriched by an occasional rodent or bird. As cities have replaced warehouses and tenements with new apartment and office buildings and have instituted rat-control programs, the supply of rodents has dwindled. More city cats may therefore have become bird specialists. But even in cities, cats and birds manage to coexist: New York recently had a much-publicized cat who set up housekeeping in the Central Park Bird Sanctuary, and the number of birds hasn't appreciably diminished.

CHAPTER 2

The Kill

To GRASP, HOLD, and kill a struggling victim, cats are equipped with two kinds of extremely efficient weapons—claws and teeth—which are specialized for hooking, stabbing, or shearing flesh.

The fore claws, razor-sharp and curved, are kept that way by frequent honing. Cats scratch trees, furniture, and sometimes even scratching posts for the same reason people sharpen pencils—to abrade the outer sheath. They chew off the outer sheaths of their hind claws. These are never as sharp as the fore claws, partly because of their inherent design and partly because they are unprotected when the cat walks and therefore become blunt. The fore claws, however, escape wear and tear because they are usually pulled into a fold of skin around each toe. They are commonly referred to as re-tractile, but the British zoologist R. F. Ewer says it would be more accurate to describe them as *pro*tractile because they are normally retracted and must be protruded by muscular action into the striking position. (See Figure 2.) In any case, the mechanism for doing this is quite marvelous:

Positioned lengthwise down the toe are three small bones. The claw is cushioned and steadied by the most forward of the three, but it is actually attached to the middle one. The linkage is made by a tendon which stretches from the top of the claw to the top of the bone and by a ligament which stretches from the base of the claw to the underside of the bone. (Tendons are tough, fibrous cords. So are ligaments, but they are more elastic than

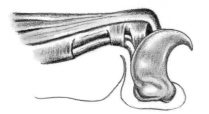

FIGURE 2. *Most cats are poor catchers of birds or butterflies because they have difficulty controlling direction and speed when their feet are off the ground. Normally retracted claws are whipped forward (right) by ligaments and tendons.*

tendons; in fact, this particular one stretches two-and-a-half times its resting length when it goes into action.) Normally, the two bones have a humped conformation—the front one angling downward, the middle one angling upward—and are held in place by the tendon above them. But when the claws are unsheathed, the ligament at the bottom stretches backward, bringing the two bones into horizontal alignment, and the claw whips forward. Other foot and leg muscles are brought into play here, too, for directional and steadying purposes, and also to spread the toes so that width of grasp will be maximal as the cat strikes its prey.

The hind claws are not as curved as the claws on the fore feet, but they are thicker and are formidable weapons in their own right. Cats rarely use their hind claws when catching mice, but may need them if they are trying to subdue a larger animal or if they themselves are being attacked. The cat's ultimate defensive tactic is to roll on its back, belly up, so the claws of all four feet can rake and stab.

The toes of the back feet are less flexible than those on the front feet, which explains in part why domestic cats are good at climbing trees but find it difficult (physically and emotionally) to make the descent. Propelled by powerful back muscles and strong hind feet and helped by spreadable front toes with claws that act as grappling hooks, a cat can get up a tree as fast as it can move on the ground. But coming down is a different matter. Cats have good depth perception, and the ground looks alarmingly far away. They don't "know" they will land upright if they fall (more about that skill in a later chapter), and they aren't used to leaping downward from any considerable height. Besides, most tree branches don't provide a steady enough surface to support a leap.

So, after spending a long time clinging to the branch, and perhaps wailing for help from humans, the treed cat will creep awkwardly down. Squirrels can descend trees headfirst because they are braced by widely spread short legs and have bushy tails to help them balance. Cats' tails are useful balancers when the running cat has to change direction during a chase, but they aren't much help—except to indicate distress—when the animal is faced with the problem of coming down a tree. A cat's legs are longer than a squirrel's, and neither knee, ankle, nor foot joints move freely in a sideways direction. If a cat were to try a headfirst descent with its hindquarters unsupported, its body weight would tumble it heels over head. The only possible choice is to come down the tree rear-end first, hanging by the fore claws. The descent is essentially a series of slides, and who can blame a cat for looking nervously downward over its shoulder the whole time?

It should be mentioned that individual cats vary a great deal in tree-descending ability. Some have slight variations in build that allow them to invert the feet a shade more than usual. It may be, too, that practice helps. Some wild cats are tree climbers by nature—the South American tree ocelot, for example. Paul Leyhausen has studied this species in detail, observing with some awe the degree to which the tree ocelot's hind feet are specialized for grabbing. The hind limbs can rotate through 180 degrees and the ankles are so flexible the paws can face inward or outward. (This is less a matter of bone structure than of modifications to the capsules of the joints, ligaments, and muscles.)

Tree ocelots spiral around tree trunks when they climb, and come down headfirst, like squirrels. The toes of their hind feet can close like a fist around a vine or a piece of cord; they can drop from one branch to another as easily as a monkey. In a laboratory cage, they hang by their hind feet from a branch and play with a spool of yarn, then swing themselves back to the branch with the ease of circus trapeze artists. Leyhausen learned the hard way not to pick them up by the nape of the neck (the best way to insure passivity in most cats). Tree ocelots swing their hind legs forward and rake their claws through even leather gloves.

As weapons of attack, cats' claws are supplemented by their teeth. There are thirty of these, twelve less than a dog has and two less than in human beings. In the center of both upper and lower jaws, there are six small, squarish incisors which the cat uses for nipping or pulling at things. Next in order are the canines, one pair in each jaw. These are large, long, somewhat flattened teeth, and sharp; they stab like daggers. Next is a line of premolars and molars, four up and three down, the last two of which have developed into very efficient shearing tools. They move against each other like scissor blades, slicing tendons and skin and cutting flesh into chunks.

The mechanical source of this motion is jaw joints aligned with the tooth row, an arrangement which causes the back teeth to mesh first. The jaw joints of rabbits, dogs, and men are placed higher, to allow all the teeth in both jaws to come together simultaneously. This arrangement is necessary if vegetable materials have to be ground before they can be swallowed, an activity that is also aided by jaws which move from side to side. Cats are primarily meat eaters. When they eat vegetable material, it has to be in swallowable form, for they have no grinding teeth and cannot move their jaws in a lateral direction. They like grass, for example, which they shear off rather awkwardly and gulp down. (Often, it doesn't stay down, and incipient hair balls come with it. Perhaps cats like grass for its emetic properties.)

The muscles powering and supporting the jaws are highly developed. The cat has a rounded head and a high braincase, which give good anchorage for muscles leading upward. The large skull also provides a firm point of attachment for neck muscles which must absorb backward-traveling shock when the canine teeth encounter sudden resistance from an animal that is struggling to get free.

Natural selection has bred into each of the predators a specific orienting reaction which directs the attacking bite toward whatever spot is most fatal for the prey. In the case of cats, small mammals are the preferred prey and the nape of the neck is the preferred target area. The main "cue" which guides the cat is a visual one: the indentation between a head and a body. Leyhausen once had a young wild cat named Bueno whose first prey was an empty pop bottle. Bueno spotted the bottle standing upright, knocked it over, threw himself on it, and bit furiously at its neck.

This innate directional sense is so strong that even cats who are thoroughly experienced hunters often apply the nape bite to animals that are more easily killed some other way. The big cats—lions, for instance—sometimes attack animals that are larger than they are, pull them down, and tear at throat or flanks; but even so a lioness often delivers a *pro forma* neck bite to a dead victim. When attempting to kill a snake, a domestic cat tries to get behind it and bite at the base of the head. Many chickens have survived neck bites that would speedily have dispatched a chipmunk because the nape of the neck is not a chicken's most vulnerable spot. The same is true when the contest is between bird and cat. A bird is vulnerable to a bite at a spot between shoulder and neck, and indeed this is where cats often seize it. Yet they frequently postpone killing while trying to shift the bird into position for a nape bite, in the course of which the bird may manage to free itself. A guinea pig can have the same good fortune if it crouches when attacked, pulling its head and limbs inward until it is roundish all over and the neck indentation is hidden. A cat will then seize it somewhere in the region of the shoulders, giving it a chance to escape.

Another cue which guides a cat's "decision" to deliver the killing bite is the texture of its prey. There is an innate feline response to fur, one that is sometimes elicited even if the prey isn't alive and struggling. Many cat owners have discovered that a cat in a hunting mood will fiercely pounce on fur-trimmed coats or hats which have been left unguarded by household visitors (who, in consequence, may become former household visitors).

If live prey cannot be dispatched immediately, it can be shaken until its neck is broken, and many predators do this. It is a usual way for dogs to kill rats, for example. In contrast, cats toss away their prey with a sideways, swinging movement which makes the captured animal so dizzy it loses its postural and spatial orientation and becomes immobile for the few moments a cat needs to kill it. Some wild cats repeat this maneuver many times, so forcefully that their victims are actually battered to death against trees or stones, but such behavior is not characteristic of domestic cats. In general, they use the technique of stunning prey when it is an unfamiliar kind of animal, has been grabbed at some point other than the neck, and is putting up a fight.

Tossing-away is a modifiable behavior pattern. The South American tree ocelot, by nature a bird fancier, doesn't release its prey with the intention of attacking again, for to do so would be to let loose its dinner. Nor does the Asian wild cat that is called "the fishing cat" release its initial grip: fish are as hard as birds to catch a second time. There are many anecdotes about domestic cats who fish successfully in rivers, ponds, and home aquariums; like bird-catching cats, they have adapted their hunting techniques to the preferred prey.

The ordinary cat who is an experienced hunter, is after its ordinary prey, and whose chase is attended by good luck will have no need to stun its prey. It attacks its mouse from above and behind, seizes it at the nape of the neck, and bites through to the spinal cord before the mouse has a chance even to squeak. And how precise that bite is! Cats hit the spinal cord with just *one* bite in such a high percentage of cases that Leyhausen believes something more than good aim is responsible.

He says that both the shape of the canine teeth and their position in the jaws must be adapted to the "lie" of the muscles, tendons, and ligaments as well as to the direction of the planes of mice vertebrae—a complementary relationship, like the fit of a key into a lock—so that any one of the penetrating teeth will almost automatically be guided into an intervertebral space. The tooth then inserts itself between the vertebrae like a wedge, forces them apart, and severs the spinal cord. Leyhausen says, "This hypothesis alone seems to me to explain why one rarely finds any damage to the vertebrae themselves. The canine teeth are exceptionally well suited to forcing things apart but certainly not to biting firmly with their tips on something hard. As one can discover from skulls in museums as well as from badly treated zoo and circus animals, the canine teeth splinter lengthwise relatively easily."

There are a great many touch-sensitive nerves at the base of the teeth. These may provide what Leyhausen calls "the last fine adjustment." Once the tip of a tooth touches a vertebral bone, these nerves may enable the cat "to feel around a little until the point glides into a gap, and only then bite harder. The 'automatic pilot' assumed above would then need to guide only as far as the vertebral bones and not so incredibly precisely as to [enter] between two vertebrae."

Either way, the feat is astounding.

Ordinarily, cats do not eat prey the minute they have killed it. They step to one side and groom themselves, then go back to their mouse and drag it by some indirect route to a protected place. This behavior is so deeply ingrained that even caged cats, whose quarters generally lack anything even faintly resembling a protected place, nevertheless go through the motions. Cats also carry prey by the neck, even if the dead animal is so large and heavy that it would be more easily transported if held at some point farther back on the body in order to distribute its weight more equitably.

Domestic cats are much more tolerant of feathers and fur than are some of their wild relatives, who pluck their prey of all feathers and some or all fur before they start to eat it. In eating, cats use one side of the mouth only, head tilted down in that direction, with frequent changes of side. The ear muscles are coordinated with the jaw muscles; sometimes both ears lie flat to the skull, sometimes only the ear on the chewing side. The big wild cats lie down to eat, holding their kill with their paws, but the small cats eat in the same posture they use when drinking—forequarters down, hindquarters up—and almost never use their paws to hold their food.

Cats usually eat their catch from the head end. Leyhausen found the explanation for this behavior by an experiment in which he turned the skins of half-grown rats into sausages by filling them with chopped meat. They were presented in various forms: with and without fur, with and without heads or tails, and even with heads stitched onto the hind ends. The lie of the fur, which ordinarily slopes away from the head, was the cats' orienting cue; they did not, for example, go for the head when it had been stitched onto the rear of the rat's body. Birds' feathers are used by predators in the same way; although, as R. F. Ewer says, "Working 'against the grain' may lead either to the head or to the base of the wing, and in fact a cat may start to eat a bird at either the head or the wing base." She notes that the habit of going against the lie of fur or feathers probably evolved originally in relation to scales—reptiles use this orienting device too—and was simply carried over into mammalian behavior.

As a prelude to killing small rodents, cats sometimes "play" with their prey, tossing and catching it repeatedly, sometimes permitting it to run free between tosses, but never far enough to prevent easy recapture. (There is a famous embroidery which hangs in the bedroom that Mary, Queen of Scots, occupied at Holyrood. It pictures a cat playing with a mouse, the cat being Elizabeth I and the mouse being Mary.) Play with prey is extremely offensive to human observers and is the source of the cat's long-standing reputation as a bloodthirsty beast that kills for the love of killing. Other predators, as a matter of fact, are equally or more "cruel" to their prey than cats are, but human beings seldom witness their hunting and killing behavior. Cats, in contrast, *live* with us; perhaps we have come to believe that after centuries of close association they should have acquired some of our own standards and values. The first edition (1771) of the *Encyclopaedia Britannica* states that the cat "does not properly pursue; he only lies in wait, and attacks animals by surprise; and after he has caught them, he sports with and torments them . . ." Feline behavior is largely motivated by patterns that were evolved a million years ago. As far as cats are concerned, a "proper" pursuit is not one governed by a code of fair play but one that results in a kill.

Leyhausen classes play with prey as of three kinds, each of different intensity and each occurring under different circumstances. The first of these is essentially exploratory behavior. Upon sighting a strange new toy or a strange new bug, the cat approaches hesitatingly, crouches at a safe distance, then extends a closed paw and dabs at the unfamiliar thing. (The mood is one of wariness; fear lurks just behind.) If the object or animal moves, the cat backs up or jumps away from it in a startled sideways leap.

That kind of play can escalate into something rougher and more damaging, however. To deal with small animals that refuse to be caught but can't hide or escape, a cat sometimes dispatches the animal with a series of closed-paw blows. Some cats also use this technique as a preamble to killing unpalatable prey. One of Leyhausen's wild cats, for example, didn't like white rats, eating them only when she was extremely hungry and with obvious distaste. She deliberately postponed killing them, batting each rat into insensibility before she killed it. (It is difficult *not* to impute human motivation to such behavior, for the picture which immediately comes to mind is of a child postponing the eating of disliked food by pushing it around and around on his plate.)

The second kind of play with prey is the lethal game of catch, so repulsive to human beings, which has already been described. Although such play is not unknown in wild cats, it is especially characteristic of domestic cats. They perform it with such exuberance—in the style of kittens playing with toys—that Leyhausen thinks it represents a retention of juvenile behavior by the species, a theory that will be discussed in more detail in a later chapter on domestication.

The third kind of play occurs only with dead animals. It is a frenzied, leaping dance in which the cat executes a series of high, arching leaps over and around its victim. This behavior, which occurs in both wild and domestic cats, usually follows a long, exhausting battle with a big and dangerous animal. Cats must overcome great fear of such prey in order to continue the fight, and the riotous following dance works off the tension. Sometimes, too, a cat rolls around with its dead prey, embracing it or kicking at it (if it is large) with its hind claws.

To understand the motivation for this and other actions in the cat's hunting and killing repertoire, one must go to the writings of Konrad Lorenz and other ethologists. They believe that each of the instinctive actions of the higher animals has its own source of neural energy, an assemblage of brain cells which trigger only the actions for which they are specific. Each of these assemblages generates energy for performing a particular movement—chasing, for example, or catching, or killing.

This is a process which creates *readiness*. Readiness increases by regular increments which are proportional to the time since the action was last performed. In addition, each neural assemblage accumulates readiness at a different rate. A mouse might be the common stimulus, but the response to it will vary in accordance with which of the cat's neural "reservoirs" is most ready for action. Readiness to catch, for example, accumulates rapidly, whereas readiness to kill accumulates slowly. This is due to the fact that in the natural situation the animal must be prepared to hunt more often than it kills. Leyhausen estimates that domestic cats lose two mice for every one they catch, and the chase-to-kill ratio must be much higher among the wild cats.

In the most perfect of feline worlds, these various accumulations of neural energy would be at the correct level of readiness whenever the cat has an opportunity to perform the action for which each is specific. But that rarely happens. A cat may chase and catch but not kill because the level of readiness for killing is too low. Or a cat may catch its prey so quickly it doesn't use up all its readiness for catching. It is under such circumstances, Leyhausen says, that cats play with prey before they kill it: they must release their unexpended neural energy. (He has also observed wild cats in zoos playing with the dead animals given them as food, or even with inanimate objects, presumably also to discharge an overabundant amount of readiness for catching, an activity denied most caged animals.) Conversely, if readiness to kill has built up to a high level—perhaps because the chase has been long and the prey has been elusive—the cat will dispatch its victim as fast as it can. There is no relationship between the need to kill and the need to eat, which is why cats sometimes do not eat their catch.

The theory of individual readiness levels for different actions also explains the apparently purposeless behavior of a house cat who suddenly leaps from a window sill, races up a staircase and down a hallway, makes a skittering turn, and whizzes back downstairs. It is a chase without a chasee, and one can see why superstitious people might believe that such a cat is possessed by the Devil. They'd be right if a devil within can be defined as an over-full reservoir of readiness for the chase, some of which *has* to be expended in order for the cat to be psychically comfortable.

CHAPTER 3

Seeing

CATS HAVE EXCEPTIONALLY large eyes in relation to their head size. Because they resemble human babies in this respect, it is understandable that people find cats' faces so appealing. But those large and lustrous eyes are also the most functional of tools. They are the cat's primary sense organs, the product of millions of years of adaptation to a particular way of life.

Any hunter must correlate its activity pattern with that of the creatures it hunts. Cats prey on some animals that are active by day and some animals that are active by night, so their eyes are adapted for both bright and low levels of illumination. The pupils are extremely sensitive to degrees of brightness: in very dim light, their diameter can be as much as half an inch; and in very bright light, they can become thin slits with only pinpoint apertures at top and bottom. The operating mechanism is a figure-eight arrangement of muscles in the iris. The pupil itself is inflexible along its vertical axis, and the muscles either spread it sideways in dim light or squeeze it shut in bright light.

The pupils of all mammalian eyes respond to sensory stimulation other than light. Pain, for example, causes them to dilate, and certain drugs cause them to constrict. Recent work by the University of Chicago psychologist Eckhard Hess and others has indicated the extent to which the pupils of the eye respond to the thoughts or feelings of the individual. If a person samples several beverages, his pupils dilate when he sips the one he prefers. And if a hungry cat is shown its customary feeding dish, its pupils may dilate to four or five times the size they were a moment before—this under conditions of constant illumination. Cats' pupils also dilate somewhat when they see a photograph of another cat and much more so when they see a moving picture of cats.

However, it is the light-responsive aspect of the feline eye that most impresses cat watchers, and has for centuries. That is why legends have linked the cat to the sun or the moon; and once the linkage was made, all manner of fantastic tales could be spun. Cats' eyes wax and wane with the moon, Plutarch said, and W. B. Yeats celebrated that ancient belief in his poem "The Cat and the Moon." Because the moon controls the tides, some people have believed that the constriction and dilation of cats' eyes mark the tides' ebb and flow. Or, if the sun was the master, then cats' eyes could serve as clocks. A French missionary priest traveling in China in the nineteenth century reported that when he asked some village children to tell him the time of day, they produced some cats, pried open their eyelids, and announced that it was not yet noon. They told their visitor that cats' eyes grow constantly narrower until twelve o'clock, "when they become like a fine line, as thin as a hair drawn perpendicularly across the eye," and that after twelve the dilation recommences.

The way a cat's eyes shine at night is an even more exotic attribute. Writing in the eighteenth century, the Count de Buffon said that cats' eyes "sparkle like diamonds, and seem to throw out, in the night, the light they imbibe during the day." The color of night shine varies from yellow-green or blue-green (in cats with gold- to copper-colored eyes) to red (in cats with blue eyes). So impressive is this phenomenon that the French coined a word to describe it: *chatoyer*, "to shine like cats' eyes." It has come into English as "chatoyant." If a jeweler displays "an unusual chatoyant aquamarine," the truly knowledgeable customer knows that it is one with a changeable luster or color.

There have been sinister explanations for night shine, too. The witch hunters of the Middle Ages, knowing that cats were agents of the Devil, believed that the night shine of their eyes sprang from the fires of hell. In his *Historie of Foure-footed Beasts* (1607), Edward Topsell said that their "eies glitter above measure . . . when a man commeth to see a cat on the sudden, and in the night; they can hardly be endured, for their flaming aspect." And, indeed, what modern motorist does not shiver a bit when his headlights reflect myriad flashes of yellow fire from the eyes of animals in the roadside brush?

The fact, however, is that night shine is a reflection from a mirror in the cat's retina. The retina is at the rear of the eye—it lines the back part of the globe—and in its upper half it contains a triangular patch of cells called the tapetum lucidum. These cells are composed of up to ten layers of a crystalline substance which is partly zinc and partly a protein; they reflect back into the eye any light which was not absorbed the first time around. The tapetum enables cats and other night prowlers to use every bit of light in their surroundings. Night shine occurs only when a sudden blaze of light falls upon pupils which are wide open because the animal has been in the dark.

There is a fluorescent quality about the resultant glow. Its source—at least in some animal eyes, and probably in the cat's—is riboflavin. Riboflavin absorbs light of low wavelength and reflects it at a longer wavelength. Antoinette Pirie, an Oxford University ophthalmologist, has studied the tapetum in many animal eyes, especially the lemur's (which has a tapetum of pure crystalline riboflavin), and believes that "the wide distribution of riboflavin or of a blue fluorescing material [as yet unanalyzed chemically] in other animal eyes makes one suspect that fluorescent materials, like the tapetal mirror, may be an effective visual aid."

Folklore claims that cats can see in total darkness, which is not true. But they *can* see in surroundings that human beings would describe as totally dark. Another British ophthalmologist, Ralph Gunter, once trained cats to choose a door with a lighted panel rather than one with an unlit panel, the reward being a saucer of milk behind the lighted door. The light was gradually diminished until the cats could no longer discriminate between the two doors. Human beings were tested at the same time. The cats kept going longer: they picked the right door even when there was only one-sixth as much illumination as was required for the human observers to see it. This was an eerie experience for Gunter, who reported that he watched his cats give consistently correct responses to an illuminated panel invisible to himself. There are a number of reasons why cats' eyes are so sensitive to low light levels; two of the most important, Gunter believes, are the tapetum lucidum in the retina and the large size of the fully dilated pupil. "A comparison of the 'f' value (signifying speed) of the human eye with that of the cat's eye shows that the efficiency of the latter is markedly superior," he says.

Of course, to admit a lot of light is not in itself sufficient to produce a good image. Light must be collected and refracted, and this is done by the cornea, the transparent outer coat of the eyeball, and the crystalline lens, which is behind the pupil. Together, they help to focus an image on the retina, the "photographic plate" of the eye. It would have been a great selective advantage, when animals capable of good night vision were evolving, for their corneas and lenses to become relatively larger than those of animals which hunted only by day, but not if the whole eye enlarged, in which case light admitted through the front of the eye would simply diffuse over a correspondingly enlarged retinal surface. So, natural selection being a good designer, the eyes of cats and other animals that are active at night have remained the same size in back as those of diurnal species of comparable build, and a large cornea has been added. The cat's is extremely convex—170 degrees of arc—and because of this curvature sits far in front of the pupil. The lens, too, is large and curved. Because the forward placement of the cornea has in effect moved the lens farther back in the "camera," the lens can project a very bright image onto the center of the retina. This image is five times brighter than any the human eye is capable of forming.

But the image is not as sharp. The lenses of our eyes and of cats' eyes both change shape—the process is called accommodation—in order to bring objects into better focus. Human beings do this twice as well as cats (although cats compensate somewhat by constricting their pupils, an action which reduces the amount of accommodation necessary for the production of a clear image). Human beings and other diurnal animals also have an indentation in the center of the retina (the fovea) which, for a reason to be explained shortly, registers a highly defined picture. Cats' eyes are less well developed in this respect; they see less clearly at the center of the retina but more clearly on the periphery.

Since peripheral vision serves them well much of the time, cats focus their eyes far less than people do. The result is the "gaze into space" that cat watchers often find odd and unsettling. People with a taste for the occult may decide that Puss over there on the tabletop—"perfectly alert, mind you, but she isn't *looking* at anything!"—must be communing with otherworldly spirits. People who keep cats for company interpret this apparent withdrawal as a sign of aloofness. But it's simply the normal way for many animals to use their eyes.

Konrad Lorenz says that when an animal "does fix his eyes carefully and for a long time on some part of his surroundings, he is either afraid of it or he has some special design on it, usually no good one. The fixation of the eyes in such an animal is almost equivalent to taking aim." Paul Leyhausen adds that cats don't like to be stared *at*, either. "If a cat is creeping up on prey and realizes that another cat is watching, it will straighten up and act disinterested," he says. "When meeting on friendly or neutral ground, one cat will stop its approach if the other looks at it directly. In courtship, the female looks about casually; if she looked directly at her partner, it would stop the action. . . . When rival cats fight, however, they *do* look directly at each other."*

The light that enters the eye may come either from a primary source, such as the sun or a lamp, or it may be reflected from some surface. Because reflected rays differ in intensity or wavelength from unreflected light in the same vicinity, the viewer can perceive the object from which the light is being reflected. When a mouse, for example, leaves the opening of its burrow, light reflected from its body alerts the waiting cat. If the reflected rays keep changing their angle or intensity, the cat will rightly interpret what is happening as movement, and will act accordingly. One of the cat's greatest areas of visual sensitivity is to movement.

In fact, movement is the basic stimulus to chasing behavior. Leyhausen has observed that kittens who have had no contact with other small animals and lack experience as hunters do nothing more than sniff at a mouse—if it's quiet. But if it should run, and especially if it should run *away* from the kitten, the kitten will pursue. This is an innate response to seeing something move across the cat's path or away from it, and whether the moving object is a crumpled ball of paper or a live animal is immaterial. Leyhausen once tested the relationship between directionality of movement and cats' chasing responses by using three wind-up toy mice. One of them ran in a straight line, one described a circle, and one turned and twisted in an erratic pattern. His cats chased the mouse that ran in a straight line, but only followed the

---

*The direct gaze is the lion tamer's most valuable tool. "All one has to do in order to control a lion is to be brave enough to look at it eye to eye," Leyhausen says, but cautions that this trick works only so long as the lion considers the lion tamer to be another lion.

other two mice with their eyes, backing away from the erratic mouse whenever it headed in their direction. Not until the last two mice were "dead" (had run down and stopped moving) did the cats approach them and bat them around.

Light reflected from any object, moving or not, strikes photoreceptors in the cat's retina. These are of two kinds, rods and cones. Both have pigment which absorbs radiant energy, converts it first into chemical and then electrical energy, and sends it on to the brain. Rods and cones have different thresholds of sensitivity, however; the rods respond to light of low intensity and the cones to light of high intensity. They function in what one physiologist has called "a staggered shift system," the rods being used in dim light and the cones in bright light, with a gradual rate of changeover as light intensifies.

Nobody seems to know precisely how many of these photoreceptors a cat's eye has, although there are millions. The rod-to-cone ratio is about 25 to 1. The rods are arranged so that many thousands converge on the same nerve cell, and these cells in turn converge on other nerve cells that lie farther along the pathway to the brain's visual center. The result of this summation is that the energy in tiny amounts of light is consolidated, a great advantage in conditions of very low illumination. But there is a penalty: when depending on their rods, eyes do not see very acutely. Acuity of vision depends on the eyes' ability to distinguish which particular receptors are responding to light; and if many receptors are acting in concert, the exact location of the light source cannot easily be determined. That is the function of the cones. They have a one-to-one relationship to the nerve cells which link them to the brain, and therefore they transmit individual messages. It is no accident that the cones of an animal that is active mainly by day are packed thickly into the fovea of each eye (the spot upon which the retinal image is focused). This enables the animal to accurately gauge the position of its prey at any split second of movement.

Cones also respond to specific wavelengths of light, and thus make color vision possible. In the normal human eye, the cones differ by the kind of pigment they contain. There are three kinds, respectively absorbing light from the red, the green, or the blue regions of the spectrum. Human eyes have more cones than cat eyes—one cone to twenty rods instead of one to twenty-five—and they are distributed differently in comparable parts of the human and feline retina. One area in the cat eye has no cones at all. Nevertheless, cat's eyes *do* have cones. Why, then, has it been so widely believed that cats cannot see color?

Back in 1915, the University of Colorado's J. C. DeVoss and Rose Ganson set up a testing device which consisted of two jelly glasses lined with paper, one gray and one colored. Every effort was made to use papers of identical brightness (that is, whose surfaces were equally reflective) and thus assure that the cats would be discriminating between different wavelengths. Both jelly glasses contained fish, but the cat got that reward only if it picked the colored glass. Nine cats spent eighteen months on this chore, making a total of more than 100,000 tries. The record showed that they could discriminate between two grays, but when the choice was between gray and either yellow, green, violet, red, or blue, the cats could make the discrimination only half the time, the level of pure chance. The investigators therefore concluded that cats are color-blind.

No one challenged that conclusion for more than twenty-five years, and the challenge, when it came, was from the neuroscientists. Cats' brains have been studied more exhaustively than those of any other animal, and from the 1940's onward a lot of physiological evidence began to accumulate. By planting electrodes in various parts of the cat's visual system, the electrical impulses from the eye to the brain can be monitored. One researcher recorded from the retina, another from nerve fibers in the optic tract, a third from the visual center in the brain, and all their data showed sensitivity to light of different wavelengths. Quite recent work indicates that cats have two kinds of cones; in time it may even be shown that, like human beings, they have three kinds.

What all this evidence adds up to is the conclusion that cats *should* be able to distinguish colors. So the behavioral scientists decided that the methodology of testing must have been responsible for their negative results. Perhaps earlier investigators had not managed, after all, to eliminate brightness factors? Perhaps the shape of the objects which cats were asked to choose between had somehow confused them? Several scientists then tried again. Their experiments (mostly in the 1950's) were carefully controlled, but the results were still negative. Well, then, perhaps the cats used in those tests had not been trained for a long enough period of time? Or perhaps they had been deprived of food to the extent that they couldn't concentrate on the job? (Cats must be hungry enough to seek the food reward that follows a correct choice, but they must be adequately fed between tests or they are as unable to perform difficult intellectual tasks as is any undernourished schoolchild.) In short, researchers tried to think of all the variables that might be affecting the outcome of the tests. It was annoying to have the physiological evidence and the behavioral evidence refute each other. And they couldn't blame the cats' failure on contrariness, for the same cats who weren't able to identify colored objects were quite capable of discriminating between a bright one and a dull one.

Finally, in the mid-1960's, half a dozen scientists managed to get all the test conditions right, and proved that cats *can* see color. But in every case it took the animals a tremendously long time to learn the discrimination; in one report, the researchers said their cats required from 1,350 to 1,750 tries before they grasped the idea that the solution to their problem was the *color* of a door or a dish or a toy. R. F. Ewer, in summarizing these studies, says the need for such prolonged training indicates that responses to colors are no part of a cat's normal behavior. It has to train its brain to use the information from its eyes in an entirely new way. Its cones may not normally convert wavelength into color; in Ewer's words, "The cat may not care whether the grass in which a mouse is hiding is bluish green or yellowish green—but it may care very much whether it can or cannot see clearly towards the blue end of the short wave length."

To protect all the delicate optical equipment inside them, eyes have eyelids containing glands which secrete a lubricating fluid to smooth their movement across the eyeball. Tear glands are set into the edges. To the human observer, cats' eyelids don't look much like eyelids because they are covered with fur (which sometimes projects outward in stiff little eyelashes on the top lid). Cats' eyes also gain additional protection from the so-called third eyelid, the nictitating membrane. This thin pliable sheet of tissue unfolds from the inner corner of the eye and spreads outward. It may possibly have a role in light control, as well: some arctic animals, whose eyes must withstand glare ice, also have nictitating membranes. Human beings have a vestige of the same structure; it survives in us as a small pinkish triangle in the inner corners of our eyes.

Cats' eyes are set far forward in the head, side by side. The resultant binocular vision is characteristic of hunting animals; it provides a slightly different image from each eye, then fuses them into a single retinal image. This stereoscopic action assures accurate distance and depth perception. Cats have binocular vision across a range of about 120 degrees and monocular vision for another 80 degrees on each side. This leaves a blind area of about 80 degrees in back, for which cats compensate somewhat by moving their eyes and rotating their necks. Hunted animals, in contrast, can't afford blind areas. Their lives depend on their seeing a predator before it sees them; therefore they have panoramic vision. Rodents and rabbits have eyes set on the sides of their heads, an arrangement that gives them only 10 degrees of binocular vision but more than 170 degrees of monocular vision on each side—and virtually no blind spot.

In birds, fishes, and reptiles, the optic nerve fibers of the right eye lead to the left hemisphere of the brain, and those of the left eye to the right hemisphere of the brain. In the mammalian eye, that wiring pattern has been modified, and to a degree that correlates with how far forward the eyes of a given animal are positioned. In horses, which have eyes on the sides of their heads, about 15 percent of the optic nerve fibers in each eye connect to the hemisphere on the same side of the brain as the eye. In rats, the percentage is 20 percent; in dogs, 25 percent; in cats, 35 percent; and in human beings, 50 percent. Because this arrangement provides a link between each eye and the visual centers in *both* hemispheres, it enables an animal better to coordinate the binocular movements of its eyes.

CHAPTER 4

The Other Senses

BARTOLOMEUS ANGLICUS, whose thirteenth-century Latin was later translated into English, said that a hunting cat "lieth slyly in wait for mice, and is aware where they be more by smell than by sight, and pounceth on them in privy places." The good monk of course had no knowledge of rods and cones, of convex corneas and binocular vision, but even so he would have hit closer to the mark if he had chosen hearing as the sense that enables cats to pounce on mice in privy places. For cats, hearing is almost as important as seeing.

How important has been demonstrated by scientists who have trained animals to discriminate between two boxes, using a buzzer or bell as the clue to the box that will produce a food reward. Jonathon C. Wegener reports that in separate but similar experiments, it took monkeys an average of 437 trials to equate sound with food, whereas cats averaged only 33 trials before they grasped the connection. This disparity is not surprising when one considers these animals' differing ways of life. Because cats hunt mobile prey by night, hearing is an essential adjunct to vision. Monkeys are active by day and they're vegetarians, besides; what they hunt doesn't move or make noise. The monkeys in the above tests must have been as puzzled as were the cats in the color-vision experiments described in the previous chapter. How could anything as irrelevant as *sound* be the clue to finding food?

Sound is like light in that it proceeds from its source in the form of waves. When a mouse scuttles across a barn floor, the force its body exerts on the immediately adjacent air particles compresses them and then, as the moving body pulls away, allows them to spread apart again. Because these molecules strike the molecules adjacent to *them*, the original pulsation is duplicated and reduplicated by air particles progressively farther from the sound source. The extent or amplitude of the resulting wave of pressure change is heard as loudness. The rate at which the molecules are vibrating (that is, the frequency of their back-and-forth movement) is heard as pitch. Slow frequencies sound deep or low; high frequencies sound shrill. Natural sounds are usually blends of several frequencies, each of which is heard as a tone. If one sets up a laboratory experiment in which two sounds differing by only one-fifth of a tone are directed to a cat's ears, it can discriminate between them.

The mammalian ear is a marvelously engineered organ. Waves of pressure change, originating with a moving object, first pass through a resonating channel to the eardrum, travel next along three chained bones suspended in the fluid of the middle ear, and finally arrive at the labyrinth of the inner ear. Here, auditory receptor cells transmute the incoming vibrations into nerve impulses which journey on to the brain. When these are received, the animal "hears."

Cats and human beings perform equally well in the lower and middle ranges of the sound spectrum—from about 20 cycles per second to 20,000 cycles per second (the latter being the rate at which the high notes of a violin vibrate). Cats' ability to hear high notes declines with age, as ours does; but when compared with human beings at relatively the same stage of life, they consistently hear sounds of higher frequencies. They have at least 40,000 fibers in the auditory nerve, as against our 30,000. Cats' upper limit seems to be around 50,000 cycles per second. This does not place them exceptionally high in the mammalian hearing hierarchy; mice, with an upper limit of 95,000 cycles per second, hear better. Bats hear sound-wave frequencies up to 120,000 cycles per second, but porpoises seem to be the champions, at 150,000 cycles per second.

Nevertheless, cats hear quite well enough for the serious purposes of their lives. Most cat owners upon returning home are accustomed to finding their cats waiting just inside the front door, having been alerted by the sound of a footstep or the key being inserted into the lock. Some people say their cats can distinguish the sound of one car motor from another. And Margaret Cooper Gay tells a marvelous story about seagoing cats' dependence on their ships' whistles to get them back aboard on time:

> The half hour whistle called the crew aboard. The fifteen minute whistle summoned stragglers. The final toot, five minutes before casting off, was the cat's whistle. Then war [World War II] silenced the whistles and cats who depended on their ears were marooned in every port. In March, 1942, the New York papers printed photographs of a sea cat named Minnie whose paw was sought by the masters of sixteen United Nations ships, their own cats having been beached in other silent ports. I heard of one cat stranded in Panama for months, who lived on the docks, waiting for her ship. She refused dozens of seductive offers to sail with other vessels, and when her own ship did come in she was first aboard.

Ears evolved from organs intended to help animals keep their equilibrium, and a part of the bony labyrinth in the inner ear still serves this purpose. If it is disturbed by movements which cause the head frequently to change its position relative to the body, motion sickness can result. Human beings are susceptible to this malady and so are dogs, but for some reason cats are not. When traveling by automobile, however, cat owners are not noticeably better off than dog owners: a cat who yowls throughout the journey can be as unwelcome a passenger as a carsick dog.

Since ears are separated by the head, the split-second differences in the timing and intensity of the sound received by each ear help the hearer localize the sound's source. Human beings can differentiate between sounds whose sources are only three degrees apart, and cats can resolve a difference of about five degrees. They would probably do a better job of triangulation than we do if their heads were as large as ours.

The function of the external part of the ear, the curved plate of cartilage which is properly called the auricle, or pinna, is to collect the sound waves. In human beings, this appendage is shaped like a cup handle, lies close to the head, and is thick. In contrast, cats' pinnae are cone-shaped, upstanding, and very flexible. It's a rare human being who can wiggle his ears, but cats have more than twenty muscles in their pinnae and can sweep them through an arc of approximately 180 degrees.

A cat will turn its neck and point one or both ears in the direction it thinks a sound is coming from. Because the pinnae curve inward so the edges overlap the opening of the ear canal, they literally funnel the sound downward. It bounces back and forth among the ridges on the inner surface, acquiring variations in its quality which help the cat to pinpoint the source of the sound. There is a fringe of hairs on the inner edge of each pinna (the edge toward the nose) and a little tuft of hair at its base, which together help to keep wind-borne particles out of the ears.

Incidentally, the size and shape of the pinnae indicate the kind of climate which is native to an animal. Those who live in the arctic cannot afford heat loss from large exposed surfaces, but the reverse is true of animals adapted to hot climates. Most domestic cats descended from African wild cats, hence the upstanding pinnae. Persian cats, however, are thought to be descended from the steppe cat, or at any rate to have a sizable inheritance of its genes. This species, which lives in rocky, arid, cold areas of Central Asia, has long fur on the underparts of its body—good insulation when lying in snow or on frozen ground—and small pinnae, no higher than the top of its head, a characteristic also of the modern Persian breed.

The relationship between hearing and touch is sometimes very close. In their psychology textbook, Donald Dewsbury and Dorothy Rethlingshafer say that hearing is properly defined as "the awareness of vibrations in an elastic medium, and a sound that is airborne is not qualitatively different from one that is waterborne or earthborne." They suggest that vibration should be thought of as *repeated* touch. It may be, then, that a cat "hears" with the soles of its feet as well as its ears when a mouse scampers across a cellar floor.

Folklore is rich in examples of animals that are said to have warned their owners of impending earthquakes or volcanic eruptions. Although sensitivity to advance tremors need not be the only explanation for such behavior (atmospheric pressure changes being another), the possibility should not be discounted—and it will be discussed in greater detail in a later chapter. "Many animals are much more sensitive to substrate variations than humans are, with the result that we have not been properly aware of its significance in the animal world," say Dewsbury and Rethlingshafer.

The cat's whiskers are part of a complement of coarse, stiff hairs which extend well beyond the body and which are called vibrissae. Some grow in tufts; others are individually set. They act like levers, pivoting at the surface of the skin, and thus translate their slightest contact with an object to a bulbous root which is rich in sensory nerves. In most mammals, vibrissae occur on the upper lip (it is this group to which people refer when they speak of a cat's whiskers), on the chin, under the chin, over the eyes, and far back on the cheeks. Cats, however, lack vibrissae under the chin, perhaps because they don't hunt food by nosing about in the soil. They also have additional vibrissae on the back surface of the fore leg; one naturalist has correlated hairs in this location with an animal's use of fore legs for grasping as well as for locomotion.

Vibrissae are important supplements to vision. Those on the upper lip are arranged in four rows, of which the upper two can move independently of the lower two. Since they extend sideways beyond the head and can be fanned out, they help a cat decide whether a small opening offers enough clearance for its body. They can also be used to feel around on the ground or floor to locate a piece of food that is so close to the nose the eyes can't bring it into focus. But vibrissae need not be in physical contact with an object in order to "feel" it; they also detect the tiny variations in air currents that are deflected from solid objects and therefore help the cat move around in the dark without bumping into things.

Edward Topsell told his seventeenth-century readers that "if the long haires growing about her [the cat's] mouth be cut away, she looseth her corage." More modern researchers have also tried to discover the effect on cats of having their whiskers cut off. The main finding is that they compensate by sharpening other senses. One group of kittens who lost their whiskers when they were eight days old lost neither their courage nor their ability to move about in space. In situations where the use of whiskers is usual, they were observed to be relying on vision several days earlier than a control group of kittens whose whiskers were intact.

Scattered among the rows of whiskers on the upper lip is a series of dark spots. These have been used by Judith Rudnai, a zoologist at University College, Nairobi, to identify lions in Nairobi National Park. She bases her system on the number and location of spots in the first row relative to the spots in the second row. After photographing and making whisker-spot charts of twenty-one lions, she discovered that each pattern was as wholly individual as a human being's fingerprints. No one has yet applied her system to domestic cats; however, since whisker spots are common to all cats, it is likely that the individuality of their arrangement is too.

The vibrissae and the softer hairs of the cat's pelt are no more than extensions of the skin, which is pebbled with "touch spots" of great sensitivity. When one flips a wet hand at a cat—to discourage thievery from a kitchen counter, say—it is not the wetness that disturbs the animal but the domino effect of the droplets. They trigger a whole series of tactile pads, causing the skin to ripple along the full length of the cat's body. There are from seven to twenty-five of these touch spots per square centimeter of skin.

A cat's skin, incidentally, is a bigger envelope than is necessary to hold the flesh and bones inside it. It is so loose, an old-time naturalist once said, that "it can be pulled halfway around the body without tearing." That's an exaggeration, but it *can* be gathered into folds, especially at the back of the neck. Should a cat become prey instead of predator, this looseness may be lifesaving; it gives the cat a better chance to slip out of its captor's grasp. The skin on the back of the neck is also five times thicker than it is on the hind legs.

Despite its exquisite sensitivity to touch, however, feline skin is markedly *in*sensitive to temperature. Elizabeth Brearley, Dan R. Kenshalo, and others at Florida State University have run a series of tests to determine a cat's reaction to heat or cold on different parts of its body, and have found that sensitivity "is rudimentary at best" on the back, the inside of the hind legs, and on the foot pads. At those sites, cats do not feel uncomfortable until they are touched by an object whose temperature is 124 degrees Fahrenheit. (Human beings feel pain at 112 degrees.) An object applied to the skin of its back has to be cooled by as much as sixteen degrees before the cat notes the change in temperature.

There is one exception to this general pattern. The lightly furred skin around the nose and the nose itself are very sensitive to changes in temperature. The cat's upper lip responds to an increase in warmth of less than two degrees and to an increase in coolness of less than one degree, so it is an accurate thermometer. When a cat lowers its nose toward a piece of just-cooked food and then draws back, it is not smelling the food but is taking a temperature reading which indicates that the food is too hot to eat.

Cats are not fond of cold weather, but manage to survive if they are forced to live outdoors the year around. Their fur coats also insulate them against excessive heat. They snuggle up to radiators that are too hot for a human hand to touch, stretch out on the metal parts of gas-range tops which are warmed by pilot lights, and even sit on stoves with a burner lit—at least until the smell of singed fur alerts some human occupant of the house to a danger of which the cat seems unaware.* In the early Middle Ages, when cats were still a novelty in Europe and were in demand as mousers, the price of a cat dropped in proportion to the number of scorched spots on its fur. Potential buyers reasoned that a cat who spent a lot of time indoors in front of a fire couldn't be a very eager hunter.

The various senses cannot be compartmentalized, for an animal's sensory system is a cooperative one. The palatability of food, for instance, is mutually determined by touch, smell, and taste. Touch helps the cat evaluate texture—to decide, say, whether feathers should be swallowed or spit out. Smell is the chemical analysis of airborne substances; a cat's nose can tell it that a particular kind of food will not sit well in its stomach. Taste is the chemical analysis of saliva-borne substances. The salivary glands secrete enzymes which break down organic material into a semisolid form that is easy to swallow, at the same time releasing molecules to whose chemical properties the taste buds respond. These lie at the back of the tongue, and from each of them, thousands of nerve cells carry the taste message to the brain.

For many years, it was believed that there were only four taste modalities—sweet, sour, salt, and bitter—but it is now known that water should be added to the list. The nerve fibers responsive to water can modify or mask some of the other tastes, and in cats this may explain why they don't seem to like sweets. Almost all other mammals are fond of sugar; cats are known to have taste-bud cells which respond to sugar (not many such cells, but some); so why are they indifferent to this taste? Scientists who have managed to suppress the water taste in liquids by adding small amounts of salt to a solution which also includes sucrose (sugar) have found that cats prefer the sucrose solution to an otherwise identical solution without it, and will drink it greedily.

* Cat owners are annoyed and embarrassed by this feline habit, but most can't break their pets of a fondness for stove-top lounging. In a recent issue of *Cats Magazine*, a readers' symposium on the topic included a report from a woman whose deterrent weapon was syrup, applied to the range top until her cats ceased to sit there. This remedy would strike most housewives as being worse than the disease.

Those dominant water-taste nerve fibers obviously serve an important function, however, for too much sugar is bad for cats. L. M. Bartoshuk, an expert on the chemistry and neurophysiology of taste, reported in one paper that his cats drank so much sucrose solution from which the water taste had been eliminated that they got severe diarrhea. They remembered the cause of their distress, too: a week later, when Bartoshuk returned them to the job, they flatly refused to drink the stuff.

Cats have individual food preferences. They catch all species of mice, but often refuse to eat one kind, the deer mouse. Moles and shrews are equally unpalatable. In fact, it is so unusual for a cat to eat a shrew that in 1945 the *Journal of Mammology* published a short note from Frank B. Mc-Murry (whose analyses of cat stomach contents were described in Chapter 1) telling of a feral cat whose stomach contained three shrews. The species, in case shrew specialists are reading this, was *Cryptosis parva*. "They had been chewed, but were mostly entire," McMurry said, an indication of how hungry the cat must have been. Snakes, frogs, and toads are only rarely eaten. Leyhausen found that his house cats would eat jays but not black-birds; three of them ate fox meat but one refused it.

Farm cats and feral domestic cats are dependent on whatever they can catch. Cats who live intimately with people are not only provided for but also have an opportunity to develop catholic tastes. Lafcadio Hearn, the writer who spent many years in Japan and there shared his life with a tor-toiseshell cat, said it "ate beefsteak and cockroaches, caterpillars and fish, chicken and butterflies, mosquito hawks and roast mutton, hash and tumble-bugs, beetles and pigs' feet, crabs and spiders, moths and poached eggs, oys-ters and earthworms, ham and mice, rats and rice pudding—until its belly be-came a realization of Noah's Ark." Cats continue to provide their owners with opportunities for one-upmanship: to counter the Petersons' Persian who adores asparagus, the Bairds have a Blue Point with a craving for canta-loupe and the McElroys a Burmese whose passion is olives.

A cat's tongue is a multipurpose organ. Thin and pliant around the edges, it curls inward to make a little spoon for holding liquid. (Cats take four or five laps of milk before swallowing.) The tongue thickens in the cen-ter, however, and is there overlaid with dozens of horny projections whose hooked points extend backward. Like a file, they are used both to rasp meat from bone and to remove loose fur from the coat.

The French philosopher Hippolyte Taine once described the cat's tongue as "sponge, and brush, and towel, and curry-comb; poor little wash rag." Cats cannot use their paws to wash their faces because the pads are so close-set and their claws might protrude, so they use their fore legs, transferring moisture from tongue to fur and then to face. James C. Boudreau, the University of Texas neurophysiologist, believes that cats secrete a special "detergent cleaning fluid" for this purpose—perhaps from glands other than those that produce saliva, because the fur after grooming smells so clean and fresh.

Smell is closely allied to taste, since the nasal passages open into the oral cavity. Like the ear, the nose is well engineered for its purpose. The nasal cavities are filled with a series of thin bones called turbinals; acting as baffles, they provide a many-surfaced chamber into which airborne molecules can be collected. A layer of tissue containing olfactory cells covers the upper back of the nasal cavities, spreading over an area that is actually (not relatively) larger in cats than in human beings. We have an estimated 5,000,000 to 20,000,000 olfactory cells and can hardly smell at all. Cats have about 67,000,000 such cells. Dogs, those champion trackers of the animal kingdom, have between 100,000,000 and 300,000,000. Cats do not track prey, nor do they recognize it by odor.

Inasmuch as they apply their noses long and attentively to objects which are completely odorless to human beings, it is impossible to compile a complete list of substances which cats can smell. Cat olfaction has been little studied; textbooks on animal behavior content themselves with saying that cats use their sense of smell primarily to recognize sexual and food odors. More anecdotally, Fernand Méry says they "love the smell of the petrol and oil used in cars, of opium smoke, yeast, the imperceptible odor of freshly slaughtered meat, the musty chlorinated smell of household washing, plaster, fennel, ammonia, and the stagnant water from vases." Perfumes should certainly be added to the list. Many cat owners have pets like Théophile Gautier's Mme. Théophile, who delighted in "India shawls lifted from boxes of sandalwood," or his Seraphita, who "with little spasms of pleasure bit handkerchiefs impregnated with scent."

Something more than pleasure is evoked by the odor of certain aromatic herbs. Old Japanese descriptions of feline behavior mention the intoxicating effects of matatabi (*Actinidia polygama*, the silver vine, which is native to the Far East). Paul Leyhausen has described the reactions of the big cats at Osaka Zoo to experiments in which an extract of matatabi was presented to them on tufts of cotton:

> After a few experiments, the cats became so eager that the moment they saw the experimenter appear they left everything, including food [or] sexual intercourse, and just ran up to the bars and waited for this smell. . . . They rolled on their backs and stayed there for some time in complete ecstasy. I believe they became truly addicted, because they continued to react although it affected their sense of smell and in the end damaged the brain, my Japanese hosts told me.

Old European accounts mention valerian (*Valeriana officinalis*, a garden heliotrope). "Wheresoever it groweth," according to Edward Topsell, "cats instantly dig it up . . . even when hedged or compassed round about with thornes, for it smelleth marvelous like to a cat." The Count de Buffon added to the list of feline excitants the plants familiarly called cat thyme (*Teucrium manum*) and catnip, or cat mint (*Nepeta cataria*). The latter is the one of the three that is best known today. It grows as a weed or can be cultivated. It is commercially available in dried form or as an extract in an aerosol spray can.

In the 1940's, the volatile oil in catnip was analyzed and the constituent which excited cats was identified. It is a substance called trans,cis nepetalactone. (That's for short; its full name is longer.) Cats who are susceptible to it go into a frenzy of rubbing or licking a catnip-scented toy, clutching, biting, clawing, and tossing it about. They roll over and over in the dried leaves or in a growing patch, get the oil on their fur, lick it off, and start all over again. Such cats can identify the odor when its concentration in air is as little as one part in a billion.

Nor are human beings immune. Two Marquette University psychiatrists, Basil Jackson and Alan Reed, reported in 1969 that some of their young patients who were seeking an alternative to marijuana had been experimenting with catnip. Smoked in the dried form it didn't give them much of a lift, but when they sprayed tobacco with the catnip extract, they experienced both visual and auditory hallucinations. The effect was more like LSD than marijuana. R. C. Hatch, of the University of Guelph in Ontario, has noted that the molecular structure of trans,cis nepetalactone is similar to that of LSD, and suggests that cats who try to catch phantom butterflies while under the influence of catnip may also be having a bad trip.

In 1963, Neil Todd discovered through controlled breeding experiments that the catnip response is inherited—it's a dominant gene—but its expression is much modified by a given cat's age, environment, and emotional state. That was true too of the cats used by Hatch to test the effect of various drugs upon feline responses to catnip. If animals were new to the lab, "withdrawn and fearful," or if they were distracted by sudden noise or movement while they were investigating a catnip-scented toy, they would either not respond to it at all or their interest would abruptly wane.

Because the face-rubbing and rolling-over movements of cats who get high on catnip are like those of female cats in heat, Todd wondered whether the excitant in catnip might be related somehow to a sex hormone or pheromone. (Pheromone means "carrying excitation," and refers to odorous substances which are emitted by one animal and produce a particular reaction in another animal. During the past fifteen years, there has been accelerating scientific interest in these substances, of which more will be said in a later chapter.) Could catnip have the same effect on behavior as one of the cat-produced biochemicals which prime or release sexual behavior in females? And if so, why do male or neutered cats respond to catnip as if they were females in heat? Sexually aroused males never roll on the ground before or after mating, as females do.

A possible answer to the second question has been suggested by Gary Palen, of McGill University, and Graham Goddard, of the University of Waterloo. They postulate that a particular part of the tomcat brain, the hypothalamus, may be briefly "persuaded" by catnip that it is female. The hypothalamus is a structure that mediates and synchronizes many activities, the overall effect of which is to control motivation. Palen and Goddard think the hypothalamus may regulate sexual behavior through cells which have different threshold levels of responsiveness in the two sexes. The substance which elicits rolling-over in females may not be produced in males or may be produced in insufficient quantity to excite the cells which are sensitive to it. The stimulant in catnip may be powerful enough to induce such cells in male cats to mimic female behavior.

The hypothalamus also figures in speculations about the function of an auxiliary scent organ which sits far forward in the roof of the mouth and has ducts leading into both the nose and the mouth. Called Jacobson's (or the vomeronasal) organ, it is present in cats and many other animals but not in man. Its olfactory cells are not connected to the same part of the brain as the olfactory cells in the nose; instead, they connect to two different parts of the hypothalamus, one of which is concerned with motivation for feeding and the other with sexual behavior.

Animals with well-developed Jacobson's organs make a curious grimace called flehmen when they smell certain odors, especially those related to sex. (The word is German and has no English counterpart; it has been taken over intact and a verb has been derived from it.) When an animal flehms, it begins by sniffing an odorous object, touching it with its nose and sometimes with its tongue, then raises its head and inhales with the mouth partially open, the lips pulled up and back, and the nose wrinkled. The resulting facial expression has been variously described as "dopey" or "expressive of disgust." (It is especially bizarre to look at because the animal holds its breath while doing it.) What is meanwhile going on behind the scenes is a flick of the tongue to the roof of the mouth, just behind the incisors. This supplements the inhalation of airborne odorants by bringing licked material into contact with the taste buds and then with the duct of Jacobson's organ which opens into the mouth.

In sum, flehmen represents a maximal effort to examine and analyze a substance or substances of particular significance to the animal. Male cats do it more often than females, and the usual excitant is the urine of another cat. For males, it is the urine of females in heat that elicits the response. R. F. Ewer once had a tame male suricate (a small burrowing animal native to Africa) who flehmed in response to sherry, but the normal context is sexual.

That Jacobson's organ plays an important role in mating was indicated by an experiment by J. Bradley Powers and Sarah H. Winans at the University of Michigan. Using male hamsters, they found that sexual behavior was *unaffected* by partial destruction of the olfactory system; that it was *inhibited* by destruction of the nerves leading to the brain from Jacobson's organ; that it was *totally suppressed* if both smelling systems were destroyed. An experiment that ought to be done—Ewer suggested it—would involve blocking the openings of Jacobson's organ in cats and observing whether they still respond to catnip.

CHAPTER 5

Origin and Spread

THE EARLIEST KNOWN MEMBERS of the modern cat family were smallish animals, about the size of today's African or Asian wild cats. They made their appearance on earth about 13,000,000 years ago. It took another 10,000,000 years for the big cats—the lions, tigers, leopards—to evolve. Between then and the beginning of historic time, the felids spread themselves around the globe, skipping only Australia and Antarctica, Madagascar, the West Indies, and some oceanic islands.

Their time table and itinerary can be reconstructed by skeletal or fossil remains (which are scanty) or by comparing the behavioral patterns of their modern descendants. The small wild cats which are native to the Old World, for example, eat their prey's fur along with its flesh and spit out only the longest feathers of the birds they catch. In contrast, all but one of the New World cats pluck their prey before they eat it. That exception is the bobcat, which has the Old World indifference to fur and feathers. Its behavior pattern suggests that the bobcat was a late arrival to the Americas, coming across the Siberian land bridge long after the ancestors of other New World cats.

There are other differences too: the big cats of the Old World and the New World cats rest with their fore legs straight out in front of them, and they leave their feces uncovered. The small Old World cats, however, curl their paws under their chests when they are at rest, and bury their feces. This

indicates that South American pumas and African lions are more closely related than are African lions and their small jungle-cat neighbors.

Wherever the members of the cat family went in their prehistoric wan-
derings, they adapted themselves to size of prey and habitat. The lions became group-living animals, whereas most of the other cats are solitaries. The
cheetahs developed exceptionally long legs and became the fastest runners of
the family. The South American tree ocelots adapted themselves to an arbo-
real life, and the flatheaded cats of Southeast Asia became expert at scooping
fish out of shallow waters. Each discovered a unique ecological niche and
made successful use of its possibilities, in the course of which the cat itself
acquired modifications which set it apart from other cats.

Yet all of these animals are unmistakably cats. As St. George Mivart said
in 1881, "Cats of all kinds agree so closely in structure, and differ so decid-
edly, in that respect, from animals that are not cats, that they are universally
admitted to form . . . a group of animals easily characterized." Basic feline
design is, in fact, so stable that bones of small wild cats dating from a million
years ago cannot be distinguished from those of modern wild cats. Even the
domestic cat, the newest member of the family and one which is still evolving, is remarkably resistant to the tinkering of man. Although dogs have been
bred in a great variety of types, cats are of approximately the same size,
shape, and temperament.

> But though it is very easy to say whether an animal is a cat [Mivart
> continues], it is often exceedingly difficult to determine what kind of a
> cat it is. The lion, the tiger, the leopard, the puma, and the cheetah
> . . . are well-marked forms. No one can mistake any of these animals
> from one another, but there are a great many smaller cats which are in
> a very different case. Many of them vary much in colour (and somewhat
> in shape and more in size) from individual to individual. Certain kinds
> have received from different naturalists more than one name, and it is
> often a task of much difficulty to find out which is the proper name
> which any given kind ought to bear.

All cats belong to the class Mammalia, to the order Carnivora, and to
the family Felidae, but from that point on there are almost as many genera
and species as there have been classifiers. The family has in the past been
divided into as many as twenty-three genera. Even today, some textbooks
list six genera and others list four. Everyone seems to agree that the cheetah,

which has departed farther than any of its relatives from the traditional cat form, should have a genus of its own *(Acinonyx)*. The big cats are assigned to the genus *Panthera;* the small cats to the genus *Felis;* the lynxes, bobcats, and caracals to the genus *Lynx;* and a couple of Asian cats float between *Felis* and genera of their own.

The problem of classification becomes even more difficult when one begins to name species, especially when dealing with some of the small wild cats. There are, for example, eight species of European, African, and Asian wild cats which are so similar except for variations in habitat and fur patterns that some zoologists believe they are merely geographical and ecological variants of a single species. It is from this group of cats that the domestic cat, *F. catus*, descended.* But from which of them?

The likeliest ancestor is the African wild cat, *F. libyca*, which is also called the Egyptian cat or the Kaffir cat. It is larger than the average domestic cat (about three feet long, nose to tail tip) and has longer legs, a lean and sinuous body, and a long, thin tail. The back of its ears are a bright-rust color, and its coat ranges from reddish or sandy buff to gray-brown depending on habitat. It may be almost solid color or there may be thin broken stripes on the body. The eyes are rimmed with dark "lining," which makes one think of Nefertiti. (Perhaps the order should be reversed. Fine Egyptian ladies, during the period when cats were symbols of fertility and happiness, may have lined their eyes to resemble those of their cats.)

There have been supporters of the theory that the domestic cat descended instead from *F. silvestris*, the European wild cat. Grayish-brown in color and with a striped body, it is about the size of *F. libyca*, but its face is wider, its fur longer, its tail bushier and more blunt, with black rings around it. Its fur pattern appears in the most common kind of modern cat, the tabby. (The word "tabby" describes pattern and not color. There are orange as well as gray tabby cats, and the tabby pattern underlies most apparently solid-color coats. The word comes from Attabiya, a quarter in old Baghdad where striped or watered silk taffeta was originally made.)

On the basis of appearance, then, *F. silvestris* seems to be a good candidate to head the domestic cat's family tree. But appearance isn't everything.

---

* The species name *catus* was given to the domestic cat by Linnaeus in 1758. Other names have since been used, among them *domesticus* and *domestica*, and subspecies names have been tacked on in an effort to classify domestic cats by coat color or pattern, but most zoologists have now reverted to the original nomenclature.

F. silvestris is quite untamable; even if raised from kittenhood by human beings, it remains fierce and intractable. It is hard to imagine any European wild cat developing the docility which must be a preamble to domestication. Its African cousin, on the other hand, tames easily. Furthermore, the oldest records of domesticated cats are Egyptian. So it is now believed that the tabby pattern was contributed by *F. silvestris* to long-domesticated descendants of *F. libyca* when they finally made it to Europe. (See Figure 3.)

Inasmuch as no animals have been domesticated in modern times, scientists have had to guess about the process. To use a tamable species would be only the beginning, for there *is* a difference between a tamed wild animal and one that is domesticated. The difference has been described by R. H. N. Smithers, who kept tamed specimens of *F. libyca*. Their offspring were as wary of human beings as if they had grown up in the wild; they dived for cover whenever people approached. It was impossible to train them not to steal food from the table; and when Smithers smacked them, they didn't jump down as domestic cats do, "but stood their ground, laying their ears back, spitting, showing their teeth, and trying to bite." When he crossed African wild cats with domestic cats, however, the progeny "turned out to be splendid house cats, great hunters, easy to handle."

No such happy outcome attends the crossing of the European wild cat with the domestic cat. Frances Pitt says,

> These two cats will mate and their offspring are fertile, but the hybrids show almost complete dominance of the wild-cat type. They are rusty-hued tabbies with thick tails ringed with black, which tails terminate more abruptly than the domestic cat; and they inherit the . . . disposition of the wild cat, besides being nervous and queer-tempered. My crossbreds could not be trusted free after they were half-grown, because they attacked poultry and ducks. Had I not shut them up, they would have been off to the woods.

Domestication, then, involves a genetic change. It obviously did not occur in *F. silvestris*, but is dominant enough in the domestic cat to override whatever equivalent gene or genes are present in *F. libyca*. Mutations that result in behavioral changes are poorly understood, but it is postulated that the probable mutation was one that suppressed the development of certain adult behaviors. The wild cat is an asocial animal except when mating, moth-

FIGURE 3. *Top: African wild cat (F. libyca); center: European wild cat (F. silvestris); bottom: domestic cat (F. catus). The African wild cat is believed to be the progenitor of the domestic cat, which may have acquired its tabby stripes from the European wild cat.*

ering a litter, or growing up in one. Leyhausen has noted that house cats' overtures to human beings come largely out of the repertoire of feline behavior associated with those periods. In the ancestral line, a gene or genes that normally controlled a maturational process must have been defective, thus producing an animal that was not afraid of human beings and could adapt to their ways.

Such a change would not necessarily have been a disadvantage in the wild. Modern cats have been much more changed by domestication—their legs are shorter than those of their wild relatives, their skulls and dentition are a bit different, and they breed more often—but even so they can look after themselves with fair success when they are abandoned by man. So it is reasonable to suppose that the basic alteration in some African wild cats' attitude toward human beings could have long gone unnoticed in the wild population.

Dogs have been domesticated for at least 10,000 years; cats, for no more than 5,000 years and probably much less. There are Egyptian representations of cats from as early as 2600 B.C., but there is no way to tell whether they were domesticated. Better evidence comes from a tomb dating from 1900 B.C. in which the bones of seventeen cats were found along with a group of little pots for offerings of milk. Positive evidence of domestication is abundantly available from 1600 B.C. onward. Many tomb paintings show cats sheltering under their owners' chairs. They are pictured eating fish, gnawing bones, and playing with other animals. In one painting, a cat is tied to the chair leg with a red ribbon.

As F. E. Zeuner points out, by 1600 B.C. the Egyptians had been taming and using wild animals for more than a thousand years. If there had been available to them a species of cat capable of being domesticated, they would surely have used it too. So the late appearance of house cats in Egypt may mean that the mutation which made domestication possible occurred in just one place and took many years to spread or to be noticed by human beings. Zeuner says the Egyptian cat may have been "for a long time an intruder who entered human habitations in search of small rodents, and was suffered in the villages because of its usefulness, without being bred in captivity." Indeed, it is quite possible that cats domesticated themselves, doing exactly what the other cats of history had done: finding an unexploited ecological niche and making it their own.

That explanation, although in the form of a fable, was put forth by Kipling in his *Just So Stories*. It is a shame that Kipling's cat that walked by himself is remembered primarily as the prototype of feline independence and aloofness, because the substance of the story makes another point. The domestication of Man, Kipling says, was the doing of Woman ("Wipe your feet, dear, when you come into the Cave, and now we'll keep house"). Woman also domesticated Wild Dog, Wild Horse, and Wild Cow, all of whom cheerfully bound themselves over to their new masters in exchange for food and shelter. Wild Cat was different. He insinuated himself into the Cave, where he was initially unwelcome, by amusing the baby and by killing mice. He exacted payment (the right to sit by the fire for ever and ever and the right to be given milk there) but refused to give up his freedom as the other animals had done.

Whenever it was in real and not imaginary time that the Egyptians recognized the domestic cat as a new species, they must have felt as if they had received a gift from the gods. Cats were kin to lions, and lions had long been venerated for their ferocity and were also identified with the sun god. On a crystal cup dating from 3100 B.C., there is a picture of the lion-headed goddess Mafdet, and in papyri of later dates the sun god Re appears in the form of a giant cat with a knife in his fore paw; he is beheading Apop, the serpent of darkness who was believed to try each day to swallow the sun and therefore deprive mankind of its benefits. (See Figure 4, p. 77.)

From around 2000 B.C., there were two lion-headed goddesses, both daughters of Re. Sekhmet had dominion over the destructive aspects of the sun, therefore she represented wrath and vengeance. Her sister Bastet, who came more and more frequently to be depicted with a cat head, stood for the benevolent aspects of the sun and by extension oversaw the welfare of all growing things. One prayed to Bastet for fertility in fields and women, and also for good health.

Apparently, Bastet was just one of a crowd—and the Egyptian pantheon was indeed crowded!—until pharaohs of Libyan origin, who worshiped Bastet, ascended the throne about 1000 B.C. They made the city of Bubastis (today, Tell Basta) their capital and the center of Bastet's cult. Domestic cats therefore became sacred to her, and were memorialized in every imaginable pose and medium. The museums of the world are full of 3,000-year-old cats painted on papyrus and plaster, engraved on ivory, sculptured in gold, bronze, stone, wood, or faïence. In size, these images range from monumental temple figures to tiny pieces used for the ancient Egyptian equivalent of chess. Cats appeared in bas-relief on amulets which young married women hung as icons on the walls of their houses, praying to Bastet for the same number of children as the cat on the amulet had kittens. Cats were valued so highly that to kill one was to court the death penalty oneself.

And when, in the fullness of time, these holy cats *did* die, they were buried with the same ceremony accorded human beings. Patricia Dale-Green, in *The Cult of the Cat*, describes the procedure: "The cat's body was placed in a linen sheet and carried amidst bitter lamentations by the bereaved to a sacred house where it was treated with drugs and spices by an embalmer." A poor man's cat, she says, was rolled in a piece of plain linen, "but the rolling was carefully and respectfully carried out." A rich man's cat was encased in strips of colored linen, wound and pleated into elaborate patterns. The head was covered with a papier-mâché mask whose eyes were sewn-on linen disks; ears were formed from the midribs of palm leaves.

The body then went into a mummy case, sometimes with a painted cat face at the top, the eyes of crystal and gold with black obsidian pupils. Kittens were buried in small bronze coffins. And since cats as well as human beings were expected to live on in an afterworld, food was interred with them. Mouse and shrew mummies have also been found in ancient tombs. Collections were taken up among the populace to pay for the sumptuous funeral rites of cats who had served in temples.

The most famous of the cat cemeteries was, of course, at Bubastis. The Greek historian Herodotus visited the city in 450 B.C. and described the magnificence of its temples and ceremonies. He reported that it was the usual practice for Egyptians to send their cats there for burial, but a much later historian disagreed. In 1841, the British archaeologist J. Gardner Wilkinson said, rather testily, "Bodies of cats were embalmed and buried at Thebes and other towns where the rites of Pasht [Bastet] were duly observed: and if some individuals preferred, from a bigoted fancy or extravagant affection, to send the body of a favourite to the Necropolis of Bubastis, it was merely a caprice, in no way arguing a common custom." No one today knows how many cats were buried there or at Beni Hasan, the location of the other major feline cemetery. But it is a good thing that some people did place their pets in family vaults, for the cats in the great necropolises had a demeaning end.

William Martin Conway quotes an eyewitness to the 1888 discovery of the Beni Hasan cats, who were exposed when a farmer happened to dig into their burial ground. Village children helped themselves to the contents, taking the mummies down to the riverbank to sell them to passing travelers, "often playing or fighting with them on the way [until] the path became strewn with mummy cloth and bits of cats' skulls and bones in horrid profusion, and the wind blew the fragments about and carried the stink afar."

The bulk of the cemetery's contents, however, was sold for fertilizer. "Men went systematically to work, peeled cat after cat of its wrappings, stripped off the brittle fur, and piled the bones in black heaps a yard or more high, looking from the distance like . . . rotting haycocks scattered on the sandy plain." The British Museum today has a skull specimen taken from a consignment of nineteen tons of mummified cat bones which were sent to England for conversion into fertilizer. It has been estimated that if each skeleton weighed about eight ounces, that consignment alone represented nearly 80,000 cats.

The earlier Egyptians, however, had not only cherished their cats—they had guarded them. Although some were smuggled out of Egypt along the trade routes, their export was in general prevented for at least a thousand years after they are known to have been domesticated. (An ivory statuette *c.* 1700 B.C. has been found in Palestine; a fresco dating from 1500 B.C. and a somewhat later terra-cotta head have been found in Crete; and there are representations of cats in Chinese art from about 1100 B.C.—but there is no certainty that any of those pictured cats was domesticated.) Zeuner says that Egyptians traveling abroad acquired any cats they found in other countries and brought them back to their homeland.

The house cat seems to have been unknown in ancient Greece. At least, the language had no word for "purr." At most, cats were novelties; else why would Herodotus have been so fascinated by their place in Egyptian life when he visited there in the fifth century B.C.? Ferrets were kept as mousers, and in fact it is the Greek word for that animal—*ailouros*—which has somehow been transmuted into the English words for cat lover (ailurophile) and cat hater (ailurophobe). The first evidence of domestic cats in

Greece appears on a marble bas-relief dating from 500 B.C., which is now in the Athens Museum. The cat is on a leash, as is the dog which it is confronting. The owners of the animals and two bystanders are leaning forward with such eager interest that it is obvious none of them is quite sure what will happen when cat meets dog.

There is no record of cats in India until after the second century B.C., and not until the first century A.D. do European writers make much mention of them. One has to conclude that the embargo placed on the export of cats was highly effective. Even after the Romans completely subdued Egypt, the cat was not well known in Italy. A first-century mosaic from Naples shows a cat attacking a bird, but there is no proof of its domestication. No feline remains were found in the ruins at Pompeii. As late as the fourth century, in fact, the Roman writer Palladius was recommending cats—in the spirit of a housewife who has discovered a useful new product—as an alternative to polecats (a relative of the ferret) for ridding artichoke beds of moles. He would not have done so had the cat been commonplace.

There are tales of cats being taken to the British Isles and western France by seafarers from the Mediterranean, but no remains have been found that predate the Roman settlements. Cat bones from the fourth century have been dug up at Silchester in Hampshire, where cat footprints were also found on tiles that had been laid out to dry by the kiln. Another cat from the same period was discovered at a Roman townsite in Kent; a fire had destroyed the house of its owner, trapping the cat in the basement. Because most of the skeleton was preserved, that find was useful in assigning a rough timetable to the progress of domestication. The mummified Egyptian cats are approximately the size and structure of *F. libyca*, but this British cat of about 1,200 years later is somewhat smaller and its skull is beginning to show the foreshortening that is characteristic of modern domestic cats.

Because it took such a long time for cats to appear in any significant numbers in Europe, present-day scholars believe they were never bred and sold as a commercial commodity like horses or cattle. Some, of course, were taken to distant places by colonists. But from either an original or a new home spot, they then distributed themselves by "moving from house to house, from village to village, until they gradually took possession of the whole continent." (The words are Konrad Lorenz's.)

A group of modern geneticists would agree. They are reconstructing the migrations of long-ago cats by comparing the color, type, and patterns of feline fur in different populations today. This is possible for three reasons: the majority of cats do not stray very far from their place of birth—a few miles, perhaps, but not hundreds; the majority of cats make random choices of mates and in that respect resemble any wild population; and all cats, like all people, carry in their chromosomes exact duplicates of genes which were also carried by their ancestors of thousands or even millions of years ago. By comparing related species, one can identify some of the genes which have been added, subtracted, or changed by mutation in the course of descent from a common ancestor.

The fur color which is most common in wild carnivores is agouti, each hair being brown or black with a yellow tip; the overall effect is a uniform gray-brown color. (The fur of such animals is called "ticked.") To this was added, at some point in prehistoric time, a gene for dark spotting in the fur of cats, and in some of them it later mutated into a gene for striping. (Such mutations would have been, and are, good camouflage for forest-living animals.) Later yet, a gene arose which prevents the formation of pigment and therefore causes white spotting. These are only a few examples of the many genes—perhaps forty—which control some aspect of fur color, pattern, length, or texture. In cats, it is primarily such variations that distinguish one individual from another.

Every animal inherits two forms of any gene, one from each parent; these are called alleles. External appearance depends on which of the two genes for any trait is dominant and which is recessive. The gene for white spotting in cats, for example, is dominant. Regardless of what partner gene is present, a cat who carries the allele for white spotting will show it. In contrast, the "Siamese" gene is recessive. It can be overridden by any dominant allele, and only when a given cat has two "Siamese" genes does it have the light body, dark tips, and blue eyes which are characteristic of the breed. (That's why a purebred Siamese female who manages to get out of the house when she is in heat and mates with a black tomcat will not produce any Siamese kittens—unless there are some recessive Siamese genes in the tom's lineage.)

Given a random sample of cats from a certain place, one can compute gene frequencies for the entire population of the area. About thirty years ago, the British geneticist J. B. S. Haldane suggested that this should be done on a world-wide basis, using a number of traits whose mode of inheritance is well known. A. G. Searle launched the project with a study of London's cats in 1949, then did a similar survey of Singapore's cats in 1959. Since then, many other scientists have followed suit. Gene frequencies have been recorded for cats in Great Britain, France, The Netherlands, Italy, Greece, Cyprus, North Africa, Turkey, Iceland, the United States, Mexico, Brazil, New Zealand, Australia, and Thailand. There are still great geographic gaps, however; for one example, no censuses have been taken in the great land mass stretching between Turkey and Malaysia.

The census takers have roamed far afield, none farther than the French zoologist Philip Dreux, who made several trips during the 1960's to the Crozet Archipelago in the South Indian Ocean to help plan a scientific research station on Possession Island. The majority of research outposts in the French Southern and Antarctic Lands are on Kerguelen Island in the Kerguelen Archipelago; about ninety people are stationed there. When Dreux's ship stopped over at Kerguelen, he took the opportunity to count cats.

On Courbet Peninsula alone he saw thirty-six cats, all wild, of whom thirty-five were black or black with white spots. Dreux believes that they descended from a cat—one pregnant female would have been enough—or cats who were washed ashore from a wrecked ship. The single cat who differed from the others was a gray tabby. This one, Dreux thinks, may be the result of a mating with a pet cat currently in residence at the research station. The others exemplify animals' ability to adapt themselves to a harsh environment quite unlike the one in which their species evolved.

Dreux did his sightings from a helicopter; the other cat watchers have sat in public parks, in village plazas, on the docks of seaside towns; have examined cats in city pounds; or have conducted door-to-door surveys in suburban areas. The censuses that have been taken during the past few years have been correlated by Neil B. Todd of the Carnivore Genetics Research Center at Newtonville, Massachusetts. Much material remains to be analyzed, but some differences have already been recorded which support the theory that feline migrations have been largely self-propelled, unless the hand of man has intervened.

Consider, for example, the mutation that produces cats with six or more toes (polydactylism). This gene is carried by about 4 percent of Salem cats and 7 percent of Boston cats, but in New York and Philadelphia the frequency is respectively .01 percent and .09 percent. Todd believes that the mutation appeared in the Boston area in the early eighteenth century, and since then has been slowly diffusing beyond the borders of the original Massachusetts Bay Colony. The New York and Philadelphia figures indicate just *how* slowly a mutation normally spreads.

Another mutant gene whose rate of travel can be documented is "blotched" tabby, an allele of the ancestral striped tabby pattern, in which the stripes are very broad and are often broken into whorls and spirals. (See the middle cat in Figure 11.) Blotched tabbies were common in England in the seventeenth century and were therefore among those brought to New England by the colonists. In modern Boston, 42 percent of cats have this gene. But in the San Francisco area and in Dallas, the corresponding figure is 27 percent, in Houston it is 29 percent, and in Mexico City it is 23 percent. Only in the relatively new Western cities that were settled by Anglos— Phoenix, for instance—is there a high frequency of blotched tabby. In Mexico, in the old Texas towns, and along El Camino Real, modern feline populations derive from cats imported to the New World from Spain in the sixteenth century, and in sixteenth-century Spain there were very few blotched tabbies.

The place of origin and rate at which this particular pattern has spread have been traced by the cat census takers. Consider its geographic distribution in Europe: 81 percent in London, 78 percent in Paris, 60 percent in The Hague, 47 percent in Rome, 29 percent in Vienna, 26 percent in Athens, 15 percent in Ankara, and 33 percent in Izmir. The blotched tabby allele must have originated in England and has been spreading eastward ever since. Todd says the rate of spread suggests that the mutation dates from the tenth century.

But, wait: the census figures show a discrepancy. Izmir and Ankara are about equidistant from Istanbul (the presumed port of entry for cats coming from Europe), so why is blotched tabby twice as common in Izmir as in Ankara? The probable explanation lies in the fact that Ankara is inland and Izmir is a seaport. It must have acquired a pool of new genes from cats whose home ports were in northwestern Europe but who jumped ship in Turkey.

Indeed, there is always a strong presumption that human beings were the agents of transport when a given genetic trait is much more common in one locality than in adjacent areas. That is probably why there are exceptionally large numbers of six-toed cats in Nova Scotia and New Brunswick. In Halifax, for instance, the frequency of polydactylism is 7 percent. It is believed that the gene was carried to the Maritime Provinces by Loyalists who emigrated to that part of Canada after the Revolutionary War, bringing pets along with their household goods. In New England, it has taken more than 200 years for the gene, transmitted by cats moving at a walking pace from village to village, to travel 300 miles. Had it not been for the ships that bore their common ancestors to Canada, that particular line of cats wouldn't have made it to Halifax until at least the twenty-fourth century.

CHAPTER 6

Ups and Downs

THE ANCIENT Egyptians and Chinese both created lovely onomatopoeic words to label the cat: in Egypt the word was *miu* and in China it was (as it still is) *mao*. In early Latin, the word was *felis*, but it did not mean "domestic cat" because the species wasn't common in Italy until well after the beginning of the Christian era. By the fourth century, when it had become desirable to distinguish domestic cats from other kinds of cats or from other kinds of mousers, the word *cattus* was coined. It is thought to derive from the Nubian word *kadis*, as would have been appropriate, considering the domestic cat's place of origin. The modern Arabic word is *qittah*.

In all but one of the European languages, the word for "cat" has a similar sound. The fourth-century Greek *katta* has become *kata*, and the *Kazza* of Old High German is today's *Katze*. The Old English *catte* has lost a couple of letters, but the Old French *chat* is intact. In modern Spain, the word is *gato*; in Italy, *gatto*; in Poland, *kot*; and in Russia, *koshka*. The exception occurs in Romania, where the word for cat is *pisicca*. Etymologists believe it to be a derivative of *pis*, a call word for cats, like the English "puss." As for "puss," it is thought to come from Pasht, another name for Bastet. And there we are again, back in Bubastis, in 1000 B.C.!

It wasn't until the end of the fourth century A.D. that Bastet was officially swept away, when Theodosius I outlawed paganism. But each religion absorbs elements of the religion it replaces, and Christianity was no exception. It incorporated into the character of the Virgin Mary the benevolent qualities of Bastet and the other fertility goddesses: their chastity, their love of women and children, their concern for the welfare of the family. Bastet's cat was Christianized too. It appears often in paintings of the Annunciation and of the Holy Family (this latter because an old Italian legend says that a cat gave birth in the Bethlehem stable at the same moment Mary did). It became the "good" cat of Christian myth, the animal created by God in response to the Devil's creation of the mouse.

Christianity also incorporated a "bad" cat. Not that it had started out that way; in its original form, it was as benign as Bastet's cat. The moon goddess Diana had created it, the story went, in response to the creation of the lion by her twin brother, the sun god Apollo. To ridicule his beast, Diana made a miniature copy of it, the cat. (See Figure 4.) It was this cat, identified as Diana was with the radiance of moonlight, which figured in other myths as the cat-moon who devoured the gray mice of twilight.

With time, however, Diana also came to represent the dark phase of the moon. She acquired the attributes of Hecate, the goddess of the underworld, who presided over the evil deeds that were committed when the earth was wrapped in darkness. This association was to become an unfortunate one for Diana's cat when it became a part of Christendom; *its* fate was to appear in pictures of the Last Supper, sitting always at the feet of Judas.

During their early centuries in Europe, cats, being scarce, were perceived by man in their "good" aspect. There remains from about the fifth century in Ireland a list of goods which were considered to be especially useful to housewives, and cats appear on the list. There is also a picture of a cat in the *Book of Kells*, which dates from the ninth century. Cats were much more pleasant than ferrets to have around the house, and they caught mice with great enthusiasm and skill. As Chaucer said:

> *Lat take a cat, and fostre hym wel with milk*
> *And tendre flessche, and make his couche of silk,*
> *And lat hym see a mous go by the wal;*
> *Anon he weyvith milk, and flessche, and al,*
> *And every deyntee that is in that hous,*
> *Swich appetyt hath he to ete a mous.*

FIGURE 4. *Top: Egyptian papyrus depicts the cat as sun, the serpent as darkness. Center: The moon goddess Diana creates the cat to mock the sun god Apollo's lion. Bottom: The Halloween cat represents wicked deeds done in the dark of the moon.*

In tenth-century West Wales, a hamlet was legally defined as a place that contained nine buildings, one herdsman, one plow, one kiln, one churn, one bull, one cock, and one cat. Thus the authorities provided for the shelter of the people, the safety and proliferation of their livestock, the planting of their crops, the protection of their harvest. The value of their cats was codified too. From birth until its eyes opened, a cat was worth a legal penny; from then until it began to kill mice, it was worth two pence; and as a seasoned mouser, it was worth four pence. (Bear in mind that the penny was the value of a lamb, a kid, a goose, or a hen.) If a husband and wife separated and they owned only one cat, *he* got it. If convicted of killing someone else's cat, the offender had to give its owner either a sheep with her lamb or the amount of corn that would cover the cat when its corpse was suspended by the tail with its nose just touching the ground. In Saxony, in the twelfth century, the king set a fine for the same offense and in the same currency: for the loss of an adult cat, its owner got sixty bushels of corn. It could not be coincidence that the payment was in grain, the crop that cats protected from mice and rats.

The legend of Dick Whittington fits nicely into the history of a continent where rodents were a plague and cats a rarity. Although the English version of this tale dates from the sixteenth century, there are variants which go back to Venice in the twelfth century and perhaps even to tenth-century Persia. But it is the English Dick who is familiar to most of us, poor-but-honest Dick Whittington who went to London to seek his fortune, married the boss's daughter, and rose in wealth and status to become the Lord Mayor of London.

Whittington was a real person; he lived between 1358 and 1423. But no one knows whether he really owned a cat for which a king in Barbary, whose realm was infested with rats, paid a fortune in jewels. Whittington's cat didn't turn up in print until a hundred years after Whittington's death. Historians now tell us that small coal-carrying coasters were once called cat boats, and that Whittington's wealth may in fact have been built on Newcastle coal which he shipped to London. In support of this theory, Carl Van Vechten quotes a riddle which used to be current among North Sea pilots. "When did the mouse catch the cat?" it asks. The answer: "When the cat [collier] ran aground on the Mouse [a sandbank in the estuary of the Thames]."

The cat in the Whittington story is realistic, but it has the literary company of many cats who are cats in name only. As embodiments of human virtues or vices, they walk and talk their way through fables and folk tales which go back a thousand years. In the earliest of these, cats are not stereotyped as villains. Aesop's cats, for example, appear in their natural roles as predators. (His most famous cat is the one whom a group of young mice decide to bell, as a warning device for them, until a sage old mouse asks which of them will do the belling.) And in the twelfth-century beast epic whose central figure is Reynard the Fox, the cat character is a naive and trusting soul named Tybert, who is easily outwitted by the fox.

By the seventeenth century, however, the cat had become the sly creature personified in Charles Perrault's "Puss in Boots," that clever rogue who turns a nobody into a nobleman and marries him off to a princess. At about the same time, and also in France, the poet Jean de La Fontaine had begun to publish his *Fables*. Although based on Aesop and other traditional sources, La Fontaine's fables are much more sophisticated than any of the originals and often carry morals which apply to the seventeenth-century political or social scene instead of merely to individual human behavior.

One of La Fontaine's memorable cats, for example, is a judge who is asked by a weasel and a rabbit to decide which of them has the better claim to a particular burrow. The cat, saying he is old and hard of hearing, persuades the animals to come close to him, then kills and eats them both. La Fontaine concludes the fable by saying that this is what sometimes happens to the rulers of small countries when they ask the rulers of larger and more powerful ones to arbitrate their cases.

La Fontaine also gives us the rascally but stupid cat who is conned by a monkey into pulling hot chestnuts out of a fire. The monkey eats them all and the cat singes its paws. Moral: "So too with princelings when they undertake/ To burn their fingers for a monarch's sake." Today, there aren't many princelings of the sort La Fontaine had in mind, but there are plenty of second-echelon corporation executives who are wary of "pulling someone else's chestnuts out of the fire" and who understand very well what it is to be a "cat's paw."

In the nineteenth and twentieth centuries, human caricatures in cats' clothing became less stereotyped. There are good cats and bad cats, bold cats and gentle cats, dreamers and schemers, in works by Balzac, Stahl, Hoffman, H. H. Munro, Colette, and Don Marquis; and in children's books by Lewis Carroll, Beatrix Potter, and A. A. Milne.

Many generations of children have also recited

> Hey diddle diddle,
> The cat and the fiddle,
> The cow jumped over the moon;
> The little dog laughed
> To see such sport,
> And the dish ran away with the spoon.

Why a cat with a *fiddle?* Was the idea inspired by The Cat and Fiddle inn sign, one of great antiquity in England? Among the hostelries that still display the sign is an inn located in a Hampshire town called Hinton Admiral; Frederick Sillar and Ruth Meyler say this inn was listed in the *Domesday Book* (1085) as the home of one Catherine la Fidèle. Another possible source, also an inn, was owned by a Frenchman who named it À la Chatte Fidèle, after his pet cat, Mignonette. Well, perhaps . . . but inasmuch as cats with fiddles appear frequently in medieval church wood carvings, one suspects that the pairing had some religious symbolism. St. Catherine (she who broke the wheel) was an exceedingly popular saint during the Middle Ages, and would surely have merited the adjective *fidèle.*

The animal fables are moral tales, intended to instruct and amuse. They are quite distinct from the horror stories in which cats also figure. In some of these, cats materialize out of darkness, the personified agents of evil. Both King Arthur and St. Brendan had to conquer such monster cats. Demons in feline form appear too in Japanese folklore, an Oriental equivalent of Western Europe's dragons, demanding from the populace the tribute of a lovely maiden. In many countries, cats were said to lead the souls of the dead to the underworld; or they came up from the underworld to identify the wicked, Poe's black cat being a modern example.

Such tales arose from the myths which connected Diana to the dark phase of the moon. Any devotee of Diana could also change form, just as the moon does. The world's folk tales are full of women who change themselves into cats, roam abroad through the night, and at dawn slip back into bed in human form. Most of the women in these stories are practicing simple deceit (they are usually off to meet a lover), but such tales of transformation contain the basic material for converting the wanderers into witches with wicked designs on others.

In the early centuries of the Christian era, the Church correctly considered the beliefs embodied in such stories as remnants of paganism which could best be discouraged by labeling them as superstition. There was plenty of *that*, as indeed there still is; our collective subconscious clings stubbornly to beliefs bred into us before the dawn of time. In both Europe and Asia, superstition maintained the link between cats and the aspects of life which the cat-goddesses had once controlled. Both the Scots and the Japanese discovered that tortoiseshell cats could foretell storms. The English discovered that cats could sour milk and bring down plagues of insects to destroy the crops. The Indonesians used cats as rainmakers, carrying them in procession three times around a parched field and then dunking them in water to be sure they understood what was expected of them. Western Europeans assured themselves of good harvests by burying a living cat in each newly planted field. Eastern Europeans believed that lightning bolts were the efforts of angels to exorcise the evil spirits which took possession of cats during thunderstorms. Cats were therefore hustled out of doors as soon as a storm broke; if the angels were going to hit anything, it had better not be the house.

To believe in witches was equally fanciful, said the early Church. But the later Church said just the opposite. By the thirteenth century, witches were *real*. This switch came about because people had begun to lose faith in the structure of medieval thought and therefore in the structure of society, and the Church needed a scapegoat for the things that were going wrong with the world. It hit on witchcraft, lifted it to the level of an organized conspiracy, and thereby transformed witches from legendary dabblers in sorcery into dangerous enemies of the state. Cats became guilty by association.

The war against the Devil was not a cynical tactic for controlling the masses; it grew out of a gradually developing paranoia which gripped the ruling classes as firmly as the peasants. At the height of the European witch hunts, *everybody* wondered whether an unfamiliar cat on the premises was just a cat or whether it was a witch who had come to cast a spell on someone in the household.

The order of Knights Templars was among the earliest victims of the new demonology. This great charitable foundation, organized in the twelfth century to protect pilgrims to the Holy Land, later separated itself from Church control, became rich and powerful, envied and hated. It was pulled down in the fourteenth century by accusations of heresy, treachery, and immorality. Among the charges to which its members pleaded guilty was that they worshiped the Devil in the form of a black tomcat.

In the course of the next three centuries, Europeans hunted witches from Scandinavia to Spain and finally in Colonial America. There *were* heretical sects whose members *did* use cats in their ceremonies, but the heavy hand of the Inquisitor landed also on individuals who were easy targets for denunciation simply because they were old or ugly or defenseless. In seventeenth-century Denmark, for example, a young woman was prosecuted for bearing a child with the head of a cat. The baby probably had that congenital malformation of the brain which is called anencephaly, but in the supercharged atmosphere of the witch hunts, such a deformity could easily have "proved" that the mother had consorted with the Devil.

And in the Swedish town of Mohra, more than 300 children were hailed into court in 1699 as witches. According to Agnes Repplier's account, they testified that

> the Devil gave to each of them . . . a young cat, its duty being to steal the butter, cheese, milk and bacon which constituted their simple offerings to the Prince of Darkness. These thievish cats accompanied them to the palace of Satan, and shared such entertainment as was given them. Fifteen children were executed, thirty-six were whipped every Sunday for a year before the church doors, and others were punished with varying degrees of severity.

Inasmuch as torture was allowed when examining accused heretics, witches invariably confessed to their alleged crimes, and these confessions further bolstered the public's belief in witchcraft. There are thousands of trial transcripts from the sixteenth and seventeenth centuries which make it perfectly clear that the ability to change one's form from human to feline was accepted as fact, and was also accepted as evidence of witchcraft. On the witness stand, witches were compliant, even garrulous: they repeated the incantations by which they transformed themselves into cats or turned their cat-familiars into demons. An English witch confessed to attempting to shipwreck King James and Queen Anne while they were en route to England from Denmark. (The reason she was unsuccessful was that their faith was stronger than her evil will.) Other witches admitted to the destruction of farmers' livestock, to rendering women infertile, to killing children by sucking away their breath. When they were finally burned at the stake, it surprised nobody to hear that a black cat had leaped out of the flames.

A cat didn't even need a particular witch as a sponsor to find itself suspected of an affiliation with Satan. Cats provided sport and an ecclesiastical lesson for the populace at the coronation of Queen Elizabeth I, when a dozen or so were stuffed into a wickerwork effigy of the Pope, paraded through the streets, and then flung into a bonfire. Their dying shrieks were interpreted as the language of the devils within the body of the Holy Father. All over Europe, on St. John's Day, cats were put into sacks or baskets and were burned in bonfires, the ashes of which were then taken home by citizens as good-luck charms. (The practice continued in France until almost the end of the eighteenth century.) Alternatively, a town could celebrate a holy day, symbolically ridding itself of evil, by tossing cats from a church belfry or putting them into casks which horsemen would run through with swords.

Nor were people cruel to cats alone; they used them to inflict pain on human beings. Several old accounts speak of convicted murderers being put in iron cages or sacks, together with a dozen cats, and then burned to death or drowned, the human victim's death agonies being intensified by those of the cats. Slave owners also practiced a punishment known as "cat-hauling." The miscreant was held or tied down, a cat was placed on his or her bare shoulders and dragged by the tail down the slave's back, of course leaving deep gouges with its claws.

In sum, the overall effect of the witch hunts was to devalue *all* cats. As Edward Topsell said in the seventeenth century, "The familiars of Witches do most ordinarily appear in the shape of cats, which is an argument that this beast is dangerous in soule and body." His contemporaries would have laughed at a law requiring the killer of a cat to pay its owner sixty bushels of corn. Nobody cared if children tied cats together by their tails, hung them over poles, and watched with glee while the frantic animals clawed each other in attempts to escape. In archery, it added an extra dimension to the sport if one confined a cat in a leather case and used it as the target; in *Much Ado About Nothing*, Benedick (describing the punishments he would accept should he forsake bachelorhood) says, "Hang me in a bottle like a cat, and shoot at me."

The cat organ was an even more refined torture. Agnes Repplier says this ingenious device was invented in 1549, in Brussels, for a festival in honor of Philip II. A Spanish nobleman in the royal party reported that "it was carried on a car, with a great bear for the musician. In place of pipes, it had twenty cats separately confined in narrow cases, from which they could not stir. Their tails were tied to cords attached to the keyboard of the organ. When the bear pounded the keys, the cords were jerked, and this pulled the tails of the cats, and made them mew . . ." A picture of a cat organ (without the bear) appears in Gaspard Schott's *Magia Universalis,* a work published in 1657, so that particular form of entertainment must have lasted for at least a hundred years. Cats were also dressed in doll clothes and trained or tricked into meowing in unison; Patricia Dale-Green says the last public cat concert was given in London in 1789.

Perhaps there were fewer witches in France than elsewhere in Christendom. In any case, the French were the first to welcome cats back into polite society. In the middle of the seventeenth century, Cardinal Richelieu was keeping dozens of them at court, and left an endowment to care for those of his cats who survived him. In the early years of the eighteenth century, the Queen—Maria Leszczynska, the Polish princess who married Louis XV—and other titled ladies were lavishing attention and indulgences upon their pampered felines. Medals were struck in their honor; tombs were erected to hold their mortal remains; salons were held to discuss their mysterious attractions. Fashionable French painters—Watteau, Boucher, Chardin, Fragonard—added them to sylvan or boudoir scenes.

But probably the most grandiose effort in their behalf was that of the French astronomer Joseph Jérôme de Lalande. Voltaire had once said, "How can we be interested in an animal who did not know how to achieve a place in the night sky, where all the animals scintillate, from the bears and the dogs to the lion, the bull, the ram, and the fish?" Lalande tried to remedy the oversight.

He was a collaborator of J. E. Bode, the astronomer who headed the Berlin Observatory and who in 1795 began to issue an astronomical atlas in several volumes. Lalande placed hundreds of stars on Bode's charts, and by 1799 had decided that "the large number of stars I supplied to M. Bode gave me some right to shape new constellations. There were already thirty-three animals in the sky; I put in it a thirty-fourth one, the cat." And there it is, in Bode's 1799 volume: Felis, crouching in an astral space between Hydra and Antlia Pneumatica. (See Figure 5.) Lalande said his inspiration for this addition to the zodiac was "a charming poem" about a cat.

Bode's atlas, and therefore Lalande's cat, can still be found in the library of the Paris Observatory, but Felis has vanished from the heavens. In fact, it didn't even last out the nineteenth century. In 1882, in *Les Étoiles et Les Curiosités du Ciel*, Camille Flammarion wrote, "Lalande's cat—the latest constellation created—is more than superfluous and it has disappeared . . . from modern charts. The small stars which were used to form it have returned to Hydra and to the Air Pump [Antlia Pneumatica]."

Across the Channel, cats were also faring better by the end of the eighteenth century. William Hogarth's 1742 painting of the Graham children includes a lively tabby and thus documents British acceptance of cats as members of the best families. (Of that portrait, Kenneth Clark says, "Hogarth enjoyed painting the cat so much that the Graham children look hollow and lifeless beside her. She is the embodiment of cockney vitality, alert, and adventurous—a sort of Nell Gwynn among cats.") People began to tell mawkish stories about cats; for example, that the black cat which had been the stablemate of the great Arabian stallion Godolphin had kept vigil over the horse's body when it died in 1753 and then itself slunk off to die alone in a hayloft. George Stubbs, the great English painter of horses, memorialized that friendship by including the cat in his portrait of Godolphin.*

In the nineteenth century, the sentimental memoir became an established literary form, and many "gentle furry ghosts, lifted to immortality by the human hands that fondled them in life" can still be recalled from works by Théophile Gautier, J. K. Huysmans, Charles Dickens, Thomas Carlyle, and Agnes Repplier (whose words are those quoted just above). She dedicated one of her books to the memory of her cat Agrippina. Queen Victoria's White Heather had her biographers, and so did Theodore Roosevelt's Tom

---

* Race horses still have pet cats. Arthur Thompson, the stall superintendent at Arlington Park Race Track near Chicago, says, "Just about every stable has a pet of some kind, ranging from goats to poultry, but the most popular pet is a cat. They sleep under the feed tubs and nap on the horses' backs. It seems to me that horses and cats have a special affinity for each other." And P. G. Wodehouse's last novel, *The Cat-Nappers*, pitted Bertie and Jeeves against some people who were trying to fix a horse race by kidnapping the favorite's companion cat, the theory being that the horse would then be too despondent to run well.

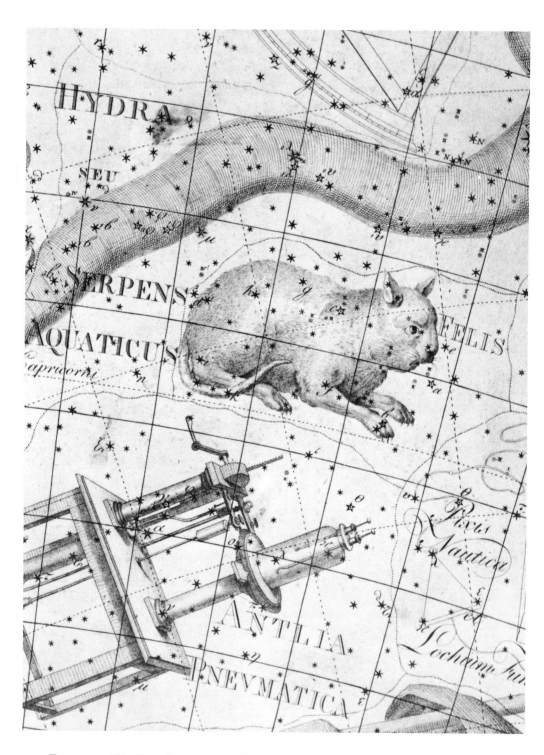

FIGURE 5. *The French astronomer Lalande put a cat into the sky, but his constellation did not survive the nineteenth century. (Photo, from J. E. Bode's 1799 volume of* Atlas Coelestis, *by J. Counil, Observatoire de Paris.)*

Quartz (named after the original in Mark Twain's *Roughing It*). Twain himself had cats with fancy names like Appolinaris and Zoroaster ("to practice the children in large and difficult styles of pronunciation").

But at the same time that the nineteenth-century family magazines were printing sentimental tributes to Our Friend the Cat, the societies for prevention of cruelty to animals were being organized. True, it was the plight of work horses that first excited the humane instincts of animal lovers; in 1900, for example, the A.S.P.C.A. in New York City intervened on behalf of almost 7,500 horses or other large animals which needed to be "suspended from labor" or humanely destroyed. But that same annual report says that 92,721 "small animals, homeless or disabled past recovery," were also destroyed. If modern figures can be applied, approximately half of those animals were cats. *Their* furry ghosts had certainly never been fondled in life by loving human hands. Cats, in short, had acquired their present multiplicity of relationships to people: used by many, loved by some, ignored by most.

Cats had fared better in Asia. As Adolph Suehsdorf says, "Cats do not engage in witchcraft in areas where people do not believe in witches." Outside of Christendom, they were never caught in a crossfire between God and the Devil. In Asia, their main supernatural power was to act as occasional tabernacles for the souls of the dead. The Eastern religions were more aware than Christianity of the unity of man with nature, more concerned with the attainment of virtue than in punishing a lack of it.

The Moslems in particular had a tender spot in their hearts for cats, thanks to Mohammed's being so fond of his cat that he cut off the sleeve of his robe, upon which the cat was sleeping, rather than disturb it. One of his followers, a thirteenth-century sultan who lived in what today is Cairo, bequeathed to the neighborhood's indigent cats the revenue from his orchard. A daily dole, in the form of scraps from local butcher shops, was distributed at the hour of afternoon prayer by each subsequent owner of the property until (it is said) well into the nineteenth century. In Moslem folk tales, cats have the guile of children, never the deceit of habitual criminals. For example: Why do cats close their eyes when drinking milk? (Actually, they keep their eyes open, but legend allows liberties with the facts.) Answer: They close their eyes because if Allah asks them whether they've had their milk they stand a better chance of getting more because they can truthfully answer that they have not seen any.

Chinese astrology features twelve animals whose characteristics infuse an astrological cycle of the years. The cat replaces the rabbit in a related system from Vietnam which Suzanne White explains in her *Book of Chinese Chance*. She says that people born in a Year of the Cat are refined and virtuous, lovers of tradition, discreet, clever, and altruistic. They may also be pedantic, aloof, devious, and oversensitive. Cat people can successfully marry Dog people but not Rat people. The most recent Year of the Cat was 1975; we are now well into the Year of the Snake, and cats must wait until 1987 to control once more the fortunes of human beings.

The Japanese, who imported cats from China in the tenth century, restricted their ownership to the nobility for several centuries and thoroughly pampered them. Lafcadio Hearn says the common name for a pet cat was *tama*, which means "jewel." Although Japanese folklore includes some demon cats, it is far richer in tales of cats who perform deeds of kindness for men or whose presence in a house brings good luck. There have never been cats as sensitively and lovingly drawn as those by Japanese artists. Still in existence in Tokyo is a cat cemetery over which the spirit of a famous folkloric cat presides. She is depicted in endless procession on the temple façade, sitting up and with her right fore leg raised in a gesture of benediction.

Today, Asian cats are no better off than cats anywhere else in the world, but at least they have no history of being tossed into bonfires or stuffed into leather bottles for people to shoot at.

CHAPTER 7

Earning Their Keep

FROM HORSES WE GET leather; from cattle, milk and meat; from sheep, meat and wool; from poultry, eggs and meat and feathers. But cats have virtually no value as commodities.

True, they *have* been eaten. There is, for example, the testimony of Mr. Brooks, the pieman in *The Pickwick Papers*, who "made pies out of everything." During the summer, he told Sam Weller, "fruits is in, cats is out." During the winter, however, all his pies were made from "them noble animals, seasoned for beefsteak, veal, or kidney, 'cording to demand." Cats are probably still eaten in poor countries, whenever people can catch them. But there is no commercial market for cat meat.

Their fur is equally without value. Agnes Laut, an expert on the North American fur trade, said in 1921 that more than 3,000,000 cats were annually being used as trims for cheap coats. (Blacks and browns were the favorites; pelt prices ran from 15¢ to $1.15 according to grade.) Today, given the fact that federal labeling laws require the fur on a garment to be identified, not many women would comfortably wear a coat or suit edged with cat.

There *is* a market, exotic rather than commercial, for cat skin. The Japanese shamisen, a kind of lute which originated in the seventeenth century and is still made for lovers of traditional music, has a squarish body that is covered top and bottom with cat (or dog) skin. William P. Malm, the University of Michigan's expert on the music of the Far East, says that some modern makers of the shamisen have experimented with plastic covers "but that animal skins remain the best for sound."*

Laboratory cats, those which are dissected in college biology classes, and cats used for bioassays should probably be classed as commodities because expendability is inherent in such use. During World War I, Carl Van Vechten says, cats went to sea in submarines as animate detectors of foul air and were introduced into the trenches in France in order to give early warning of gas attacks. Today, they appear in toxicological manuals as the organism of choice for the diagnosis of a little-publicized but prevalent tropical disease, ciguatera poisoning.

There are more than 300 species of tropical fish which at certain seasons of the year become highly toxic, probably as a result of feeding upon certain kinds of algae. Reported as long ago as the sixteenth century, ciguatera poisoning causes severe intestinal pain, general weakness, blurred vision, and sometimes paralysis; the mortality rate is around 7 percent. Bruce Halstead, in summarizing for public health doctors what is known about ciguatera poisoning, assures them that one cannot detect a poisonous fish by its appearance, and advises that a small sample of the fish be fed to a kitten. If the animal is still healthy twelve hours later, the fish can be presumed safe to eat. For this purpose, a mongoose will also do; that's what was used in June of 1974 to diagnose the ailment which felled half the guests at a Hawaiian wedding party for which the menu included kahala sashimi. (Kahala is amberjack; sashimi is sliced raw fish.)

If but a poor case can be made for cats as commodities, can a stronger one be made for them as chattels? Yes, but chattels of an odd sort. We house and feed them, pet them, claim them as ours—yet have no real control over them. We have never been able to breed them to do specific jobs, as we have dogs. Unlike horses, they aren't competitive enough to race or tractable enough to harness. They can't be herded like cattle or sheep. They *do* catch our rats and mice, but at their pleasure, not ours. They also keep us company, when they feel like it, and delight our senses, when they're around. People who are fond of them are happy to settle for what they get.

But many people don't think that's enough. Off and on, for some 200

* If anyone wonders why a reference to stringed instruments does not include mention of catgut, the reason is that the gut used for musical instruments, surgical sutures, and tennis rackets comes not from cats but from sheep. The "cat" in catgut is an Anglicized version of the Arabic word "*kit*," the name of a stringed instrument.

years, they have been saying that cats should be banned from human society, either because they have unpleasant personalities or because they are only marginally useful to us—or both. If these attitudes do not wholly derive from eighteenth-century ideas about the relationship of animals to men, they have certainly been reinforced by them. The sixteenth- and seventeenth-century naturalists viewed animals as animals and men as men; there was a vast distance between them. In the eighteenth century, however, animals began to be anthropomorphized. They began to be judged by the same standards and valued for the same reasons as human beings.

Eighteenth-century intellectuals set great store by "sentiment," that quality of tender and sensitive feeling which opposes itself to cold and calculating reason. The thinking man is an incomplete kind of fellow; he should also be conscious of the emotional needs of others and be generous in his efforts to satisfy them. Eighteenth-century intellectuals also believed in the perfectibility of society via the education of its citizens. They thought that people could be *taught* (generally by example) to become more useful, more productive, more socially responsible. So it is not surprising that the Count de Buffon should have said in his *Histoire Naturelle*, "When his [an animal's] sentiment is delicate, and improved by education, he is then fit to associate with man, to concur with his designs, to aid, to defend, to caress him."

The Count de Buffon was the leading naturalist of his day. The first fifteen volumes of *Histoire Naturelle* were published between 1749 and 1767 and included chapters on the domestic animals. By the time the work was complete (1804), there were forty-four volumes. The set was so popular that it was reprinted many times (and was even reissued in the 1930's, with illustrations by Picasso). The English translation was done by the Scottish printer William Smellie, who was also the editor of the first edition (1771) of the *Encyclopaedia Britannica*. He credits "Bouffon's *histoire naturelle*" as the source of the encyclopedia's articles about animals, which closely follow the original.

Both Buffon and Smellie have good things to say about the horse, upon whom education has conferred the ability "to govern and check the natural vivacity and fire of his temper." The same is true of the dog "when his natural talents have been improved by education." He is "fierce, cruel, and voracious in a savage state; but when civilized and accustomed to live with man, he is possessed of every amiable quality." Even captured lions are "capable of culture," although one mustn't expect too much of them because "their passions are impetuous and vehement [and therefore] it is not to be expected that the impressions of education will at all times be sufficient to balance them."

But there is no excuse for the behavior of domestic cats, who equally with dogs and horses have been exposed to the benefits of association with man. Cats, Buffon says, possess "an innate malice, and perverse disposition, which increase as they grow up." They "easily assume the habits of society, but never acquire its manners." The cat "appears to have no feelings which are not interested, to have no affection that is not conditional, and to carry on no intercourse with men, but with a view to turning it to his own advantage." Furthermore, cats are "averse to any kind of restraint," "are incapable of any system of education," and "act to please themselves only." That is *not* the description of an animal of sentiment, nor of one that is trainable. Small wonder that the rewrite of Buffon in the *Encyclopaedia Britannica* begins by saying, "Of all the domestic animals, the character of the cat is the most equivocal and suspicious. He is kept, not for any amiable qualities, but purely with a view to banish rats, mice, and other noxious animals from our houses, granaries, etc."

A century later, an American ailurophobe echoed the same ideas. In 1895, the Harvard geologist N. S. Shaler wrote a book about domestic animals in which he said the cat "is the only animal which has been tolerated, esteemed, and at times worshipped, without having a single distinctly valuable quality. As it is, in a small way, serviceable in keeping down the excessive development of small rodents [and] by its caresses appears to indicate affection, it has awakened a measure of sympathy which it hardly deserves."

If Shaler had a readership among businessmen, farmers, and government officials, his low opinion of cats' serviceability must have been disputed. From time immemorial cats had waged effective war on rodents. Up to half a grain crop can be lost if a harvest becomes infested with rats or mice. It is no wonder that the farmers, millers, and brewers of the Middle Ages managed somehow to keep *their* cats on the side of the angels. For the same reason, Frederick the Great in the eighteenth century required the citizens of conquered towns to provide him with a levy of cats to protect his army's stores.

By the nineteenth century, the cat's usefulness had even increased. As cities grew, as more records had to be kept, as transportation and communication improved, rats and mice had moved into the new warehouses, railway depots, post offices, and libraries. In response, managers of such places began to acquire cats who would live and work on the premises. Probably the largest such group were the British Post Office cats, members of a corps so venerable that the Post Office Records Department has prepared a mimeographed summary of the Cat System's history. Here are some highlights:

The Cat System was inaugurated in the autumn of 1868, when the Money Order office in London asked the Secretary of the Post Office for two shillings a week to feed three cats. The Secretary authorized their hiring, but refused to pay more than a shilling a week for the support of all three, saying "they must depend on the mice for the remainder of their emoluments." Furthermore, "if the mice be not reduced in number in six months a further portion of the allowance must be stopped." The experiment was a success, either (as the Controller of the Money Order office archly suggested) because the cats knew of the Secretary's threat to reduce their rations or because of "a laudable zeal for the Service."

Many branch offices followed suit. The weekly allowance was six or seven pence per cat—not enough to feed it adequately, even in the nineteenth century, which explains why much of the Post Office's subsequent internal correspondence about cats had to do with their stipends. The branch managers always wanted an increase and the headquarters accountants always resisted one.

Among those whose suits were successful was the Southampton postmaster, in 1873. The employee who was responsible for the cat felt that extra money was needed to compensate him not only for the extra wear on his shoe leather but also for "the loss of dignity when carrying the cat's food through the streets in Her Majesty's uniform." In 1918, it was the stubbornness of the cat in the case that turned the trick. Asked for more money by a London branch-office manager, the accountant said that "an increase from seven pence to a shilling sixpence per week is rather difficult to justify. Is the milk diluted before it is given to the cat?" The branch manager replied that the cat, "having been used to milk alone, will not drink milk and water." In each of those instances, a shilling per week was finally allowed for the cat's upkeep. But not until the 1930's was there an across-the-board raise to that amount for all Post Office cats. Today, inflation has driven up the cats' salaries to £2 per week.

The position has often been hereditary. At the Headquarters Building in London, a long-lived cat named Minnie served from 1938 to 1950 and was succeeded by her son Tibs—a giant of a cat, twenty-three pounds in weight— who died in 1964. He was something of a celebrity, as were several other Post Office cats of the 1960's. They had counterparts in other official establishments—Mike, for example, who for nineteen years welcomed visitors to the British Museum, and Peter, the Home Office cat. Since 1883 there had been a series of black cats who worked in Whitehall, all named Peter. The last of that name held his job for sixteen years—from 1948 to 1964—and was succeeded by a tribute to the Women's Liberation movement, a black female Manx named Peta.

Business firms have also had their famous cats. In the United States in the 1940's, Standard Oil of New Jersey's Minnie Esso got a certain amount of publicity. So, in the 1950's, did the Georgia Power Company's Tom Kilowatt. According to *Animal Facts and Feats*, the champion British rodent destroyers were corporation cats: a female tabby who killed 12,480 rats for the White City Stadium in London during a six-year period and a male tabby who eliminated about 1,000 mice per year from the premises of Shepherd and Sons in Burscough, Lancashire, throughout the twenty-three years he worked for them.

The old order changes, however, even in Great Britain. By the 1960's, the new pesticides and municipal rodent-control programs were making it unnecessary for modern office buildings to have resident mousers. The government's famous "official" cats became little more than mascots. When they died or when they retired (as Peta did, in 1974), they were not replaced. In 1975, after weighing the usefulness of ship's cats against the possibility of their bringing rabies home from their travels, the Royal Navy banned cats from warships. There were already fewer aboard than in the days of sail and wood. Writing in the *Daily Telegraph*, Gerald Bartlett said, "With better standards of hygiene and metal plates in superstructures, the rodent population has diminished, and with it the prevalence of cats."

So there does not seem to be much of a future for cats on Great Britain's public payroll. In the private sector, there and elsewhere in the world, an enterprising cat can doubtless still make a place for itself in a restaurant or grocery store. But job opportunities are shrinking over all, at least in the industrialized nations. In their traditional role of rodent exterminators, cats may one day be as redundant as the ferrets the Greeks used to keep for the same purpose.

The first twentieth-century effort to document the cat's inadequacy as a destroyer of rodents was made by Edward H. Forbush. In 1916, after directing a farm canvass for the Massachusetts State Board of Agriculture, he reported that half of the surveyed farms had both rats *and* cats, and only a third of the cats were known ratters. Many of the rest were said by his respondents to be "absolutely worthless for the purpose"; in fact, Forbush notes that one farmer "was anxious to know about the best rat traps, as the rats had even entered the bird cage and eaten the canary."

The farm felines' record as mousers was better. "The majority apparently catch them," Forbush says in summarizing the survey. "This has been the experience of mankind for centuries, but as mice are easily caught by anyone with energy enough to set mouse traps, the principle advantage of the cat as a mouse trap is that it is 'easy to set.' "

As the State of Massachusetts Ornithologist, Forbush was chiefly concerned with demonstrating that cats are a menace to birds. The monograph in which his farm survey appears is full of pictures of traps (for cats, not rodents) and designs for devices to be installed on trees or around bushes to protect nesting birds and fledglings. The booklet is also full of prose so sonorous that it deserves a modern audience. Here is a sample:

> Animals were domesticated because of their utility to man in his struggle upward from savagery. The sympathy which he feels for his helpers and pets, praiseworthy and important as it is, is a secondary consideration. The claims of the cat to a place in our domestic life rest primarily on the fact that it is supposed to do for us the onerous, petty and disagreeable task of destroying small rodents which for centuries have elected to fasten themselves as parasites on civilization. Insomuch as the creature fails in this, insofar as it destroys other more useful or nobler forms of life, in such measure it becomes evil and a pest.

The final sentence foretells Forbush's conclusion: that cats do not destroy enough rodents to compensate for the damage they do to wildlife. The point is valid, although not in a discussion of the degree to which cats' predation benefits humans, and therefore Forbush will return to these pages in a later chapter.

In 1939–40, C. S. Elton, of England's Bureau of Animal Population, took a more dispassionate approach to the question. As part of a World War II effort to conserve for human consumption as much of each grain harvest as possible, Elton set up several rodent-control programs on Oxfordshire farms, varying the degree to which cats and pesticides were relied upon. He discovered that when a farm has already become home to both rats and cats and each species is equally familiar with the environs, the cats can prevent the farm from being overrun by the rats but cannot wholly eliminate them. If, however, a farm is cleared of rats by trapping or poisoning, the cats can then keep newcomers away from an area about fifty yards around a barn or house. Beyond that distance their policing power declines rapidly, and at distances beyond 120 yards they are ineffective.

Elton also noted that cats whose owners fed them were more dependable, simply because they stayed put. Cats who were expected to subsist entirely on what they caught had no particular reason to hunt rodents on a "home" farm and moved on to fields or woodlands or possibly to other farms. Elton estimated that the cost of keeping them was one-half pint of milk per cat per day, or twenty-three gallons per year. At 1976 farm prices in the American Midwest, that would be about $20 per year.

His conclusion was that cats should be regarded as only *one* component in a farm's rat-control program, as additions to the staff. "To the extent that they keep farm premises free of rats," he says, "they can reduce the labour required for periodic servicing of the whole farm." He also pointed out a psychological advantage of cats over human beings: cats don't get bored, whereas people in the pest-exterminating business *do*.

A related experiment was undertaken in 1957 by David E. Davis, of Johns Hopkins University. To a farm near Baltimore which was regularly used for ecological studies and had one cat in residence, Davis added three more. A system of estimating seasonal fluctuations in the rat population had already been worked out and the usual pattern was known. Davis found that the extra cats caused the rat population to decline about two months earlier than usual. He was never able to compute the actual number of rats killed by the cats in a normal hunting situation, and the same cats who left half-eaten rats around the place refused to kill rats at all when under observation in a laboratory.

No cat owner will be surprised to hear of Davis' difficulties in keeping track of his cats. One of his research purposes was to determine whether the cats' interest in hunting would diminish if they were fed commercial cat food at home. This required regular examination of their feces; but, alas, the investigators couldn't initially find any cat feces. For three months, Davis says, a fruitless search proceeded. Then it was discovered that the cats were defecating in the shavings used in the horse stalls (and these, of course, had been swept out whenever the stalls were cleaned). Sandboxes were then installed. Some of the cats used them some of the time. Finally, the cats were locked up once a week until they produced the needed scats. It then became possible to determine that feeding the cats at home did not diminish their appetite for rats and mice, and for pigeons too (especially the squabs).

In summary, then, people who use cats have confirmed the findings of Leyhausen and other zoologists who observe cats. Cats do help to control rats and mice, but they are not rodent-killing machines. People who currently keep them must therefore (1) be willing to settle for whatever amount of rodent extermination their cat or cats can provide or (2) value their cats for other reasons and consider the killing of rats or mice as a sort of bonus.

A 1964 study by Oliver P. Pearson describes the thoroughness with which a group of country cats destroyed a population of meadow mice on a thirty-five-acre tract of land near Berkeley, California. By the end of the breeding season in June, 88 percent of the mice were gone. Farmers appreciate that kind of help, so one would expect most farms to have cats. Yet only 44.6 percent of rural households in Yolo County (also in California but farther inland than Berkeley) have resident felines, according to a 1974 survey by C. E. Franti and J. F. Kraus, of the University of California at Davis. And the incidence of cat ownership is much lower in the same county's cities and suburbs. Approximately one household in four contains a cat.

Some of the geneticists involved in taking the cat censuses described in Chapter 5 have lately become interested in the sociology of cat ownership. Their inquiries have just begun, but already a pattern is appearing—and it is just the reverse of that found in a famous 1944 study done in Cardiff, Wales, by the zoologist Colin Matheson. Using questionnaires sent home with schoolchildren, he correlated cat ownership with the kinds of neighborhoods in which the schools were located. In blighted old neighborhoods, where rodents were well entrenched, cat ownership was high. Close to the Cardiff docks, for example, 74 percent of households had cats. But in parts of town where housing was newer and there were better sewers and drains, the frequency of cat ownership dropped to as little as 30 percent. The pattern repeated in the nearby town of Newport: 75 percent of households in run-down sections had cats, whereas the figure was 26 percent in a new housing development. In short, more poor people than well-off people kept cats.

In 1975, however, the University of Glasgow's J. M. Clark found cats in no more than 10 percent of households in two blighted old neighborhoods of that city. In two newer and more affluent neighborhoods, though, the frequency of cat ownership was 25 percent and 39 percent. One would expect to find more rats and mice in the two run-down neighborhoods; and, of course, one would also expect to find more stray cats in such neighborhoods. Perhaps the strays do the same work for which the citizens of Cardiff a generation ago kept their own cats. Or perhaps Glasgow's system of refuse disposal and other rat-control measures are so much better than Cardiff's in 1944 that rodents are less of a problem. In any case, people in poor neighborhoods are now less likely to keep cats than those in rich neighborhoods.

That is also true in several cities and towns which have been surveyed in the United States. The Charlestown/Somerville sections of Boston, for example, are old neighborhoods, densely populated, full of multistory, multifamily buildings. The population is lower middle class; many households depend on wages brought home by both adults in the family. Pets can thus be too costly to keep or too difficult to care for. In addition, many landlords forbid them. In contrast, Newton, Massachusetts, is an affluent suburb whose largely professional-class residents can afford the space and privacy of a single-family house and lot. In Newton, only one member of the family customarily works outside the home and the cost of keeping a pet is no deterrent. It is not surprising, then, that in 1975 Neil Todd found cats in only 13 percent of households in Charlestown/Somerville but in 24 percent of households in Newton.

On the other coast, C. Richard Dorn's 1970 survey of Alameda County (on the east side of San Francisco Bay) shows that only 4.7 percent of people who live in multiunit buildings have cats, 11.6 percent of those who live in two-family buildings, and 20.5 percent of those in single-family homes.

By job category, the survey lists 11.4 percent of "service workers and laborers" as cat owners, whereas the figure rises to 20.2 percent among those with "professional, semi-professional and technical" jobs. The percentage of households with cats also increases with the age of children in the family. Only 16.7 percent of cat owners have children under six, 22.5 percent have children between six and twelve, and 24.7 percent have children between thirteen and nineteen.

Market research firms which gather statistics for advertisers also tell their clients that upper-income families and those with older children are most likely to be cat owners.

Such households do not need cats as mousers. Perhaps these "typical" owners simply gave the kids a kitten to play with, in due course found they had raised themselves a cat, and have now become accustomed to its face. Fernand Méry reports a British survey in which cat owners, some of them giving more than one reason, said they kept cats because they were lonely (43 percent), to keep away mice and rats (26 percent), because of a general fondness for animals (21 percent), as company for children (19 percent), and "to make the place look homelike" (5 percent).

Now, what about the people who *don't* keep cats?

While doing his earlier-mentioned demographic surveys, Neil Todd interviewed 546 people who did not own cats. Eighteen percent had no particular reason ("We just don't"); 11 percent said that someone in the family was "allergic"; 36 percent couldn't have any kind of pet because of housing restrictions or some similar limiting factor; and 35 percent refused to have a cat because of what Todd describes as "antipathy, ranging from mild dislike to hate." He expects to explore more fully the basis for that feeling. He'd like to find out whether it is characteristic of particular social groups or personality types or is evenly distributed throughout society.

When Shylock was pressed to give a reason for his determination to have his pound of flesh, he said it was a "humour"; a fancy as inexplicable as the fear some people experience in the presence of a "harmless necessary cat." And indeed some portion of cat haters *can't* explain why they feel as they do. They are simply profoundly uneasy in feline company. But other cat haters are quite explicit as to the source of their aversion. It's the cat's personality. They can't stand its willful ways, its aloofness, its . . .

CHAPTER 8

How Sociable?

. . . sheer perversity.

At the Folies Bergère in Paris, Agnes Repplier once saw an animal act which included dogs, monkeys, and a cat. The cat "condescended to leap twice through a hoop and to balance herself very prettily on a large rubber ball. She then retired to the top of a ladder, made a deft and modest toilet, and composed herself for slumber. Twice the trainer spoke to her persuasively, but she paid no heed, and evinced no further interest in him nor in his entertainment."

The next day Miss Repplier commented on the performance to friends who had seen the show on other nights. One of them said, "The evening I went, the cat did wonderful things; came down the ladder on her ball, played the fiddle, and stood on her head." The other friend was astonished. She said, "The night *I* went, the cat did nothing at all except cuff one of the monkeys that annoyed her. She just sat on the ladder and watched the performance. I presumed she was there by way of decoration."

Even people who have learned to live with their cats' independence of spirit are occasionally exasperated by it, especially if there is a dog in the house. Dogs sit still when one tells them to; cats sit still only while deciding whether to jump to the mantel or into someone's lap. Dogs are ready for a romp whenever their owners are; cats chase balls if they feel like it. A chastised dog grovels and begs forgiveness; a chastised cat stalks haughtily away and grooms itself. It is easy to interpret such behavior as "obsequiousness" or "defiance," as indeed it might be if one were talking about human beings. But both dogs and cats are simply following courses that were set for them long ago by their wild ancestors. Dogs are "social" animals and cats aren't.

Dogs descended from canids—wolves, or maybe jackals—who live in packs. When the social unit is a group, its members organize themselves into hierarchies within which each individual has an established place. The phrase "top dog" is an accurate description of the dominance relationships within a pack; subordinate dogs defer to the superior one. It was easy for men to domesticate dogs because their loyalty to the leader was transferable to the two-legged leader of a different kind of pack.

Group-living animals like to do things together. If a human being yawns, so will his canine pet; it's a household echo of den behavior in the wild. Canids engage in communal yawning as a way of becoming fully alert after a communal nap. A dog anticipates with pleasure any contact with another dog, and wags its tail by way of greeting. Even if a wild canid loses a fight, it must remain associated with the victor, so evolution has built a *quid pro quo* into such animals: if a vanquished dog indicates submission, a victorious dog must refrain from further attack.

Except for lions, wild cats are loners. They don't go in for yawning or much of anything else done in concert. An encounter with another cat is more likely to generate hostility than friendliness. Cats do not wag their tails, and their behavioral repertoire after a defeat does not include ritualized gestures or postures of submission. A cat who has lost a fight with another cat may remain on the field of battle, but its mood is one of watchful waiting— defensive, not submissive—until it has a chance to escape.

Historically, cats have been reputed to be wholly self-sufficient animals, happiest in solitude, caring for none but themselves. Many textbooks say they associate with others of their kind *only* when mating or raising litters, and avoid one another the rest of the time. But no one really knows whether that is true. It is almost impossible to keep cats in the wild under constant surveillance, and conclusions about their social behavior therefore tend to be based on random rather than systematic observation. As Paul Leyhausen says, perhaps the reason many mammals are described as "solitary" is that they can be shot only one at a time. His own belief is that many species have the capacity to live either as individuals or in groups, and that local circumstances may determine what kind of social structure a population will have. He points out that the now-vanished lions of North and West Africa used to live at most in pairs; it is the plains-dwelling lions of East Africa whose prides number twenty or more.

Most of what *is* known about interactions among cats is the result of studying wild animals in captivity, domestic cats in a laboratory, or free-ranging cats in social situations which occur often enough for cat watchers to monitor a series of encounters. Information thus obtained indicates that cats do indeed normally keep other cats at a distance, but they are not complete isolates, even in the wild. If they were, zoos couldn't cage them together. A pair of wild cats can exist in a cage without harming each other, and if they were raised together they may also occasionally behave like friends.

Domestic cats are not enthusiastic about being caged, either, but domestication has bred greater tolerance into them. One can keep half a dozen or more in a laboratory colony and observe how they react to imposed togetherness. One such experiment was done in 1957 by Alan Baron and a group of colleagues at the University of Oregon. Its objective was limited and the setting was unnatural: cats who had already been trained to scoop a piece of meat out of a dish in front of a cage were put into a situation in which four cats had to compete for a single piece of meat. In each of the three groups, dominant cats emerged—an autocrat named Rum and two lesser despots named Walter and Cognac, who occasionally allowed their subordinates to share their food.

Dominance did not correlate with sex, weight, intelligence, or any other quality the researchers could measure. The dominant cats didn't win their place by fighting; in fact, Rum *refused* to fight the occasional subordinate cat who struck out at him. Two of the cats subordinate to Cognac fought each other but never challenged Cognac. The subordinate cats, incidentally, did not acquire a 2-3-4 rank order; each of these small cat societies consisted of one Chief and three coequal Indians. Nor was the ranking permanent. A month and a half after the initial trials, the experiment was repeated. Rum was still the top cat in his group, but Walter and Cognac were replaced by cats who had formerly been subordinates. It was apparent that even in confinement cats do not develop the hierarchical organization that is typical of animals that ordinarily live in groups.

Paul Leyhausen came to much the same conclusion after observing the interactions among twelve cats caged in one large room with an outside run. This was not an experimental setup like Baron's; the object was just to see how a group of cats who were forced to live together would organize themselves. In this group, two cats became dominant; they appropriated the "best" feeding bowl and the "best" sleeping places. But they did not demand subjugation from their inferiors. If a subordinate cat took a sleeping place normally used by one of the dominant cats, its owner did not drive the interloper away. When the animals were all very hungry, they rushed to the feeding bowls together and ate a little, after which the subordinates withdrew from the "best" bowl to allow the dominant cats to feed to repletion. There also developed a pattern of usage of floor space for running or play in which each cat had its "own" time, regardless of rank within the group.

The same behavior occurs in multi-cat households. The dominant cat is most likely to tyrannize the others at feeding time, and may respond to challenges from its subordinates, but does not consistently assert its authority. Dominant cats do not take caught prey away from lower-status cats; in fact, no cat steals another's catch. Boudreau and Tsuchitani note that cats "don't know how to behave toward one another while eating from the same plate [and] will often wait their turn, preferring the possibility of no food to the anxieties and uncertainties of communal feeding." The spasmodic quality of such superior/inferior relationships has led Leyhausen to categorize feline society as one in which "relative dominance" is the norm. (An exception, however, will be noted in the final chapter of this book.)

Cats who are free to roam characteristically tolerate the company of strangers in proportion to some arbitrary measure of distance from home. A cat usually has its own special resting or sleeping place (a particular corner in the barn, a particular room or even a particular chair in the house); a home range, which is the geographical area through which it regularly rambles and which it shares more or less amicably with other cats; and a territory, from which other cats are excluded. Females have small territories, perhaps no larger than the yard surrounding the house they live in, whereas males may defend five acres or more.

In the wild, there is good reason for the establishment of territories. They ensure that the holder has at its disposal an area sufficient to provide for its needs in terms of food and shelter; animals would otherwise spend so much time fighting for the available resources they might not survive. Since most domestic cats do not have to kill their own food or find a cave or cranny to live in, their territorial instincts no longer serve the original ecological function, but they are nevertheless much in evidence.

A cat's aggressiveness in defense of its own turf depends on how close to home it is. Tomcats meeting on the borders of their territories are not as bold as when one has penetrated deeply into the territory of another. In that case, the advantage is always to the cat on home ground because familiarity breeds confidence. (This is true also of a household into which a new cat has been introduced. It is easily intimidated, at least initially, by the cat who already "owns" the place.) A stranger must be exceptionally courageous to successfully challenge a resident cat. The usual outcome is a hasty retreat.

And no wonder! A cat who is defending territory can attack so fast and look so fierce that even large dogs can be routed. Screaming and spitting, ears laid back, tail expanded to twice normal size and the hair along the spine similarly erect, the cat charges the intruder like a whole troop of cavalry. Leyhausen had one cat who regularly bluffed two collies and a husky, but only, he notes, because it was not acting according to dogs' expectations of cats. The dogs, he says, "were in the same position as the cat who is faced by a brown rat. It is not anticipated that prey will attack. The same dog who flees from an attacking cat will seize it and shake it to death if he catches it when it is running away."

Cats pick fights very rarely, but when they do they create such spectaculars of sound and fury that people who are only occasional cat watchers think of them as more belligerent than they really are. Females are aggressors only in defense of territory or to protect a litter (of which, more later). Males fight for territory, as just described; but they also have another style of fighting when they are competing with another male for a mate or when the object is to determine their neighborhood ranking in what Leyhausen calls "the fraternity." When one hears a prowling tomcat making a cry with a peculiarly sweet and plaintive quality—almost a coo—one is overhearing an old boy inviting any young male in the vicinity to come out and test his mettle. The ensuing fights are highly ritualized; they have none of the spontaneous fury of a territorial defense.

The attacking cat is ordinarily very deliberate about opening the en-

FIGURE 6. *Tomcats, whether fighting to determine their own rank in the neighborhood "fraternity" or to win a mate, engage in noisy but ritualized battles. The female who is being fought over does not always choose to mate with the victor.*

gagement. He begins by straightening his hind legs so his rump is as high as possible, then exaggerates the illusion of height by selective erection of the hairs along his backbone; those toward the rump end stand higher and stiffer than those at the head end. He also bushes out his tail, which is held downward and crooked to one side, the purpose again being to increase his apparent size. He stretches his head forward, with his ears spread outward so they appear to the opponent as very sharply pointed triangles. Then he slowly approaches the other cat, all the while growling, yowling, salivating heavily, smacking his lips and chattering. In full battle dress, any cat is a daunting sight to behold; and in this kind of combat the cat who is being attacked has plenty of time to behold.

If the cat who is being attacked is an experienced fighter with a taste for the sport, he duplicates everything his opponent does; the one becomes a mirror image of the other. Cats normally avoid direct eye contact, but when they're fighting, their gaze is direct and unwavering. Taking tinier and tinier steps as they approach each other, both heads now inclined a bit to one side, they finally come abreast, brace themselves for a spring—and freeze. They may hold this adversary position for several minutes, growling and screeching and lashing their tails, but otherwise unmoving.

Finally, one leaps for the neck of the other. The attacked cat immediately throws himself on his back, grabs his attacker with his fore paws and rakes with his hind claws. (In a territorial battle, the attacking cat hits at the intruder with his paws, but in fights to establish male dominance the full arsenal is employed.) Both animals roll about wildly, biting and scratching, to the accompaniment of piercing shrieks. At some mutually sensed stopping point—a human observer can almost hear a bell signaling the end of a round—the two cats pull apart and run a little distance away from each other. Then they repeat the whole performance—a second, third, or as many times as is necessary for one of them to throw in the towel. He signals his defeat by not returning to the field of battle. Thereafter, the same two cats will probably never fight again over the issue of which one is the better man.

Some cats can live out their days without fighting. They may not be challenged or they may be too timid to accept a challenge. A cat does not have to be "dominant" in order to live a good life. The dominant cats in a neighborhood do not attempt to control other cats' activities, and in fact manage to share the common area that is their home range with more courtesy and common sense than many human beings exhibit in analogous situations.

A cat's home range has no specific boundaries; it is simply the area within which there are a number of favorite places which it regularly visits, plus a network of pathways which it travels to get to them. Country cats may range over as much as sixty acres. Suburban and city cats are much more restricted because of such barriers as streets and buildings. In either situation, though, several cats may use the same geographical area as a home range, each having its own special hunting grounds or resting places within it.

Leyhausen has watched how cats whose ranges overlap solve the problem of using the same pathways. One cat, upon spotting another moving along a path, holds back until the other cat has disappeared. If two cats see each other approaching a junction of two paths, both may sit down at a distance from the crossroads and try to outwait the other. One cat may eventually make a fast run across the junction, or both may turn around and go back in the direction from which they originally came. They try to avoid confrontation, even if one of the cats has already established itself as dominant to the other. If, for example, an inferior cat is already walking down a pathway when a superior cat approaches, the superior cat sits down and waits until the road is clear. Nor does it drive an inferior cat away from its own favorite lookout post or sunning spot.

For many small mammals, the mere sight of another of its species is not enough to evoke aggression. That cats know what cats look like has been shown by researchers who have watched feline reactions to pictures of variously shaped abstract forms and animal silhouettes. The usual behavior of a cat in this test situation is to cautiously approach the cat silhouette and then sometimes hiss or spit when the pictured cat fails to respond to its overtures. A cat who sees itself in a mirror also approaches the "animal" it has just sighted in a friendly spirit. Unable to locate a flesh-and-blood cat in front of the mirror, the real cat often searches behind the mirror, and when this fails, it rapidly loses interest.

However, if the animal in the mirror exhibits aggressive behavior, the response will be in kind. R. F. Ewer tells a marvelous story about a tame black-footed cat (*F. negripes*) that had the run of her laboratory. At night, when the room's lights were on, the windows over the lab benches made a fine reflecting surface, and once when the cat jumped onto a lab bench

. . . its own reflection appeared so suddenly that the cat bristled in defense. The reflection did likewise and the animal found himself suddenly launched into a threat duel which ran through the whole gamut of the expressive vocabulary, ending in the pose characteristic of maximal aggressive threat. With two so exactly matched rivals, there was only one possible end to the contest. . . . Having clearly met his match, the animal retreated and jumped down again onto the bench.

He then moved along to a second window, hesitated a moment, bristled slightly and jumped up on the ledge. There, of course, his rival again threatened back and the performance was repeated but this time more briefly and the retreat to the bench was made sooner.

The cat then returned to the first window, hesitated for a while and then, very cautiously, raised his forequarters and peeped over the ledge—where he was just in time to catch his rival doing exactly the same thing. He hastily withdrew and made no further attempt to renew the acquaintance.

Apparently, cats do not recognize particular other cats by sight but depend for identification on the distinctive smell of each individual. Cats who already know each other or have no reason yet to be hostile customarily greet each other with a nose-to-nose smelling ceremony which is the feline equivalent of "Do I know you?"; and then engage in a round of anal sniffing. They also sometimes greet familiar people the same way. A loving cat may stand in its owner's lap so its nose is presented to the human nose, then turn around with its tail up and hind end raised so its anus may be sniffed. People with inhibitions about that section of the anatomy usually grimace and push down the cat's rump, which is as rude as to refuse to shake a proffered human hand.

Michael Fox, summarizing unpublished work by the British scientist R. G. Prescott, says that cats possess scent glands diffusely along the tail, abundantly on each side of the forehead, and also on the lips and chin region. Inanimate objects are marked at certain places and in certain contexts with the tail and lip glands. Marking with the forehead glands accompanies friendly head rubbing. Human beings cannot smell the odors in these glandular secretions, but cats find them very informative.

There are also scent glands around the anus which are the presumed source of the odors disseminated in urine and feces. (People *can* smell these.)

They indicate to another cat whether an animal is male or female and if female whether she is in heat. Only at that time do females spray urine on objects around them, but males routinely place scent marks on trees, walls, posts, automobile hubcaps, or anything else that is stationary. They back up to the object, raise the tail, and eject a stream of urine at exactly the right level to make smelling easy for the next cat who passes by. It is not a random process; scent marks are set on much frequented pathways, at crossing points, at the cat's special places within its home range, and along the boundaries of its territory.

In whatever form, scent marks are not necessarily intimidating to other cats. Leyhausen says he has never seen a cat sniff one and then withdraw from the area. Instead, it uses the information thus obtained to decide whether to chance an encounter with whomever is ahead on the road. The mark tells the investigating cat the sex of the other, whether it is one of the regulars in the neighborhood, and how long since it passed that way.

Some of the scents that cats exude are pheromones, the substances mentioned in an earlier chapter which do more than inform; they also elicit a specific reaction in the animal that smells them. The extent to which feline behavior patterns are primed or released by these substances is unknown. Certainly, the scent of a female in heat encourages a male to pursue her. But can sex pheromones speed up a courtship, for example? Are they necessary to a mating? When Sherman Rosenfeld, a young California biologist, tested the responses of male cats to cotton balls soaked in the urine of females in heat, some uttered the distinctive chirping cry which in effect asks the female if she's ready yet. Females in heat were more responsive to male urine than other females were. Nursing mothers were not interested in the urine of mature males, but responded to that of immature cats. These responses indicate that a cat's own physical state determines its reaction to another cat's scent. So it may well be that in addition to being a general attractant or repellent, scent may play a dynamic role in starting, continuing, or stopping particular activities.

Cats are also affected by their own scent. To the animal who originally set them, scent marks tell him that he has been there before; that this is "his" place. The indoor cat who rubs its chin along the edge of a particular lamp shade is marking its territory as surely as the outdoor cat who urinates on a certain porch post. If another cat has marked the same place, he may put his scent over that of the other, to re-establish dominion. Cats become timid in areas where they find only foreign scent marks and are much readier to flee than cats who have been reassured by the presence of such marks. This is one reason why cats on their home territory have such an advantage over intruders.

Visual marking is practiced too. Both wild and domestic cats scratch trees and posts which are strategically situated along the routes they regularly travel. This urge may be reflected in house cats' predilection for scratching furniture which is high enough for them to attack in a standing position. They also use horizontal scratching posts or the undersides of sofas and chairs for utilitarian claw-sharpening purposes, but the enthusiasm with which they assault upright furniture or doorjambs suggests another motivation as well.

Both chemical and visual signals have the advantage of persistence. As Ewer says, "Like the GONE TO LUNCH note pinned on a door, their message can be read in the author's absence."

Thanks to these various ways of communicating—by fighting, by scent, by sight—the cats in a given neighborhood get to know one another and establish a loose kind of ranking order. As a result, they can meet without hostility. Sometimes they even *seek* a meeting. Paul Leyhausen has observed many congresses of city cats, usually in the early evening, in which a dozen or more members of the same neighborhood's cat population turn themselves into the kind of group that English country folk used to refer to as "a clowder of cats." They pick neutral ground—in Paris, it was a small public square—and sit in agreeable companionship for several hours. "There is little sound," Leyhausen says. "The faces are friendly, and only occasionally an ear flattens or a small hiss or growl is heard when an animal closes in too much on a shy member of the group." Such meetings, he is convinced, are purely social gatherings, a change of pace for animals that on other occasions can be seen chasing one another or fighting.

Cats also form twosomes. For example, country cats from the same household sometimes hunt "together": about fifty yards apart but within sight of each other. City and suburban cats can often be seen sunning themselves, with about six feet between them, on a front porch borrowed for the purpose. Cats who have lived together a long time, even if not blood relatives, can develop such genuine and personal affection for each other that they do not preserve distance. They engage in frequent mutual grooming, curl up in a joint sleeping place, and exclude other cats (if there are others in the household) from their inner circle. Cats can also mourn the loss of a feline—or human—companion.

This substratum of sociability is the basis of the bond that can exist between a cat and a person. Leyhausen believes that cats perceive human beings as sufficiently like themselves to make a social relationship possible, but not so much like themselves that they react to us as they would to adult cats. In maturity, the close communion of the period when kittens are being raised is overridden by such forms of personal contact as territorial defense, contests for dominance, and mating, but it is not destroyed. "The human speaks to the remains of the childish impulses and so revives them," Leyhausen says. "Thus it is possible to have a lasting friendship between man and cat."

CHAPTER 9

Sex and Reproduction

THE ORDINARY CAT FIGHT is noisy, but of relatively short duration, and it involves only two cats at any given time and place. When, however, "there be hard fighting for wyves" (Bartolomeus Anglicus, thirteenth century), the din can last for days. Perhaps because our own inclination under the same circumstances is to close the doors, pull the blinds, and converse in whispers, human beings have always been amazed and annoyed by the sound effects attending feline courtship and mating—from the seventeenth century's Edward Topsell, who said, "In the time of their lust (commonly called cat-wralling) they are wilde and fierce, especially the males, who . . . will not keepe the house: at which time they have a peculiar direfull voyce," to the nineteenth century's St. George Mivart, who, with Victorian delicacy, decried the way in which cats "are wont to give expression to their sensibility."

"Cat-wralling" occurs because a female in heat—the technical word is "estrus"—attracts males from far away, many of whom are breaching the boundaries of another male's territory. So there is double reason to fight. There is plenty of opportunity, too, because females come into heat several days before they are ready to mate. That timing is a holdover from life in the wild, where cats are widely dispersed and the two sexes might have trouble finding each other at the start of a breeding season. Under those circumstances, it would never do for the female to be sexually responsive for such a short period that she and the male might not get together in time to reproduce. Therefore, well before she reaches her peak of receptivity, the female announces her availability by "calling" and by placing scent marks in the environs. The males, once gathered, must then hang around until she is ready to mate. The intervening courtship period allows the female to get acquainted with the various males who are contending for her favors and to decide which one she likes. She will probably mate with several.

Wild cats normally have only one breeding season a year, but domestication has altered the sexual cycle. Cats are ready to mate two, three, or even four times a year, depending on geography. As with other animals, the seasonal fluctuations in the amount of daylight control the hormone production which in its turn creates sexual readiness. Cats who live in northern latitudes therefore go into heat less frequently than those who live farther south. A typical North American cat experiences a series of approximately fifteen-day sexual cycles between late January and June, within each of which the estrous period lasts about five days. For many cats, these cycles continue until September (unless some breeder prolongs them by providing twelve to fourteen hours of artificial daylight). Kittens conceived in February are born in April and reared by July, and Mama is ready to go again.

The onset of puberty varies greatly in individual cats. Females may be ready to mate at four or five months of age or not until they are a year old. Males begin to secrete androgens during the fourth month of life—these hormones play an important role in the development of the penis—but sexual maturity does not usually occur until the cat is twelve to fifteen months old. Like humans, cats are not necessarily successful as sexual performers the first time out; both sexes seem to do better in the second and succeeding seasons.

Cat owners can always tell when Kitty is in heat because she becomes so affectionate, rubbing herself more than usual on both people and objects, often chin down along the floor. Hormonal requirements differ for each phase of sexual behavior, and the hormone level builds up gradually over a three- to six-day period. At some midpoint in the process, the cat is pushing herself along the floor with her head on one side, after which she flips over into a roll, then rubs her head on a paw or grooms herself. She spends a lot of time in a head-down crouch, her rump elevated, her hind legs moving as if treading. The vocal accompaniment to all this is a low throaty call that in Siamese can be especially raucous. The cat is constantly in motion, constantly entreating; there is no letup. This is the point at which a kind owner (or one who can't endure the mounting frenzy) opens the door and lets the cat out. She will return, much calmed, two or three days later.

If there are several males waiting for her (see Figure 6, p. 105), progress is delayed while they fight it out, during which time she acts completely indifferent to the battle which is being waged over her. (The fighting style is the same as the one described in the previous chapter in which males establish their place in the tomcat brotherhood.) But even if there is only one male waiting on her doorstep, she does not fly into his arms. As he approaches, she runs away. Not very far though; if she realizes he is not following, she stops. She may roll, or may rub against nearby objects, but if the male gets closer to her than she wants him to, she spits at him and hits out with a paw. As he follows her around, he rubs his head on the places she has rubbed, and courts her with sweet-sounding chirps which are quite unlike the caterwauls he produces to intimidate his rivals.

This flight-and-chase behavior can go on for quite a time, but gradually the female allows the male to get close enough to sniff her. She may roll on the ground in front of him, purr, or pat at him playfully. But once again she repulses him if he tries to make contact with her, in Ewer's words, "flouncing off with an indignant spit and a 'never-so-insulted-in-my-life' expression." When she is finally ready to accept him, she half crouches, chin on her bent fore legs, eyes half closed, ears a little back, rump raised, and tail up so the vulva can be seen. There are even little hairs around the vulva which can be erected to make the target more visible.

In mounting, the male first grips her by the back of the neck. The skin is loose there and he holds it with a partly opened mouth, the teeth acting to restrain rather than bite. His fore legs embrace her at shoulder level and his hind legs grasp her flanks. Thus positioned, his body directly above and parallel to hers, he lowers his hind feet and begins to tread. She does the same. Meanwhile, his penis has erected and he begins a series of thrusts. When he finally makes a successful entry, ejaculation occurs in a matter of seconds.

There then occurs a reaction that from time immemorial has astonished and fascinated human observers. The female gives a loud screech and writhes out of the male's grasp, turning to strike at him with a paw before she runs a short distance away. As Edward Topsell tells it, there are two possible explanations for this behavior: "One, because she is pinched with the talants or clawes of the male in the time of his lustfull rage, and the other, because his seed is so fiery hot, that it almost burneth the female's place of conception." A colorful interpretation, that latter—but wrong. Copulation is painful for the female because the male's penis is covered with backward-directed horny spines which hurt her vaginal tissues as the penis is withdrawn.

There is a good evolutionary reason for those barbs. They help to solve the reproductive problem caused by the short life—only about twenty-four hours—of a female's egg cells. Fertilization within that period presents no difficulties to the social animals (among them, human beings) because males are always present in group-living societies. Each female produces egg cells at a certain time in her sexual cycle, whether she mates or not; she can afford to be spendthrift because a male will be available when she *does* want to mate. Females of such species are called "spontaneous" ovulators.

Solitary species, however, cannot count on the two sexes being together at precisely the right time to fertilize eggs which live for only a day. Given the problems of locating each other in the wild and of overcoming the barriers to personal contact that the solitaries impose on themselves, these species would perish if reproduction depended on coordinating coitus with a waiting egg cell. Such animals, cats among them, have therefore evolved as "induced" ovulators: their ovaries do not release egg cells until *after* copulation has occurred.

Because the penis is smooth in species which ovulate spontaneously and is spiny in species in which ovulation must be induced, the spines are believed to be important to that process. Their prickly presence in the vagina is reported by nerve impulses to the hypothalamus, which initiates a chain of hormonal reactions whose net result is the release of egg cells by the ovaries— five or six at a time. It takes twenty-four to thirty hours after coitus for this process to be completed.

Theoretically, that is time enough for fertilization to occur, since sperm cells are viable up to forty-eight hours after ejaculation. In statistical fact, however, females who mate only once may not conceive. Sperm cells are not equally viable, and the ovaries may need more than one hormonal booster. So most breeders do not separate a pair of cats until they have mated at least three times. Nor is a litter guaranteed even then. Sometimes the fertilized eggs do not implant in the uterus. Sometimes the implanted eggs fail to develop. Research labs which maintain their own cat colonies find that anywhere from 70 percent to 95 percent of breedings result in births.

After each mating, the female rolls on the ground, licks her genital region, rubs her head on nearby objects, and thus gradually works off her excitement. The male licks himself, too, and waits for her to be ready for him again. The courtship ritual does not have to be repeated after the initial acceptance, and the two cats mate many times in the course of the following twenty-four (or more) hours. When they are fresh, they may copulate as often as eight times in a twenty-minute period, but as time goes on, the intervals between matings gradually lengthen. The male tires faster than the female; in fact, their roles change as they proceed and she ends up wooing *him*.

Finally, there comes a time when he is satiated (not tired of sex, but tired of sex with her, for his interest will revive if another female is presented to him). Should he lose interest before her estrous period ends, she mates with other males. That's why the kittens she eventually produces may not all have been sired by the same father. It is only in the controlled conditions of the breeder's cattery or in the laboratory that pedigrees can be established.

One can therefore see why brothels are sometimes called "cathouses," and why consummate promiscuity in human males is referred to as "tomcatting around." Yet it must be said in fairness to cats that many estrous females do not couple indiscriminately with all comers and not all male cats tomcat around. Leyhausen has noted that male cats have periods of greater or lesser readiness for mating, that "they are always capable but not always eager." Patricia Scott says it is much harder to get male cats to perform under laboratory conditions than it is to mate females there: males are much more inhibited and will not mate at all if placed in a strange cage without their own scent marks to reassure them.

As for females, they have definite preferences as to their partners. Among both Leyhausen's caged animals and his pet cats, females sometimes choose a male who is subordinate in the cage hierarchy or one who was not the victor in a battle between toms. The pet cats also show preferences for particular males with whom they have mated before, although Leyhausen has never been able to keep them under constant enough surveillance to discover whether they go to those males *exclusively*. (He thinks they do.) He reminds cat owners that there are all sorts of gradations between monogamy and total promiscuity.

R. F. Ewer agrees. She describes a male cat she once owned who brought a strange young female home with him despite the fact that there was another "reproductively fully competent" female already in the household. "Although he mated regularly with each of them," Ewer says, "his friendly behaviour was directed almost exclusively to the female of his choice; the other was no more to him than an adequate sexual object when she was on heat."

Cats are also very individualistic in sexual "style." According to Jay Rosenblatt and T. C. Schneirla, each male cat has a characteristic way of approach and mounting, a characteristic speed of intromission and ejaculation, a characteristic reaction to the female's period of after-response. Furthermore, each female "clearly differentiates among a group of males with whom she has been mated frequently and reacts differently toward each." Both sexes make mutual adjustments to the partner's style of lovemaking.

Psychologists have been interested for a long time in the extent to which the brain influences sexual behavior. In the lower animals, courtship and mating appear to be almost completely controlled by hormones, and this is true also of the female of the species in many higher animals. Surgical removal of the gonads quickly eliminates sexual behavior in female cats, but does not necessarily have that effect on males. Jay Rosenblatt and Lester Aronson once compared the sexual behavior after castration of cats who had been allowed to mate freely and cats who had never associated with females. After castration, cats in the second group showed no interest in sex but those in the first group continued for a period of weeks or months to approach females in heat, mount, and even achieve intromission. Since they were producing no sex hormones, their behavior had to be the result of learning—that is, the product of experience.

Another experiment, performed by K. K. Cooper, reached the same conclusion. After androgens were administered to castrated males, it was those who had had sexual experience before castration who most enthusiastically sought out and mated with estrous females. Many scientists have also attacked the same problem from the other end of the animal. When certain areas in the cortex (the "thinking" part of the brain) have been made nonfunctional, males can't mount; sometimes they can't even find the female.

People who believe that any alternative to heterosexuality is shameful will sometimes whisper to their veterinarians that Buster has lately been acting "in a very peculiar way." Perhaps the cat in question is a young male who has been observed trying to mount another male. This is the most common form of feline homosexuality; it appears among adolescent cats as a kind of practice run for the real thing. Females also occasionally attempt to mount other females, but this occurs only when both are in heat and no male is available. Some really rare aberrations have also been reported, all involving adult males: rapes of females, attempts to copulate with kittens, adoption of toys or other inanimate objects for purposes of masturbation and against which the confused male ejaculates. One cat has even been immortalized in scientific literature because it had spontaneous emissions during sleep. Most of these examples of hypersexuality, it should be noted, have been observed in laboratory animals. There is no way of knowing how common such activities may be in the free-roaming feline population, but it's obvious from the number of cats and kittens in the world that most mature males are interested in mature females and vice versa.

And if one happens to believe that there are too many cats and kittens in the world, what then?

Aside from keeping an estrous female away from males, there is only one sure way to prevent conception: to "neuter" the cat by surgery. Spaying removes the female's ovaries, uterus, and fallopian tubes, the same operation that in women is called a hysterectomy. Castration removes the male's testes. The advantage to the cat owner is that a mature male no longer sprays indoors—the odor is singularly strong and unpleasant to humans—and a mature female does not produce kittens for whom her owner has progressively more difficulty finding homes.* But surgery has disadvantages. It's expensive—spaying a female can cost $50 or more—and it's permanent. It is unacceptable to people who want their females to have an occasional litter or

---

* Tubal ligations and vasectomies are possible also. Both operations make the animal sterile but do not affect "calling" on the part of females or fighting and spraying by males because that behavior is instigated by hormones manufactured in the ovaries or testes.

whose males are good studs; to people who still believe the myth that neutered animals inevitably become fat and lazy; and to people who equate their own sexuality with that of their pets.

In 1973, the conclusions of many scientists who have interested themselves in the psychology of pet ownership were summarized by Carl Djerassi of Stanford, Andrew Israel of Columbia, and Wolfgang Jochle of Syntex Research's Institute for Veterinary Medicine. Children's first exposure to animals, they point out, "is in the anthropomorphized creatures of juvenile fiction, thus establishing the human-like qualities of pets at an early age." Later in life, many adults see puppies and kittens as substitutes for children not yet planned; or for the small number of children planned; or for children that never arrived or have already departed; or as an unconscious protest against their own exercise in family planning.

Some male owners may want their pet roaming and impregnating as an unconscious protest against the sexual restrictions society and morality impose upon them. Many people regard their pets as family members and are horrified at the concept of "taking sex away." One veterinarian is quoted as saying that female clients show more distress when a female pet suffers from breast tumors and male pet owners tend to become more upset if a male pet develops prostate trouble than if it has suffered, say, a complex bone fracture. The latter is accepted by the owner with much more composure than imminent loss of the animal's sexual capacity.

For all such pet owners, chemical sterilants will (if and when they are available) provide an alternative to surgical procedures. Since dogs are more useful to mankind than are cats—as trackers, for example, or to guide the blind—and also because more dog owners than cat owners patronize veterinarians, most of the pet world's research and development dollars have until recently been spent on dogs. There are canine intrauterine devices intended to prevent conception, but no counterpart for cats. Besides, the problems associated with these cause scientists who are seeking ways to control animal fertility to put more faith in drugs.

The oral contraceptives, so far developed only for females, are chemically like male hormones and suppress estrus. A branded version of megestrol acetate called Ovaban has been available in England for both cats and dogs since 1969, but the Food and Drug Administration has approved its use in the United States only for dogs. Clinical tests on cats are still in progress.

Under development too are pills which will prevent conception postcoitally. They will be useful only to cat owners who have complete control over their pets' sex life. Inasmuch as pills must be given within the following twenty-four hours, one must *know* when coitus occurred.

A drug which will induce abortion has also reached the testing stage. However, as Djerassi and his colleagues point out, few people would give it to their cats at home once they realized that the abortion might take place on the kitchen floor. It is also possible to use biochemical agents to postpone the onset of puberty, and it may be possible to use them to prevent sexual maturation altogether. "Sexless" rodents have been experimentally produced.

Nor is the opposite problem being ignored. A fertility drug for cats who have difficulty conceiving is now being tested. There is also available a perfected technique for artificially inseminating those females who can't or won't mate with the male of their owner's choice.

Most of these methods for planning pet parenthood are available to the public, if at all, in clinics associated with university schools of veterinary medicine. To develop feline contraceptive drugs is a long and costly process—six to eight years, on the average. In the immediate future, therefore, kitten production is likely to continue at its present rate of about 13,000,000 per year.

Complications of pregnancy are rare. Kitty comes home, calm and quiet again after she has mated, and for several weeks seems to be her same old self. But even before her sides begin to bulge, an alert owner will notice that she is grooming herself and is licking her abdominal and genital regions far more than a non-pregnant cat would. This behavior, probably induced by hormones, helps to focus her attention on areas which are soon going to require a great deal of licking. Gestation takes sixty-three to sixty-five days, and as it draws to a close, the cat begins to hunt for a suitable place to deliver. She may or may not show interest in the towel-lined box that is provided for her. Backs of closets, bath mats, sofa cushions, dresser drawers, or the hollow between the pillows on her owners' bed may strike her fancy instead.

Cats are highly individual in their preferences for attended or unattended deliveries. When contractions of the abdominal wall begin, some cats seek out the most sheltered and inaccessible refuge they can find. Other cats, especially those who are very affectionate toward their owners, insist on having support and sympathy as the birth proceeds. Such cats keep popping out of their boxes, meowing piteously, until someone comes to sit beside them. Some owners say their cats actually manage to postpone a birth (for a few hours, anyway) until their human companions are available to cheer them on.

The speed of delivery is also highly individual. The contraction stage can be as short as twelve seconds or as long as an hour and a half, during which the cat restlessly and repeatedly changes her body position. Her basic posture is a semisquat—fore legs straight so she can brace herself during contractions—with her rear end curved slightly around toward the front. In this position, she can see the kittens when they are born. She frequently licks her vulva, especially if there has been leakage of amniotic fluid. A flood of fluid also accompanies the birth itself, and from then on she has so much licking to do that one wonders why her "poor little wash rag" doesn't wear out.

It can take a given kitten as little as thirty seconds or as long as fifty minutes to be born. Delivery times vary within a litter, and so do the intervals between births. Deliveries have been reported in which seven kittens were born within two and a half hours and others in which a litter of four required well over three hours. Each kitten comes wrapped in a thin transparent sac, trailing its umbilical cord. Cats who have read the textbook immediately rasp off the birth sac and lick dry the little bundle of wet fur they have exposed. First attention goes to the kitten's mouth and nose, to clear away any obstacle to breathing, and then to the rest of the body. This equivalent of a brisk toweling is necessary to start the kitten's circulation. The mother may sever the kitten's umbilical cord while she's licking it dry or she may wait until the placenta is expelled (a matter of minutes after the birth), in which case she eats it and the umbilical cord down to the spot where it is attached to the kitten.

To eat the placenta, incidentally, is common behavior among animals, even those who are normally grass eaters. It contains hormones which aid in starting lactation, and it also provides nourishment. Cats remain uninterruptedly with their young during the first twenty-four hours or so after birth, and especially in the wild the food value of the placenta spares the mother a premature but hunger-driven return to hunting.

Among cats whose deliveries do not go by the book, however, a second kitten often arrives before the mother has finished cleaning up the first. If it is a large litter, the first born may be nuzzling around in search of its mother's teats at the same time the last born is making its appearance. Given enough confusion, kittens can be ignored, sat on, or misplaced. Some cats don't seem to realize they *have* kittens, and try to walk away from them. A few don't distinguish between the end of the umbilical cord and the beginning of the kitten and eat them both.

In animal species whose young are up and around from a few minutes after birth—goats, horses, cattle—it is usual to have only one and occasionally two offspring. The mother couldn't keep a watchful eye on any more. But in species like cats, whose young are so immature at birth they must be kept in nests or dens to protect them from predators, litter sizes are large. In domestic cats, the average litter is four. This number is also the desirable maximum, according to Neal Nelson and his colleagues at a Cincinnati research institution. Between 1963 and 1968, they kept records on kittens born in their cat colony and found that the average birth weight of each was 99.2 grams when litters consisted of one to four kittens, but in larger litters there was a decrease in weight of about 5 percent for each additional kitten.

Some cats become mothers when they are only five months old. Some keep going until they are thirteen or more. The peak years of production, however, are between the second and eighth years of life. According to *Animal Facts and Feats*, the most fecund female of record was a seventeen-year-old Texas cat named Dusty who gave birth to her 420th kitten in June of 1952. The largest litter ever recorded was thirteen kittens born in April of 1969 to Boccaccio Blue Danielle, a year-old Siamese Blue Point who lived in Australia. If all survived, Danielle must have had a difficult logistical problem. Cats have only eight teats.

CHAPTER 10

The Young Family

NEWBORN KITTENS have flat faces, squeezed-shut eyes, and stubby ears that stick out sideways. Their legs are too weak to support them, but within minutes after birth they begin to crawl—heads wobbling from side to side, fore legs moving like paddles, hind legs pushing from the rear. (See Figure 7.) There is nothing directional about this maiden voyage; it is a random search. The small noses snuffle along the surface of the box or nest, exploring an area a few inches wide. A human observer will note that the kittens initially move away from their mother as often as they move toward her.

However, there are clues as to where they should be heading. They can smell the mother cat; they can feel the warmth which radiates from her body; and they can hear the continuous rumble of her purring. (Possibly, they feel its vibrations; no one is quite sure how well newborn kittens can hear.) Their mother also makes it easy for them to locate the right part of her: she lies down in a crescent shape, facing into the area where they were delivered. The kittens therefore climb aboard more or less in the region of her abdomen, nuzzle around in her fur until they locate a teat, and start to suck. All this normally happens within an hour after a given kitten has been born.

By the second or third day of life each kitten in a litter has laid claim to its "own" teat, and thereafter suckles from it exclusively. To be able to differentiate one teat from another seems a miraculous accomplishment.

Recognition cannot be visual, for kittens that young cannot see. Possibly there is a spatial component, but there is no evidence for it. All the evidence points instead to identification of individual teats by odor. If one washes the mother cat's underside, thus rendering it odor-free, her kittens temporarily lose their ability to find their "own" teats; and when that portion of the brain which registers smell is oblated, they permanently lose their ability to nurse from their mother. J. K. Kovach and A. Kling, who did the latter experiment, say that destruction of the smelling center in the brain does not interfere with kittens' ability to suck from a bottle; it merely prevents their finding their mother's teats, presumably because they can't smell them.

Even when a litter is small and there are more teats than kittens, individual kittens tend to restrict themselves to just one. There is a good evolutionary reason for such fidelity. As Ewer says,

> Once ownership has been established the speed with which the whole litter settles down to a feed is striking. Waste of time and energy in fighting is negligible; within less than a minute of a mother's lying down to nurse, each kitten is in position and sucking vigorously: a kitten whose teat is not very easily accessible because of the mother's position only rarely wastes time in fruitless endeavours to dispossess another, but seeks until it finds its own. Such economy of time may be of importance in natural conditions, where much of the mother's time must be spent in hunting. . . . In addition, teat constancy ensures that at least one mammary gland per kitten is kept functional by regular milking. Without such organization, the weakest kitten might begin by taking what was left after its fellows had fed. This might suffice for a few days but the leavings would get less and less and the weakest would presently die of starvation.

The onset of lactation is not dependent on kittens' suckling, but its maintenance *is*. Right after the kittens are born, the pituitary gland releases a substance which causes an increase in pressure in the mammary glands; they respond by ejecting milk. At first, the milk comes as fast as the kittens can ingest it, and they use their paws only to steady themselves or to spread their mother's skin away from the teat. But within a few days, as their appetites grow, they develop the "milk tread," a series of back-and-forth movements in which the fore paws push alternately against the mother's belly. This kneading stimulates milk flow. It also remains in the cat's behavioral repertoire throughout life. Many an old cat, when it finds itself on something soft and warm—such as its owner sleeping under a napped wool blanket—repeats the milk tread of its infancy, complete with purrs.

If a mother cat absents herself for a long time, newborn kittens have some nutritional reserves to draw upon. For at least a few days of inadequate feeding, they can use glycogen (a carbohydrate stored mostly in the liver) to maintain their energies. They also arrive in the world outside the womb with safeguards against certain other possible hazards. For one example, they are able to withstand lack of oxygen longer than a human baby. The chemical reason is that enzymes can break down that reserve of glycogen without the presence of oxygen in the bloodstream and thus maintain life processes. So, if a mother cat doesn't get a kitten out of its birth sac and lick it into respiratory life immediately upon its delivery, the kitten can survive the time lag. According to the English scientist E. M. Widdowson, kittens' tolerance for lack of oxygen is also the reason it is so hard to drown them.

She also points out that kittens (in common with the newborn young of many other small animals) are spared the necessity of maintaining their body temperature at the adult level of around 100 degrees. To do so would require such active metabolism that they would burn up their body tissues. Kittens therefore are equipped to withstand a sizable fall in body temperature right after birth, a greater fall, in fact, than an adult cat could survive. When huddled together in the nest, they have body temperatures of about 80 degrees, and even then they are pooling each individual's warmth. By the time they are two weeks old, their temperature-controlling mechanisms will function like those of adults, but it is fortunate that during their first days of life the mother cat spends so much time curled cozily around them. In her absence, it is instinctive for them to cluster. When bestowing that instinct upon them, a canny Mother Nature also seems to have included a bonus: kittens whose immediate response to the departure of their mother is to seek contact with a littermate's body are not likely to stray out of the nest.

Kittens nurse, initially, for as much as eight hours a day in sessions that may last as long as forty-five minutes. They grow fast. They have no initial weight loss, double their birth weight (about four ounces) in a week, treble it in two weeks, and quadruple it in three weeks—females being heavier on the average and growing faster for the first month of life, after which males take the lead. Human infants grow more slowly, doubling birth weight only in the fifth or sixth month. There is an old theory that rate of growth correlates with the percentage of protein in a mother's milk, and this holds true of cats and humans. Feline milk is about 10 percent protein, whereas the protein content of human milk is only a little more than 1 percent.

Here is a chart listing the most important components of mother's milk in four kinds of animals. (The ranges given for dogs are due to breed differences.)

Species	Percentage of Protein	Of Fat	Of Lactose (Sugar)
Dogs	5.4 to 10.6	8.5 to 13.6	2.5 to 4.2
Cats	10.1	6.3	4.4
Cows	3.2	3.6	4.7
Human Beings	1.2	3.7	6.8

It is easy to see why orphaned kittens do poorly on fresh cow's milk but thrive on the evaporated version, in which the amount of protein is doubled.

Kittens are born with many of their physical and sensory systems undeveloped. They cannot urinate or defecate for the first two weeks of life and depend upon their mother's licking of their genitals to stimulate these processes. They are blind for about the same amount of time (and when their eyes do open, they are milky blue, changing color later). Their claws are not yet retractile, and they have no teeth. The milk teeth begin to erupt in the second or third week; the incisors first, then the canines. Kittens have no molars; they come in, along with the other permanent teeth, at about the age of six months.

But kittens are less helpless during this first fortnight than one might think. If separated from their mother, for example, newborns respond with a peculiarly shrill and incessant wailing which is quite unlike any sound they will later emit. Furthermore, this sound is necessary to their mother's finding them. Leyhausen has done a number of experiments in which a kitten was removed from its mother, the object being to study her retrieval behavior. If an absent kitten is quiet, she doesn't miss it. Only when it wails does she search for it. Michael Fox has made spectrographs of kittens' distress meows, and says that each kitten's voice is different, but no tests have so far been made to find out whether a mother cat "knows" that Kitten A rather than Kitten B is calling for help.

When they are about a week old, more mobile than at birth but still unable to see, kittens may wander away from a home spot that does not have protective barriers. But, barring a fall, they quickly learn how to find their way back. Jay Rosenblatt has chronicled the development of this ability as observed in his laboratory:

One day after birth in a cage thirty-six inches square, a kitten can distinguish between its home cage and a strange one. Put in a strange cage, its intense wailing moderates only when it is returned to the cage in which it was born. It cannot find its home corner (usually at the back of the cage) if placed elsewhere; it simply crawls in circles around the spot where it is put down. By the end of the first week of life, however, it can find its home corner if placed in the corner directly opposite it at the front of the cage (thirty-six inches away); and by the end of the second week it can find its way home from the corner diagonally across the cage (fifty inches away).

Again, odor is the guide. Kittens who had already proved that they could make it home from the directly opposite corner of the cage would not do so when Rosenblatt washed their home corner. They came to an abrupt stop when they reached it, backed away, and chose instead a part of the cage where the family odors had not been eradicated. Nor did their reliance on their sense of smell vanish when their eyes opened and they could presumably see where they were going. Rosenblatt found that three-week-old kittens were still disoriented and likely to become lost if they were denied olfactory cues to point the way home. Only if visual cues were made very prominent—by adding a black-and-white checkerboard pattern to the floor of the home corner, for instance—could the kittens locate their home corner. In natural settings, of course, there are no black-and-white checkerboards to act as homing devices, and kittens are dependent for quite a long time on the guidance provided by odor trails.

The first three weeks of a kitten's life correspond to the first eighteen months of human infancy. Human babies who are inadequately mothered during that period tend to reach maturity with emotional and personality defects, and the same is true of kittens who do not get their full three weeks of concentrated maternal attention. In 1959, the psychiatrist Philip F. D. Seitz raised a group of motherless kittens from the age of two weeks and an-

FIGURE 7. *Blind and as yet unable to stand, a newborn kitten pushes and paddles toward its mother, guided by her scent and purr. Within three days after birth, kittens each choose an "own" teat and thereafter nurse from that one exclusively.*

other similar group from the age of six weeks, and found that those earlier separated from their mothers were the more fearful, suspicious, and aggressive as adults. They were less purposeful in their activity, more easily frustrated, more randomly active—in sum, just plain disorganized.

The initial period of intensive mothering is nature's way of forging so strong a social bond between mother and kittens that the family will stay together long enough for her to rear them. Her interest in her offspring is presumed to be of hormonal origin because it is non-specific: she doesn't respond to kittens as kittens and certainly has no awareness (as a human mother does) that they are unique entities. Instead, her response is to kittens as small, animate creatures. This is the period—right after she has given birth—when she will indiscriminately mother the young of other species, even rats. A few weeks later, after she has become familiar with her kittens as individuals, she will no longer accept other young. That period, too, is short; as soon as the kittens become active enough to leave the nest, she ceases to differentiate very sharply between them and any other kittens. At that stage, two mother cats living in the same household will allow each other's kittens to nurse from them. Between these two periods, mother cats may go through an ambivalent stage. For example, a cat observed by Ewer was friendly toward a strange kitten if she approached it from the rear, in which case she began toilet-licking; but if she met it head-on and smelled its face, she hissed at it.

It is asserted by some cat fanciers that mother cats occasionally chew off kittens' whiskers in order to keep them from straying, or as a sign of affection. In *Cats in the Belfry,* Doreen Tovey says, "I nearly fainted on the spot when Solomon marched proudly into the living room with his whiskers sprouting on one side as exuberantly as a gorse bush—and the other side completely bare . . . We didn't know that Siamese mothers sometimes did that to their favorite kittens when they were particularly pleased with them."

Perhaps some Siamese (or other breeds) do nibble on their kittens' whiskers. The zoologists' and veterinarians' literature is silent on the topic. Bonnie Beaver, of Texas A & M's College of Veterinary Medicine, has heard the story and has seen short-whiskered kittens but says, "I haven't been able to conclude to my own satisfaction whether these kittens are born with shorter whiskers or whether the queens have chewed them off. I strongly suspect the former." Neither Paul Leyhausen nor Jay Rosenblatt has witnessed the alleged behavior by mother cats. Leyhausen thinks that broken whiskers in a kitten are more likely to signify a calcium deficiency than maternal love.

There is also a much older and more widely reported tale to the effect that male cats eat their young. In his *Historie of Foure-footed Beasts*, Edward Topsell tells it most eloquently; he even gives a reason for it. "The male," he says, "is most libidinous, and therefore seeing the female will never more engender with him during the time hir young ones sucke, hee killeth and eateth them if he meet with them (to provoke the female to copulation with him againe, for when she is deprived of her young, she seeketh out the male of her own accord). . . ." As often with Topsell's explanations, the conclusion is wrong but the observed facts are correct. Male cats do sometimes kill and eat kittens. However, according to Leyhausen, the action is not deliberate; it results from a misapprehension.

When kittens are a few weeks old, a mother cat may behave as if she were in heat again. If this is a pseudo estrus, as is often the case, she repulses any male cat who shares the same household quarters. Leyhausen says the male then looks for a substitute, which he may find in the young just leaving the nest. They look flattened to the floor, as a submissive female does, and the sexually excited tomcat may try to mate with one of them. "Failure here makes him even more excited," Leyhausen says. "His hold at the base of the neck becomes firmer and he may kill it, and afterwards eat it." Occasional incidents of this sort are probably the basis for the belief that male cats commonly eat their young, if given a chance to.

But such behavior is very unusual, and instances of it can be countered with numerous examples of loving attention to kittens by tomcats. Siamese males in particular are notable for grooming and playing with their kittens in a fatherly fashion that any psychologist would approve of in a human family. Sheila Burnford's Simon (upon whom the Siamese cat in *The Incredible Journey* was modeled) "had a maternal attitude toward all young things. Once he licked into shape, literally and figuratively, an Abyssinian kitten with pneumonia and a young Irish setter pup which had no training." He also became the self-appointed foster parent of kittens born to another Burnford pet, a white cat named Annabelle—"a good time girl who cared only for a roistering life on the tiles, as fecund as she was feckless, and a terrible mother." It was Simon who "washed, warmed, protected, and purred over" Annabelle's offspring.

At about three weeks of age, kittens begin to use their paws to pat at things that excite their interest. Soon they will be hooking objects toward them for closer inspection. Most kittens develop paw preferences which do not change throughout life. In 1955, the Oxford University physiologist J. Cole found that about 58 percent of cats prefer one paw—20 percent of them the right paw, 40 percent the left paw. (Parrots are left-handed, too. Most human beings are right-handed. Rats, monkeys, and chimpanzees are equally divided in matters of paw preference.) J. M. Warren and colleagues at Pennsylvania State University have since satisfied themselves that feline preferences for using a particular paw mature slowly but are firmly fixed by the time a cat is a year old.

Nature does a marvelous job of coordinating the development of certain behaviors with the need to use them. For example, it is not until young animals are mobile enough to be in danger of falling from a height that they develop depth perception. In the 1950's, Eleanor Gibson and Richard D. Walk did a series of studies of the genesis of that ability, using a contraption which they called a "visual cliff." They built a six-by-eight-foot table which stood about four feet high. The entire tabletop was covered with a sheet of clear glass. On half the tabletop, directly under the glass, a checked linoleum was laid; but on the other side there was no visual barrier to seeing through the glass to another piece of the same linoleum on the floor below. The investigators found that animals which cannot yet walk show no fear upon being moved from the "shallow" side to the "deep" side of the table, but by the time they are capable of independent locomotion their optical systems have matured to a sufficient extent to make them balk. Human babies begin to crawl at six to ten months of age, and cannot then be enticed to move onto the sheet of glass through which they can see the faraway floor. Kittens behave the same way at three to four weeks, when *they* are fully mobile.

At about the same age they also learn to bury their own feces and urine. During the weeks when they cannot get out of the nest, and odor would be an invitation to predators, the mother cat licks up their excrement. But once the kittens are on their feet and able to go abroad, they search out suitable latrine facilities some distance from the nest. The routine involves digging a hole in the dirt with the front feet, standing with the hindquarters above it, then covering the urine or feces by scratching dirt into the hole. Household cats who regularly go outdoors have special spots for urination and defecation; indoor cats have less choice because their owners decide where a sand-box or litter pan should be located.

Kittens require virtually no toilet training by humans, so inborn is the urge to dig-and-bury and to use a customary place. However, it is not one of those stereotyped behaviors which animals sometimes perform out of context. A caged squirrel, for example, will try to bury a nut even if it can't dig a hole for it, but kittens dig only if they have something to dig in. Cats who have been raised on hard floors in laboratory cages relieve themselves anywhere. (Scent-marking, especially by males, is, of course, an exception to the otherwise general feline practice of burying excrement.)

It is also during the third or fourth week of kittens' life that their mother suddenly decides to find a new home for them. Most animal behaviorists believe this to be a throwback to life in the wild, an insurance against predators. Paul Leyhausen disagrees; the captive wild cats he has observed are (except for the black-footed cat) usually content with one nesting place. For whatever reason, though, the practice is common among domestic cats. The mother may or may not pick the new home spot before she starts to transport her young; sometimes she initiates her search with a kitten already dangling by the scruff of its neck from her mouth. A cat who is raising her first litter may grab her offspring at any handy spot, but the old hands know that kittens instinctively hang motionless when held by the nape of the neck and are therefore easier to lug around. Some cats are satisfied with one change of nest; others shift their young several times. And each time, after she has moved the last kitten, the mother cat makes a final trip to the abandoned nest to do a visual check—so it is obvious that cats can't count.

When the kittens can walk well, they learn to follow their mother on short journeys of discovery. However, she does not take them far from the nest and immediately retrieves any who are bent on independent exploration. They must be kept together and close to a place of refuge because she cannot protect them individually from a really determined predator. They are too young to flee from danger and therefore neither can she. The resultant blocking of her normal flight responses creates a high degree of excitability; she is prepared as she never will be at any other time to attack other animals.

A cat in this emotional state presents a truly frightful aspect to any animal or human being who comes close enough to her kittens to be considered a menace. She shoots out of the nest, screaming like a banshee, her back arched, her body and tail twice normal size because the hair is all erected, ears laid back, mouth wide open, teeth bared. She seems to be coming at the trespasser from two directions: her hindquarters are swung around to one side (to make her total body mass look as large and as intimidating as possible), yet all four legs are galloping forward. This arched-back, sideways-slanted assault is used by cats only when a sudden attack is the best mode of defense, and particularly when the enemy is a larger animal.

House-reared kittens seldom or never need this kind of protection, but their mothers nevertheless develop extreme readiness for aggressive behavior on their behalf, and sometimes can't contain it. Ewer once had two mother cats who were so eager to attack something that they made themselves an opportunity to do so. A neighborhood dog happened to wander into the garden and made some sound which alerted them to his presence. Whereupon:

> As though actuated by a single switch, the two cats leapt up from their litters, neck and neck they raced for the door, neck and neck they jumped a small fence separating themselves from their objective and hurled themselves upon what was to them a superb releaser for their pent-up fury rather than a danger that had to be faced. The wretched dog, taken completely by surprise and utterly demoralised by this unprovoked assault, turned tail and fled, yelping like a hurt puppy, with one cat still on his back, raking him with her claws like a jockey flogging the last ounce out of his steed.

In other circumstances, Ewer says, the same cats would never have attacked the dog.

In short, the first month of a kitten's life is one of dependency, changing from total to partial as the days go by, with the mother in almost constant attendance. The second month is equivalent to a human being's young childhood. The bond between mother and offspring is beginning fractionally to loosen; the foundations are about to be laid for the formal lessons of late childhood and the maturing experiences of adolescence.

CHAPTER 11

The Older Family

MONTH-OLD KITTENS HAVE shining eyes in pansy faces, spiky little stand-up tails, fur so soft and downy-light it makes an aureole around their bodies. This is the age at which they begin to be lifted out of the nest by people who coo at them and call them Sweetums. And like children at the same stage of growth, they do their best to squirm free, the world being full of much more interesting things to do. They are enchanted by leaves and feathers and the twitching tails of other cats, and although they still tend to fall over when changing direction while running, such misadventures do not diminish their exuberant approach to life.

The feline family has by now acquired a new character. The kittens no longer do everything together and differences among them have become apparent. A hierarchy has begun to evolve; there is almost always a dominant kitten in a litter. At any given moment, particular kittens may be engaged in grooming each other, perfecting their climbing techniques, or exploring some mini-wilderness a yard away from home. Whereas it used to be their mother who signaled that it was time to eat, by lying down and nudging them toward her, it is now the kittens who initiate suckling. To be precise, one of them does. The first kitten who starts to nurse alerts the others with its purring; they come running and they too begin to suckle. (Ewer calls this "the dinner-gong function" of purring.)

Their most important developmental job during the next two or three weeks is to become skilled at play. *Skilled* at *play?* To many humans, the two words are antithetical. Play is trivial and purposeless, an amusement, nothing one *works* at. Yet play is an apparently essential activity in the development of the higher animals. No one understands why this should be so.

A common explanation for the value of play is that it allows young animals to practice adult behaviors; yet adult behaviors obviously require no practice because they are performed as well by animals without play experience as by those who have had such experience. Play makes the player physically fit; but animals can be physically fit without playing. Play provides information about the environment and also enables young animals to learn what their own capabilities are; but animals who don't play are as much at home in their environment and as capable of judging their own limits as animals who *do* play.

Nevertheless, since nature is never frivolous, there must be a good reason for play. Ewer suggests, first, that it occurs especially among animal species whose mode of life requires quick movement, accurately oriented to a goal, with the failure of a first attempt carrying a heavy penalty. (As, for example, a cat's need to find immediate refuge from a pursuing dog.) Secondly, the species that play are the more intelligent ones—the primates (apes, chimpanzees, monkeys, man), the cetaceans (whales, dolphins), and the carnivores (cats, dogs). These animals all experience childhoods under adult protection, a period which allows more time for brain development than occurs in species whose young are launched into the competitive business of real life almost from birth, and whose actions are therefore mostly instinctive. Animals who have time to play learn from it how to make judgments based on experience.

Kittens, for instance, do not have to be taught to initiate a chase; they are innately programmed to pursue small objects which are moving away from them. But to chase is not to capture. In play, they learn how to adapt their speed to the varying speeds of moving objects. (Problem: If a Ping-Pong ball decelerates in regular increments as it rolls away from one, how must the chase technique be altered in order to capture an erratically wind-driven leaf?) Play also teaches kittens how to gauge expenditure of energy relative to the distance which must be covered. (Problem: If one wishes to knock a littermate down and a pounce from a foot away only staggers him, from what distance should the attack be launched and how much force should be put into a second try?) Accurate judgments of this sort are indispensable to a grown cat who wishes to intercept a running mouse before it reaches its hole.

Although almost all the action patterns a cat will use in maturity appear in kittens' play, they are performed out of context. As Ewer says,

> Two kittens may chase each other in play, but the one that flees is not terrified and the pursuer is not bent on . . . driving him away: the roles of pursuer and pursued can alternate as rapidly as in a children's game and, indeed, at the end of about seven weeks, kittens begin to play running games with such enthusiasm that what starts as a chase may end up with several of them galloping more or less abreast. Similarly, in play fights, biting and scratching are not carried out at full strength and it is quite obvious that there is no intention of wounding or killing the opponent.

In the language of psychologists, kittens' play is not goal-directed; they seem to be pushing buttons at random on some behavioral console.

Leyhausen believes that the reservoirs of neural energy (see Chapter 2) which create readiness to perform particular actions have themselves matured but have not been linked to any of the others. Such linkages do not develop, he says, until genuine motivation for a certain behavior develops. When kittens finally discover that mice are to be killed, they perform prey-catching actions in the proper sequence, but before that point has been reached, and whenever peak readiness to perform a given action accumulates, they expend the energy in each neural reservoir on the single action for which it is specific. Because playful behavior declines with age (although it never wholly vanishes), the assumption is that a change in the organization of the central nervous system occurs with maturation.

In 1974, the Cornell University psychologist Meredith West observed twenty-eight kittens from the time they started to play (at about three weeks of age) until their play became sporadic (at approximately eighteen weeks). She identified eight motor patterns in the basic repertoire of play, some of which are shown in Figure 8. They developed in this order:

Timing	Pattern	Description
21–25 days	Belly-up	Kitten lies on its back, all four legs up, the back legs making treading movements, perhaps, while the front ones paw the air.
23–26 days	Stand-up	Kitten stands near or over a kitten in the belly-up position and aims "bites" at its head or neck. The outreached paws of the belly-up kitten then pull the stand-up kitten down. The two then tumble around, alternately assuming the stand-up and belly-up positions.
32–34 days	Side-step	Kitten arches its back, curls its tail upward and toward its body, and walks sideways toward or around another kitten or object.
33–35 days	Pounce	Kitten crouches with its head held close to the ground, its tail straight back (but perhaps twitching). Then it wiggles its hindquarters back and forth and thrusts forward from its hind legs.
35–38 days	Vertical stance	From a sitting position, kitten rocks back on its hindquarters, lifts its body so its forepaws are at right angles to its body: the boxer's stance.
38–41 days	Chase	Kitten runs after or away from another kitten.
41–46 days	Horizontal leap	Same body position as the side-step, but the kitten jumps off the ground instead of merely walking.
42–48 days	Face-off	A kitten sits near another kitten, watching it intently, its body hunched forward, and tries to hit the other kitten on the head with its paw. This is usually a game for two.

When they first emerge, all patterns except the stand-up are performed alone, sometimes a dozen times in a row. Initially, only two kittens play together and only one motor pattern is used. After a sequence of belly-up and stand-up play, for example, the two kittens quit. From five weeks on, more than two kittens often play together and several motor patterns are combined in a single play sequence. Those favored as openers change and so does the proportional amount of time spent in doing any one. At six weeks, for example, there's a lot of pouncing, but very little at twelve weeks. By then, much more time is spent in chasing.

Play also serves the same purpose as the newborn kittens' huddling together in the absence of their mother: it keeps the litter together and reduces the likelihood of their individually straying far from the nest. Its frequency declines as the kittens become increasingly capable of looking after themselves and as adult activities begin to supervene. The hyperkinetic activity of young kittenhood disappears; between the eighth and twentieth week of life, for example, West's kittens doubled the amount of time they spent in just sitting and looking at things. When they were eighteen weeks old, those dozen of her young subjects who were home-reared were spending most of their outdoor time in exploration and hunting.

Play begins and proceeds spontaneously, without adult encouragement, but other activities require the guidance of the mother cat. She must, for example, teach her kittens to recognize danger. Their only instinctive fear response is to cringe in fright if a large object comes at them from above (a month-old kitten is terrified if an open umbrella is moved over it), but otherwise they are fearless. Young kittens assume that all other animals are cats, approach them with jaunty friendliness, and invite them to play. So one of the mother cat's responsibilities is to identify potential enemies—from the indoor vacuum cleaner to the outdoor dog—for them. They soon learn that a special kind of growl is an order to scatter and run for cover. If their curiosity gets the better of them and they don't obey fast enough, she supplements her growl with a good strong bat to get them going in the right direction.*

* It is well known that both animals and human beings require particular kinds of experience during "critical periods" of development. Human babies, for example, must learn to trust other human beings when they are infants if they are to be emotionally whole in maturity. This does not seem to be true of kittens. A cat who is mistreated in youth can still become friends in adulthood with people or other animals.

FIGURE 8. *A chronology of kittens' play patterns: the stand-up and belly-up positions (top) emerge in the fourth week; the side-step and the pounce (center), in the fifth week; the chase and the leap (bottom), in the sixth week.*

A second responsibility of a mother cat toward her kittens is to wean them. This process begins in their sixth week or thereabouts. From then on, the mother makes herself less and less accessible to them. When the kittens want to suckle, they must persuade her to lie down so they can nurse comfortably. If she refuses to do so, they suckle while she is sitting or standing. The less she encourages them, the more eager they become; often, when she terminates a feeding session, the kittens are still hanging to her underside like little sausages.

As with human babies, there is no sudden cutoff point after which suckling ceases. Kittens learn to eat solid food by following the mother to her feeding dish. Although their object is to nurse from her, they may get their feet in her food and acquire a taste for it as they lick themselves clean. Their owner may put down a saucer of milk for them, into which they first stumble and from which they then learn to drink. (For a while, there is a lot of sneezing and shaking of whiskers because kittens can't at first gauge how deep to dip their noses.) But even after they are getting most of their nourishment from solid food, they continue to suckle—if their mother allows it. Leyhausen says there is a correlation between litter size and such permissiveness. As the kittens get older, they bite as well as suck: the more biting the mother cat has to endure the sooner she is ready to write *finis* to that aspect of motherhood.

Developmental stages are nicely timed. A kitten who is ready to eat solid food is also ready to learn to catch it. Mice, of course, play no part in the diet of cats who spend their lives indoors, and their kittens graduate from mother's milk to canned cat food or fine-cut meat provided by their owner. In contrast, kittens whose mothers are allowed to go out to hunt are exposed from about their fourth week of life to a series of experiences whose object is to turn them into accomplished predators.

To chase and catch is inborn, but killing must be learned. So must the knowledge that mice are good to eat. The mother cat sees to it that her kittens have the opportunity to learn these things, but she is not a teacher in the human sense. She makes no assignments, asks no questions, does not correct mistakes. What she *does* is to structure an environment in which the kittens' responses automatically lead to learning.

Lesson One, for example, could be called Prey Recognition. It consists of the mother cat bringing dead prey back to the nest and eating it in the presence of her kittens. She does not urge them to eat; she merely calls their attention to her catch. This takes the form of a keening cry which is unlike any other sound in her repertoire; it is not a cry of alarm but one of such urgency that even the human ear can distinguish its special character. Initially, its message is "Look! Here is something interesting!" Later, after the kittens connect her cry with the appearance and odor of prey, they interpret her signal as "Look! Here is a small harmless animal!" (mouse) or, if her cry is more intense, "Look! Here is a big dangerous animal!" (rat). She may toss it about before she eats it, while the kittens watch warily.

They soon learn to come running when she announces a catch, and in time are emboldened to pat at it or pounce on it themselves. By the sixth week, they know what mice or rats smell like, and the bolder kittens among them may also know what prey tastes like. Toward the end of this stage, the mother cat does not herself eat her catch but leaves it for the kittens.

Her behavior is quite remarkable, when one thinks about it, for she must first inhibit her own desire to eat prey at the place of capture and then she must forgo eating it at all. Motivation for doing so cannot be under hormonal control, since cats who are not mothers often bring *their* catch to other cats' kittens. Scientists therefore believe that the young themselves are the stimulus; that their size and behavior at a certain developmental stage trigger the carrying activity in adults. Ewer once had a cat who was raising foster young along with her own, the adopted kittens being older. The cat brought prey to each group of kittens, but on a separate timetable.

Neutered cats even transform their human companions into proxy kittens, bringing prey home and depositing it at their owners' feet. "She wouldn't leave me alone," people say, "until I had patted her and told her what a good hunter she was." According to Leyhausen, praise is not what the cat is looking for. It simply wants assurance that its kitten substitutes are sufficiently interested in prey to have "learned their first lesson."

The second lesson, beginning late in the kittens' second month of life, introduces them to live prey. By now, they have perfected their play pounces and play chases and are ready to apply them to a practical problem. Their mother brings back to the nest a mouse she has wounded during capture, and which is therefore a slow-moving target, and turns it loose. She sits watchfully by, ready to recapture and return it to the arena if it appears likely to escape, but only occasionally (for example, when she has a litter of only one or two kittens) does she herself participate. And even when she does join in, her object is to entice the kittens into the game, not to resolve it.

Gradually, as more mice are provided for the kittens to practice on, the motor patterns they have been performing in play become organized into the proper sequence for successful prey-catching: ambush, slink-run, lunge, seize. To those are added the nape bite, which does not appear in play. Once again, nature has been wise: the nape bite is too dangerous a tool to be used except in earnest. Some kittens do it correctly right from the start; others get only so far as the catch and are unable to bite into a mouse's neck with sufficient strength to kill it. According to Leyhausen, this is a common problem among the subordinate kittens in a litter. Perhaps the dominant kitten inhibits them. In any case, such kittens must engage in extended and vigorous competition with their littermates, or even with their mother, before they can work themselves into the state of hyperexcitability which must precede a first kill. Some never do.

Writing with Konrad Lorenz in a book about the motivation of animal behavior, Leyhausen says,

> Time and again the impression is forced on the observer that after having killed for the first time the cat is quite astonished by its achievement; it seems unable to comprehend why the dead animal no longer moves. It sometimes takes a while before the cat realizes that this can now be eaten, and certainly it must kill several times before it grasps in full the connection between the nape bite and transformation of a live animal into food.

He says that experiments have been done comparing the behavior of kittens whose sole solid food had consisted of prey animals with that of kittens who had never tasted prey before they made their first kill. The kittens in both groups were equally good hunters, but only those in the first group immediately ate their prey. The others had to be taught that mice or rats are edible by having their catch cut open for them so they got the direct smell of raw meat. And even that didn't persuade them to eat if they had not previously been fed raw meat. It is quite possible, in short, to raise a cat who is a good mouser but prefers to eat Kitty Krunchies out of a box. Nor will hunger "teach" an inexperienced cat to kill. Only those cats who have already made the connection between killing and eating go outdoors with the intention of catching themselves a meal.

Once a kitten has learned to kill, it is an enthusiastic practitioner of the art. It goes by the book at first, attacking only when a mouse is running away from it and striking on a slant from above and behind. Then it begins to experiment. It grabs a mouse on the flank—and gets its nose bitten. Ergo: there is no substitute for a good nape bite. By such trial-and-error learning, a kitten discovers that it can aim that bite from a direction other than above and behind; that it can use its paws to maneuver the prey around; that certain strategies are better than others for outflanking a fleeing mouse. Finally, the kitten becomes brave enough and experienced enough to kill prey that fights back.

In the wild, a young cat hunts with its mother and therefore learns to prey on the same kind of game. Some bobcats, for example, kill deer and others do not. Lions in different parts of Africa hunt different prey. The domestic cat, however, has too many kittens in a litter to engage in group hunts, and each kitten is free to develop its own specialty—unless its mother interferes. Leyhausen has had kittens who were developing into good ratters but whose overprotective mothers wouldn't allow their little ones to attack so ferocious an animal.

In summary, then, a cat becomes a predator by using its innate or learned responses in a series of prey-catching situations, carefully graduated in difficulty, which are provided for it by its mother. But *must* a kitten have that experience in order to learn to kill? What about apartment-reared kittens whose mother cannot bring them prey at the time nature has set for this kind of learning? Is there a "critical period" in kittenhood when a cat must learn to kill or forever be unable to do so?

There was a time when the answer to that last question was yes, thanks to a famous experiment which was done in 1930 by Z. Y. Kuo. He raised kittens in three different circumstances: with a mother who killed mice or rats in the presence of her kittens; without a mother from time of weaning and without ever seeing an animal killed; without a mother from the age of one week but with the company of a small rat or mouse. Results? All but three of the twenty-one kittens in the first group became enthusiastic hunters and killers. Only half of the kittens in the second group ever killed a mouse and none attacked a rat. In the third group, only three of the eighteen kittens who had been raised with rodents would later kill one, and those three would not kill the kind of rodent they had grown up with.

But in recent years it has become obvious that some cats without a proper bringing-up *do* learn to catch mice. Many millions of house-reared kittens are dumped in adolescence along country roadsides, and some of them manage to survive in the wild. (It may be, of course, that they subsist entirely on garbage, or become scavengers of other animals' catches.) Leyhausen says that cats can learn to kill for the first time in adulthood "but that far stronger stimuli are needed than with kittens" before the first nape bite can be performed. Warren P. Roberts and Harold Kiess have used electrical stimulation of the cat brain to trigger chasing, seizing, or killing of prey in animals that do not normally hunt, so it is apparent that the necessary motor patterns are present and in working order in the central nervous system of mature cats. Therefore, an earlier generation's belief that predation is learned in kittenhood or not at all has now been qualified. "We simply do not know enough about the way in which prey-killing and hunting develop to establish a firm conclusion about critical periods," Jay Rosenblatt says.

For whatever reason, the urge to chase and kill its normal prey can be absent or muted in individual animals. Genuine friendships are possible between dogs and cats in the same household, and mutual tolerance is commonplace. Cat-mouse friendships occasionally occur and are always good for a newspaper story with an accompanying photo of the mouse sitting on the cat's head or sharing its food dish. By and large, though, alliances between these natural enemies are tricky to establish and difficult to maintain. By way of illustration, here is a tale from Leyhausen:

He once had a wild cat named Tilly, whose diet included live rats. One of them managed to escape being caught by hiding under the cat's sleeping box. From there it made forays into the cage, nipping at Tilly's heels in a most unsettling manner. (Rats aren't supposed to be aggressors.) Finally, Tilly decided it was a "pet" rat and not a "food" rat, and gave it the run of the cage. She went about her daily business of killing food rats without ever mistaking her pet rat for one of them. In fact, the two of them came in time to eat fresh-killed rats together.

Tilly never struck at or bit her pet rat, even when it snatched food away from her, and eventually it moved from under her sleeping box *into* her sleeping box. Tilly slept holding it to her breast with her fore paws. This idyllic comradeship lasted four months, at the end of which Leyhausen took the rat away from her. Three months later, he returned it to her cage. Tilly showed no sign of recognition, and started after it. It had turned into a "food" rat. The rat, too big now to hide under the cat's sleeping box, jumped into its one-time refuge. But the appeal to auld lang syne was fruitless: Tilly leaped into the box and killed and ate her former friend.

At five months of age, kittens are young adults, as ready to make it on their own as they will ever be. In the wild, the feline family stays together longer, for there is only one litter a year. Domestic cats, however, go into heat again within six months of producing a litter, and may then turn hostile toward their kittens—hissing, growling, chasing them away. At the same time, the kittens become abrasive to one another. If they remain in the same household, a semblance of closeness may remain for a few months, but this too disappears. Year-old cats behave toward their mother or their littermates as they do to unrelated cats. Mother mates with son, daughter mates with brother, brothers fight one another. There is no memory of clustering together to pool their warmth, no recollection of the shared excitement when they saw their first snake, no remembrance of the mice their mother brought them. Now they too walk by themselves.

CHAPTER 12

The Genetics of Breed

And then?

Let us assume that the kittens of the preceding chapter were purebreds. A purebred cat is one whose ancestry is known for at least five generations and whose pedigree has been registered with an association of cat fanciers. As members of an elite group—500,000 out of the crop of 13,000,000 kittens who are born each year in the United States—most of them go to homes in which they are admired and respected. They have been conscientiously and expensively raised and are expensive to acquire. People who buy purebreds take care of them.

Cats Magazine estimates that there are about 27,000 breeders of purebreds in the United States and Canada. Some run large catteries, have national reputations, and sell hundreds of animals. Others are little more than hobbyists, limiting themselves to a local clientele and selling perhaps ten kittens a year. Although something like $25,000,000 annually changes hands over all, breeding cats is not a business that makes many people rich. As Margaret Cooper Gay says, growing potatoes may pay better. But growing cats is more interesting, and for most breeders has elements of addiction.

The females—in breeders' parlance, the "queens"—must be fed the year around, stud fees must be paid or a stud kept and fed, veterinarians must be consulted, people must be hired to keep the animals' quarters clean, piles of records must be kept. When the kittens have been "thrown" and themselves fed, there is no guarantee that they will sell, or, for that matter, even survive. Every breeder dreads the appearance of the runny noses or diarrhea which indicate that one of several highly infectious feline diseases may have gained a foothold in the colony. A real epidemic can wipe out the whole enterprise.

To sell a kitten for less than $50 is inevitably to lose money. Prices range upward into three figures, depending on the rarity of the breed or the number of relatives who have Ch. (for Champion) in front of their names. Depending on breed and bloodlines, a mature cat who is to be used by the buyer for breeding can cost anywhere from $200 to $1,000. If one can believe *Animal Facts and Feats*, "the most valuable cat in the world" (at least in 1967) was a champion white Persian tom whose English owner refused a $4,200 offer from an American breeder.

The world of the Cat Fancy is small, close, and competitive. It is composed of regional clubs which are affiliated with one of eight fanciers' associations whose aggregate membership is about 10,000. Clubs also exist to promote interest in particular breeds (including one devoted to non-pedigreed animals, the Household Pets). All of them sponsor shows at which cats compete for prizes in a variety of classes and gradually accumulate enough wins to become Champions, multiple Champions, or (in another scoring system) All-American Cats. Owners, devotees, and breeders meet one another at these shows, buy and sell, swap information, lobby to get show rules or breed standards changed, and otherwise "advance the interests of the Fancy." It is a growth industry: between 1900 and 1957, only about 100,000 cats had been registered with the largest of the groups, the Cat Fanciers Association. These days, the CFA is registering cats at the rate of 10,000 per year.

Breeds? At present, there are at least twenty-six: Abyssinians, American Shorthairs, Balinese, Birmans, Bombays, British Shorthairs, Burmese, Chartreux, Egyptian Maus, Havana Browns, Himalayans, Japanese Bobtails, Korats, Lavenders, Maine Coons, Manx, Persians, Ragdolls, Rex, Russian Blues, Scottish Folds, Siamese, Somalis, Sphinxes, Tonkinese, and Turkish Angoras. Not all of them have been accepted for registration by all the fanciers' associations or admitted to championship competition; not all of them will be described in the pages to follow; and the detailed standards which determine each kind of cat's prizeworthiness will not be included.*

Inasmuch as the development of breeds depends upon a knowledge of genetics, let's start with chromosomes. Each chromosome is filled with nucleic acid which itself is composed of molecular groupings called genes. Twenty-five years ago, before the structure of nucleic acid was well understood, genes were often described for laymen as beads on a necklace. Today, the necklace should be envisioned as two strands of beads which are wound around each other like two-ply yarn or rope.

Living organisms have varying numbers of chromosomes. Cats have nineteen pairs, one of each pair being inherited from the female parent and the other from the male parent. Of the nineteen, the X and Y chromosomes (which among other things determine sex) are unlike. All the other chromosomes, however, are matched pairs. The genes in both chromosomes of a pair are strung on the necklace of nucleic acid in the same order and are specific for the development of the same traits. These equivalent genes (alleles) may carry the same or different biochemical directions. In a given chromosome, for example, the gene for hair length may specify short hair and in the paired chromosome the allelic gene may specify long hair. Or the genes in both chromosomes may carry identical directions relative to hair length.

When the outward expression of any trait is brought about by just one of a pair of genes, it is said to be dominant and the overridden gene is said to be recessive. Recessive genes are externally expressed only when both chromosomes of a pair contain them. That's why one kitten in a litter of four can turn out to be long-haired despite the fact that both of its parents are short-haired. Let *A* stand for short hair (the dominant form of the gene) and *a* stand for long hair (the recessive form). Because both *A* and *a* are expressed in the progeny, both must be present in the parents, even though not visible.

The checkerboard below assumes that both parents possess one dominant and one recessive form of the gene. Readers who have hazy recollections of their high-school or college biology courses might also need to be reminded that sex cells possess only *one* chromosome from each parental pair. Which one is a matter of chance; each of the female parent's egg cells (at

---

* Grace Pond's *Complete Cat Encyclopedia* (New York: Crown Publishers, 1972) includes complete descriptions of breeds and their standards. *Cats Magazine* carries notices of cat shows and announcements by each of the cat fanciers' associations.

FIGURE 9. *There are twenty-six breeds of cats, many of them very recently developed. These three are among the oldest breeds: the stockily built long-haired Persian (top), the tailless Manx (center), and the lithe and agile Siamese, whose light body is tipped with darker color (bottom).*

left of chart) is equally likely to hold *A* or *a*, and the same is true of the male's sperm cells (top of chart).

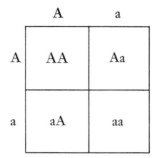

Therefore, four combinations of fertilized eggs are possible. The *AA* kitten will have short hair and will pass on only genes for short hair to its progeny. The two hybrid kittens—*Aa* and *aA*—will have short hair but can pass on either allele. The *aa* kitten will have long hair and will pass on only genes for long hair. If one wants to be sure of getting long-haired kittens, one must mate long-haired cats.

Growth and reproduction are based on the division of cells: one becoming two, two becoming four, and so on. Whenever cells divide, so do chromosomes. The two strands of beads in the nucleic acid necklace unwind, and each chain then acts as a template upon which a copy of itself is made. This biochemical duplicating process is remarkably accurate, but once in a while a mistake occurs and a gene in the new chain acquires a molecular structure which differs slightly from that of the gene upon which it was modeled. A different molecular structure conveys a different biochemical message, and whatever trait it controls will therefore be different. Such a change is called a mutation.

If its presence does not adversely affect the animal's ability to survive, the mutated gene will be copied along with the rest of its chromosome whenever that chromosome duplicates itself. And if the chromosome is in a sex cell, the changed gene will also be transmitted to another generation. This is the process which creates allelic forms of genes. In animals, breed differences are based on it.

Those differences are not as marked in cats as in dogs. There is no feline equivalent of a mastiff or a Chihuahua: all domestic cats are approximately the same size. The assumption therefore is that the genes which control size are very resistant to mutation. Genes which control skeletal formation and fur texture are somewhat less resistant, and those which control pigmentation and pattern are very plastic indeed. Cats come in a multitude of hues and tints and with various kinds of stripes and spots. Some of those colors and patterns can, in fact, be considered products of domestication. With man as its protector and source of food, a cat does not need to be camouflaged against predators. Human beings also like novelties, and the cat fanciers among them have preserved certain mutations which would be lethal in the wild.

Color and pattern are controlled by different genes, and there are also genes which mask the effect of others. The cellular environment in which a given biochemical process takes place can also affect the outcome of genetic action. These interrelationships are too complicated to describe here in full, although some will be mentioned. Suffice it to take A. G. Searle's word that the end result depends on the functioning of "a hierarchy of genes becoming active at different times and in different places or, sometimes, acting throughout the organism at the same time."

The so-to-speak "basic cat" is a shorthair. It is the cat common to every neighborhood; the kind, if adopted from a doorstep, which may be described by its owner as "just an alley cat." It may be gray, black, orange, or white; solid color, striped, or spotted; and its eyes may be yellow, orange, hazel, green, or blue. But many a similarly patterned and colored animal, different only in that its ancestry is known and that it meets certain physical standards, will be described by *its* owner as an American (or British) Shorthair. As Adolph Suehsdorf says, "Alley cat is not a breed but a condition." In 1974–75, more than 3,000 American or British Shorthairs were entered in championship competition in American cat shows.

Variations in eye color result from the amount, location, and shape of the pigment granules which are deposited in the iris or on the retina; the yellow to orange range is most common. Sometimes a particular color correlates with a particular fur color, as in blue-eyed white cats, but sometimes several colors are possible. In that case, the Cat Fancy picks just one of the possibles when setting its standards.

Both eyes and fur owe their color to the presence or absence of the pigment melanin, which comes in two types: eumelanin (brownish-black) and phaeomelanin (yellow to reddish). The fundamental kind of feline fur has hairs banded with both pigments. This coloration is called agouti, after a South American rodent of that fur type, and the gene responsible for it is dominant. In cats, agouti coloration is usually paired with a striped pattern for which there are three alleles. Two are recessive: the gene for striped tabby (see Figure 3, p. 65) and the gene for blotched tabby (see the middle cat in Figure 11, p. 180). The third is a dominant gene which produces a stripe down the cat's backbone and faint lines on legs, tail, or flanks—the pattern characteristic of the African wild cat. (*F. libyca*) and also of the modern Abyssinian breed of domestic cats.

The "Aby" was introduced into England in 1869 by the wife of an English officer who had served in Abyssinia (Ethiopia). Because its agouti coat so much resembled that of a rabbit, cats of this breed were often called "bun [for bunny] cats." Nobody knows the source of the breed; native Ethiopian cats are not Abyssinians. During a century of breeding for show purposes, certain of its characteristics have been refined. In some Abyssinians, only the stripe along the spine remains, and the fur is a richer and more ruddy brown than one sees in a wild animal with an agouti coat. There is also now a "red" Abyssinian, in which the coat is a copper color. This variation may be due to a recessive allele of the gene for black which in other cats dilutes black to brown; in the Abyssinian it allows the phaeomelanin bands on each hair to contribute more color to the coat. Abyssinians have green, yellow, or hazel eyes.

The agouti coat can mutate into one of its constituent colors via recessive alleles which affect the manufacture or deposit of the melanin bands in each hair. Some cats are black because they have two genes for *not* producing the yellow pigment that is normally present in agouti hair. As mentioned in the preceding paragraph, however, there is also a dominant gene (quite unrelated to the agouti gene and its alleles) which produces black fur. And *it* has an allele (recessive) which changes the protein framework and the shape of the melanin granule, the result being the chestnut-colored coat of the green-eyed, short-haired breed known as the Havana Brown.

A different biochemical message is carried by the "dilute" genes, all of them recessive, which also lighten fur color. They cause the pigment granules in the hair cells to clump together in irregular groups and therefore to absorb less light. Under such circumstances, pigment which would make the hair look black, if spread evenly, appears gray or blue-gray; and yellow pigment appears cream-colored.

Gray cats whose fur has a blue undertone are sometimes referred to as Maltese, a name that according to legend derives from a gray cat native to the island of Malta. There is no show breed by that name, however. All the pedigreed gray shorthairs whose fur color is a dilution of black are called "blue." The Russian Blues, once called Archangel cats because that's where they came from, are long and lithe. They have green eyes and plushy coats with a surface sheen which results from a silver tip at the end of each hair. The British Blues have shorter bodies, untipped fur, and eyes in the yellow to orange range. The Chartreux have eyes of the same color but are even stockier of build, and their fur is somewhat coarser. At one time, they were called Carthusian cats because they were introduced into France from South Africa by Carthusian monks.

And then there are the albino genes, a graded series of alleles which first eliminate the yellow (phaeomelanin) band and then the black (eumelanin) band from agouti hair. All are recessive. The so-called "chinchilla" gene, first on the list, removes the yellow pigment and thus creates white-and-black-banded hairs. The result is the silver tabby or the "smoke" longhair whose underfur is white with black tips. At the opposite end of the scale are the white-furred and pink-eyed cats who are true albinos. Few survive; total absence of pigment is usually lethal. (The fur of all-white cats with normally colored eyes is not produced by a gene in the albino series and will be discussed later.)

Intermediate in the list of albino genes are those that create the yellow-eyed Burmese and the blue-eyed Siamese. Inasmuch as the latter breed figures in the ancestry of the former, the Siamese will be discussed first. Genetically, these are the most interesting of all cats because of the several ways they differ from all the others. The Siamese is one of the most popular breeds. The cats who started the fashion were given by the king of Siam to the wife of the British Consul in Bangkok in 1884. They are lean-limbed, agile, and sociable cats; those qualities, combined with their exotic coloring, made the first pair a sensation when they arrived in England. (See Figure 9.) The early imports to the United States cost about $1,000 each, but now the breed is so common that a pedigreed kitten can be acquired for as little as $25.

The Siamese cat is a monument to the action of recessive genes, for in one of its color phases four pairs of such genes are involved. But let's start with the original—and the simplest—version, the Seal Point. A Seal Point has two genes for non-agouti (the ones that eliminate the yellow pigment from the agouti band and leave only black). To those are added a pair of albino genes whose initial effect is to bleach out almost all the color, with the result that newborn Siamese kittens are off-white all over.

These particular albino genes, however, have a peculiar property: they inhibit the making of pigment only when body temperature is above 98 degrees Fahrenheit. A cat's normal body temperature is about 100 degrees, but at the extremities it drops to 96 degrees or below. Therefore, pigment is formed on the face, ears, feet, and tail of the Siamese cat from about the fifth day after birth. The Seal Point's pigment is the extremely dark brown or black that is specified by the non-agouti gene.

The fact of temperature sensitivity and the temperature thresholds required to activate the gene were established in 1930 by the Russian biologists N. A. and V. N. Iljin, who created light hair where it would normally be dark by shaving off the first growth and applying warm bandages to the shaved spots. When the cats' new hair grew in it was white. The Iljins also discovered that the heat generated by an infection prevents the formation of pigment too.

The temperature on the surface of cats' bodies is not constant. There is greater heat loss wherever bones lie close to the surface, and therefore Siamese cats in time develop color on the body itself. A slightly pigmented band may appear along the backbone, for example, or on the flanks. There is often a faint patch of pigmented hair at the back of the neck, where the shoulder blades rise up. An Oriental legend has it that this "temple mark" memorializes the god who once picked up a sacred Siamese cat and forever left the shadow of his hands on the cat's descendants.

Such body pigmentation is less apparent on the breeds of Siamese which were developed after the Seal Point, for their pigment is lighter in color. These variants require the addition of genes which modify the basic mix of non-agouti and Siamese albino. In the Chocolate Point, for example, the basic pair are supplemented by two of the "brown" genes which are responsible for the coloration of the Havana Brown breed. In the Blue Point, the supplement is a pair of the "dilute" genes which produce the Russian Blues. And the Lilac Point has all four: the non-agouti and Siamese albino genes of the Seal Point, the "dilute" genes of the Blue Point, and the "brown" genes of the Chocolate Point. (There are also a couple of other color variations which will not be discussed here.) Given so much variety, it is not surprising that almost 12,000 cats with Siamese coloration were entered in American cat shows in championship competition in 1974–75.

Two genetic problems beset breeders. One of them is the tendency of Siamese cats to have kinks in their tails, a peculiarity which bespeaks their place of origin. Peculiarities of tail structure are common in Asian cats; Charles Darwin, in fact, said in 1868 that "throughout the Malayan Archipelago, Siam, Pegu, and Burmah all the cats have truncated tails about half the proper length, often with a sort of knot at the end." To say "all cats" was an unscientific generalization. Darwin was corrected in 1959, for part of the population, by A. G. Searle. As an addendum to his census of Singapore cats, he mentions that about a third of Hong Kong cats and almost two-thirds of cats examined in Malaysia have kinky tails.

According to legend, the kink in the Siamese tail was an amenity created by the royal Siamese cats for the princesses they attended. When the ladies went to the palace lake to bathe, each slipped off her rings and for safekeeping hung them on the tail of her cat. The cats crooked their tails in order to make their precious burdens more secure, and in time the kink became permanent. Modern scientists, ignoring the wisdom of the past, say that kinks are caused by an inherited abnormality of the caudal vertebrae.

The gene for kinked tail apparently has no relationship to the albino gene which is responsible for the beautiful coloration of Siamese cats. The latter gene is a mixed blessing, however, for it plays havoc with the neurology of the Siamese visual system and sometimes produces the breeders' other problem: cats with crossed eyes. Show standards permit neither kinky tails nor crossed eyes.

Scientists do not understand the process by which a gene that inhibits or prevents pigment formation also alters the development of the nerves linking retina and brain, but the effects of that process are well documented. Before describing them, though, it is necessary to describe how the optic nerves are normally distributed and how they *should* function:

In animals with binocular vision, the retinal nerves from both eyes ordinarily arrange themselves in a symmetrical pattern as they proceed into the brain. As mentioned elsewhere, certain nerves in the right eye go to the left hemisphere of the brain; the corresponding nerves in the left eye go to the right hemisphere of the brain; and the remaining nerves in each eye go to the same side of the brain on which the eye itself is located. Thus both hemispheres receive an equal amount of visual information from each eye.

The nerves which start in the retina terminate in a structure in the middle of the brain which is called the lateral geniculate nucleus. The nerves from one eye are connected to the top layer of geniculate cells and the nerves from the other eye are connected to the second layer. Furthermore, the nerve from a given receptor—call it Receptor A—in the retina of one eye enters its cell layer in the geniculate nucleus at the same point where the nerve from Receptor A in the other eye enters *its* cell layer. Two representations from the same retinal position in each eye are thus superimposed. Basically, each confirms the information carried by the other. That information is then transmitted to the visual cortex, the structure at the back of the brain which determines the cat's response to what it sees.

In Siamese cats, however—and in many other animals with albino genes—an abnormal number of retinal nerves cross over to the opposite hemisphere of the brain. There they pair up incorrectly with cells in the lateral geniculate nucleus. The top-layer cell which is linked to Receptor A in the right eye may, for example, be paired with a second-layer cell which is linked to Receptor K in the left eye. Because the information sent on by these differently located receptors is different, the paired cells would transmit conflicting messages to the visual cortex. The resulting confusion would be reflected in the cat's behavior: it would be unable to locate objects in space.

The conditional "would" was used just above because Siamese cats obviously *can* locate objects in space. They can catch mice, steer a safe course around furniture, and avoid falling into holes. How do they overcome the neural disability that afflicts them? The University of Wisconsin's R. W. Guillery, one of many neuroscientists who are studying abnormal optic nerve pathways in albino animals, says in a recent summary of the research that the Siamese cat brain uses one of two strategies to deal with the mismatched pairs in its geniculate nucleus. Depending on the location of those cells, the brain either suppresses the messages sent by the discordant cells in the lower layer—in the example above, the information derived from Receptor K—or it reroutes the nerves from the geniculate nucleus to the cortex in such a way that the information from Receptor K no longer arrives at the cortex jointly with the information from Receptor A.

By looking at their pets' eyes, Siamese cat owners can tell which of the two strategies is being employed. Cats who use the second strategy—who re-route the information in their discordant cells—tend to be cross-eyed. Siamese cats who restore visual sanity by suppressing the information in the discordant cells tend not to be cross-eyed. *Why* the eyes cross is unknown. Siamese kittens are not born with the condition; the squint develops during their first six or eight weeks of life. So it is clearly a response to the use of their eyes, in some way compensatory for the internal abnormality. It is also clear that capability for binocular vision must diminish in proportion to the extent that an animal's visual cortex is deprived of input from properly paired geniculate cells. Siamese cats probably do not see quite as well as cats of other breeds.

Two other peculiarities of Siamese may or may not be related to their albino genes. The scientific literature provides no explanation for the slowness with which Siamese kittens mature (relative to kittens of other breeds) nor for the distinctive quality of the Siamese voice, which is much hoarser and more rasping than that of other felines.

There is some Siamese in the ancestry of the Burmese breed, whose creation is a good example of breeding problems and techniques. The effort began in 1930 when Joseph C. Thompson acquired the female progenitor of the breed, for which he chose "Burmese" as the generic name because the sailor from whom he bought the cat said she came from Burma. The cat had the dark points and general conformation of a Siamese but her fur was much browner and her eyes were yellow. Thompson guessed that she had one Siamese gene, but what was the other one?

In the absence of any Burmese males, the next-best choice of a mate was a Seal Point Siamese. That union produced both light-furred, blue-eyed Siamese kittens and darker-furred, yellow-eyed Burmese kittens. This confirmed the presence in the dam of Siamese genes (two of which, one from each parent, are necessary to produce Siamese offspring). But since Burmese kittens were also present, that gene—whatever it was—was obviously dominant over the Siamese genes of the sire. In the following generation, adults with both Siamese and Burmese genes produced both medium-brown and dark-brown kittens. The breeders had only to keep selecting the darker animals in order eventually to create the yellow-eyed cat with sable-brown fur which is today's Burmese. To achieve a true-breeding strain took more than ten years, and it was another ten years before Burmese were officially recognized as show cats.

More important to geneticists, a new allele in the albino series had been discovered. The Burmese gene, which removes less pigment than the Siamese gene but more pigment than the chinchilla gene, now appears between them in the graded series of albino alleles. The neural miswiring which afflicts Siamese cats does not appear in Chinchillas or Burmese; it obviously correlates with the extreme loss of pigment characteristic of Siamese cats and the true albinos, the latter having pure white fur and pink eyes. (The Himalayan rabbit, whose dark points and light fur duplicate the Siamese pattern, has the same disordered neurology of the brain. So do white mink, white rats, white mice, white ferrets, and white tigers. Neuroscientists would very much like to examine the brains of human albinos, but so far have been unable to do so.)

Now let's consider the recessive genes which affect cats' fur length or texture.

Rex cats have curly whiskers and short crimped hair which makes their coats resemble Persian lamb. The rex gene eliminates the long guard hairs and most of the awn hairs that form the top layer of fur in normal cats. Only the downy underhair remains. (Rex mutants occur in other animal species, too.) Breeders distinguish between German Rex, Cornish Rex, and Devon Rex—the names indicate where the original animal of each line appeared— but only their breeders can distinguish the differences among them. At least two of them have been crossed without altering the character of the offspring. As one would expect, Rex cats are sensitive to low temperatures.

The Sphinx is the ultimate step in defurring a cat without skinning it. The genes involved act just opposite to those in the Rex cat. In the Sphinx, the downy base coat disappears in kittenhood, leaving only the guard hairs and a scattering of others. These are easily dislodged because the bulbs from which the hairs spring are malformed. So, although hair continues to grow, it keeps falling out and these cats are virtually hairless. They appeal to people who like novelties and are prepared to protect them. Lacking insulation against extremes in temperature, these cats cannot survive in the wild.

If popularity among cat fanciers had been the criterion, the long-haired

Persian (see Figure 9, p. 149) would have been the breed described first in this chapter. Persians consistently head the lists of entries at cat shows; more than 21,000 went into championship competition in the United States in 1974–75. The numbers are in part explained by the fact that there are so many show categories for Persians, since each of fourteen types can win prizes. Colors are the same as for shorthairs, but Persians are chunkier in build—"cobby" is the term used by breeders—and have rounder heads, shorter ears, and flatter faces than the average shorthair. These characteristics are the result of the intensive breeding which followed the introduction of the first longhairs to England in the nineteenth century.

What was their pedigree? One theory, as mentioned in an earlier chapter, is that Persians trace their line from the steppe cat (*F. manul*) of Central Asia. The steppe cat has a round head, short ears, and a compact body, but its hair is woollier than the modern Persian's and is not uniformly long. The wild species could have interbred with Asian domestic cats and the descendants could have found their way slowly westward from, say, Tibet to Iran (Persia) and thence into Europe. In the course of centuries, a mutation for uniformly long hair could have occurred among them.

The old cat books speak of Persians which were imported from Persia, but none of the accounts makes clear whether those cats had the flat faces and short ears which now distinguish the breed. The Count de Buffon, writing in the eighteenth century, describes Persian cats as gray ("the color of those we call Chartreux cats") but in every other respect "they have a perfect resemblance to the cat of Angora." The homeland of the Angora cat, he says, was Syria. Blue-eyed white Angoras were then fashionable in France; in fact, when they were later imported into England they were referred to as "the French cats." The Angora pictured in Buffon's book looks nothing like a modern Persian.

Like Angora goats and Angora rabbits, Angora cats have very long, crinkled, silky-feeling hair. They are big animals with wedge-shaped heads, high ears, long bodies, and great plumy tails. They enjoyed quite a vogue in England during the early nineteenth century, but they eventually lost their identity. The British, who prefer stocky cats, started to breed the silky hair of the Angora into the existing strain that was called Persian, a cat with a cobby build, flat face, and short ears. Wherever the Persian came from, it shared with the Angora an alleged origin in the romantic and mysterious East.

Maybe cat fanciers lumped the two "imported" breeds into a single category. In any case, one finds it difficult in reading nineteenth-century references to cats to know which breed is being referred to, because they are so often equated.

The English zoologist St. George Mivart wrote in 1881, for example, that "the Angora, or Persian cat is remarkable for its great size and for the length and delicacy of its hair. . . . Its temperament is said to be exceptionally lethargic; but this is certainly not always the case, and may be due to excessive petting for generations."* Agnes Repplier could have been describing either an Angora or a Persian when she said, in 1901, "Who that has ever seen the cats of Stamboul can forget those beautiful Persians, snow-white, indolent, amber-eyed, carried in the arms of Nubian slave women?" Persian, Angora, or a mix, they were exotic, and cat fanciers loved them.

Angoras themselves declined in popularity after about 1900 and have only recently made a comeback as the Turkish Angora breed. The new Angoras look like the ones which were pictured in nineteenth-century cat books but the ancestors of those now being bred in the United States were imported from Turkey in 1953.

There are other new long-haired breeds which a casual observer would class as Persians because they are fluffy. Of these, the Himalayan *does* have Persian in its pedigree; it's a cross between a Siamese and a Persian. One could describe it as a long-haired Siamese if it were not for the fact that the Balinese breed *is* a long-haired Siamese. (In other words, it developed its own mutant long-hair gene.) There is also the Birman, which has color points but whose feet are white. Maine Coon cats and Ragdolls are distinctively colored or marked longhairs but have no Siamese ancestry.

As can be seen from the foregoing, cat breeders generally have to pair recessive genes if a line is to breed true. However, that is not the case with Manx cats (see Figure 9); their taillessness results from a dominant gene. An old myth has it that the progenitor of this breed was dawdling as it went up the ramp into the Ark, and Noah shut the door on it too soon. A modern myth holds that Manx cats are "part rabbit" (which is a biological impossi-

---

* That acquired characteristics can be inherited was still widely believed in 1881. Mivart also ascribes the birth of kittens with stumpy tails to the fact that their mother had had her tail amputated.

bility) because their exceptionally long hind legs give them an odd gait which someone who is looking for rabbit ancestry can interpret as a hop.

On the Isle of Man, from which the breed derives its name, it is said that the original Manx came ashore from the ships of the Spanish Armada. Inasmuch as taillessness is not a conspicuous feature of Spanish cats, it is more likely that Manx descend from Oriental cats (among whom, as mentioned earlier, abnormalities of the tail are common). In the 1800's, English tailless cats were called "Cornwall cats." Like the Isle of Man, Cornwall is a place where ships' cats originally from Asia could have been landed or washed ashore in wreckage.

Or maybe the gene controlling the formation of the final vertebrae in the tail mutated independently.

That gene is one of several which have "incomplete penetrance"; that is, it may express itself in an intermediate rather than in an all-or-none manner. The Manx who win prizes in cat shows are completely tailless, have hollows where the tail should be, and are called "rumpies." Other Manx have short tails and are called "stumpies." There are even some long-tailed Manx. The fur is short and comes in all the standard colors and patterns.

Several other dominant genes are important to cat owners and breeders, although only one of them seems to be in the process of being developed as a distinctive breed. It causes the tips of the cat's ears—the pinnae—to fold forward and downward, an aberration which does not affect the cat's ability to hear. The mutation appeared in 1961 on a farm in Scotland; hence the name, Scottish Fold.

Another dominant gene causes polydactylism, the presence of six or more toes. Slippers, Theodore Roosevelt's famous White House cat—the one who lay in the middle of the corridor between the dining room and the East Room and forced the guests at a state dinner to detour around him—was a six-toed cat. The University of Denver's V. A. Chapman and F. N. Zeiner, in studying a large number of polydactyl cats, have found that eight different anatomical types occur. Sometimes one type appears on the fore feet and another type on the hind feet. The two scientists believe that simple dominance explains the general trait but that the details are genetically more complex.

And then there is the gene for orange, which differs from all the other fur-color genes in that it is sex-linked; it is carried in the X chromosome.

Pigment genes in the sex chromosomes override those in the body's other (autosomal) chromosomes. Normal females have two X chromosomes; males have one, plus the Y chromosome that determines maleness. If a tomcat (XY) has the gene for orange in his X chromosome, he will be orange or a tint of it, and the same is true of a female who has the gene for orange in both chromosomes.

What happens, however, if one of the female's X chromosomes carries a gene for orange and the other one carries an allelic gene which specifies non-orange? The result is a tortoiseshell, in which the two colors are blended together in a sort of tweedy mix. (The second color can be gray, brown, or black, but only black is recognized in show cats and therefore black will be the example used here.)If a gene for white spotting is also present in the animal, one gets a calico cat, sometimes called a tricolor, in which orange, black, and white appear in large patches. The presence of white is irrelevant to the inheritance of the orange-black combination and therefore what follows applies to both tortoiseshells and calicos.

According to the geneticists Willard Centerwall and Kurt Benirschke,

> Early in embryonic life and long before cell differentiation occurs, a "decision" is made for each cell as to which of its two X chromosomes will be active and which will stay in the resting stage. As the embryo matures, all cells descending from the original cluster will retain the decision made in their own ancestor cells. The result in normal females is a random mixture of cell groups through the body. In the skin, orange patches will be derived from cells in which the orange gene is active and black patches will be derived from cells in which the non-orange gene is active.

Males, however, normally have only one X chromosome and therefore should be orange or non-orange but not both. Yet there *are* male tortoiseshells and calicos—rare, to be sure, and almost always sterile. Most of them have an extra X chromosome, acquired from the sperm or egg cell which gave them life but in which the two parental chromosomes did not separate during cell division. Thus their genetic constitution is XXY. The Y still confers maleness, but the double X's cause sterility.

It has been estimated that about 6 percent of cats are tortoiseshells or calicos, and among these the ratio of males to females is 1 to 3,000. Anthologies of folk remedies sometimes include a recipe for the removal of warts, specifying that they should be rubbed with the tail of a tortoiseshell tomcat. But a warning is appended: such treatment is effective only during the month of May. One wonders if this alleged folk remedy was in fact a fifteenth- or sixteenth-century spoof of folk remedies. Country folk must have been well aware of the scarcity of tortoiseshell toms. Modern owners treasure them for their rarity if not for their medicinal or reproductive powers. Incidentally, the XXY anomaly appears among human males, also.

Centerwall and Benirschke say that the occasional appearance of a fertile orange-black male is due to "somatic chimerism." That condition results from the fusion, during the earliest stages of cell division, of two fertilized egg-embryos, which if all had gone well would have developed as two distinct individuals. The single individual who does develop, however, has an XX-XY constitution and makes both orange and black pigment. If the proportion of XY cells is large enough, the cat appears to be male; and if there are XY cells in its testes, it is fertile as well. Considering how many "ifs" are involved, one can see why such a cat is so uncommon. Its incidence is unknown. There are XX-XY individuals in the human population too.

Random white spotting on a cat's body may or may not be due to a dominant gene. Take, for example, a black cat with a white blaze on its forehead, white feet, a white tail tip, and a white spot on its belly. The lack of pigment in those spots is probably not due to a gene which prevents pigment formation but to a lack of pigment cells for genes to act upon. A developmental error is at fault. Pigment cells (as well as cells involved in the formation of the skull, skeleton, and many of the sensory nerves) originate in the neural crest, which runs along the part of the embryo that will someday be its backbone. At a very early stage of development, neural crest cells move down and around the curled-up body of the fetus, like water flowing off a rock, each finally coming to rest at its appropriate location. But if some pigment cells make a late start or are impeded in reaching the parts of the body farthest distant from the neural crest, no pigment can be made there and white blazes result.

Most white hair, however, results from gene action. Geneticists are not agreed as to whether white spotting is caused by one gene and totally white fur by another gene, or whether those different conditions reflect the action of a single gene which has a series of alleles whose effects are progressively more extreme. (That is the case, remember, among the albino genes which create the Chinchilla, Burmese, Siamese, and albino effects.) Donald Bergsma and Kenneth S. Brown, of the National Institutes of Health in Bethesda, provide support for the single-gene theory in their 1971 study of white cats, but their evidence will not be included here because those of their findings which will interest cat owners (as distinct from geneticists) have to do with the correlation of white fur, blue eyes, and deafness—a common problem among white cats.*

One hears it said that all blue-eyed white cats are deaf (or that just the males are deaf) and that white cats with one yellow eye and one blue eye are deaf on the blue-eyed side. None of those assertions is true. What appears to happen is that the gene for white is 100 percent effective in preventing the formation of pigment in fur, but in each of its other manifestations its dominance is not complete. Thus, the eye color and hearing ability of any given white cat depends on whether it has one or two genes for white and its (or their) interaction with other genes.

By interfering with the development of various structures derived from the neural crest, the gene for white can cause anatomical malformation of the ear, which results in deafness, or it can eliminate a layer of pigment which should be deposited at the back of the eye. Blueness always correlates with reduction of pigment, and in the case of white cats, also with the loss of the tapetum (the "mirror" in the retina which is responsible for the night shine of cats' eyes and which was described in Chapter 3).

If a cat has two genes for white, it is not inevitably deaf, but it is twice as likely to be deaf as is a cat with one gene for white. Similarly, cats with two blue eyes are more likely to be deaf than are cats with one yellow and one blue eye, and those in turn are more likely to be deaf than are white cats with normally pigmented eyes. One additional fact discovered by Bergsma and Brown is that the pupillary opening is larger in blue eyes of this type than in normal eyes. The effect is odd indeed when a cat has one eye of each type.

* Anyone who has a taste for scientific history and a little knowledge of genetics should read a 1933 paper by Ruth C. Bamber, of the University of Liverpool. Published in the *Journal of Genetics* (Vol. 27, p. 407), it is entitled "Correlation Between White Coat Colour, Blue Eyes, and Deafness in Cats." Bamber summarizes various scientists' opinions as to the cause of the condition, going as far back as the 1820's; in aggregate, a fine example of blind men examining the elephant, for each opinion is *partially* correct. Scientific progress often comes about via just such steps.

Cats carrying the gene for white are seriously disadvantaged. A deaf cat is everywhere in danger, and a white cat is in danger everywhere except against a backdrop of snow. The white gene is therefore selected against in nature. In the cat censuses conducted by Neil Todd and others, however, too many white cats show up to be explained by spontaneous reappearance of the mutation. In New York City, for example, more than 2 percent of cats are white, and in Melbourne they account for more than 7 percent of the feline population. Human beings obviously like white cats with blue eyes, even deaf ones; protect them; and allow them to pass on their genes to their progeny.

About 5 percent of congenitally deaf people have a condition called Waardenburg's syndrome. They have eyes of two different colors, hearing-nerve abnormalities, a white streak in the hair over their foreheads, and a tendency for the other hair to go gray prematurely. Bergsma and Brown hoped to throw some light on this condition by "using the cat as a model for genetic, physiologic, histologic, and developmental studies of hearing that could not be performed on man." It is logical to consider next the role of cats in scientific research laboratories, the Bergsma and Brown study having been a good introductory example.

CHAPTER 13

Service to Science

THERE ARE FOUR GENERAL reasons for using cats or other animals as subjects for laboratory research:

1. To enable people to observe behavior which cannot be adequately studied in a natural setting or (as in breeding experiments) to control such behavior.

2. To measure sensory, motor, or intellectual abilities.

3. To ascertain the effect of a given experience on mental or emotional health or development.

4. To advance medical knowledge or practice.

Research in all those categories has been mentioned in preceding chapters, but the object then was to report what the investigator had found out about cats. In describing scientific experiments in this chapter—and there will be examples of each of the categories just listed—the emphasis will fall on the investigative techniques employed and the human applications of the research, if any.

One of the earliest uses of the motion-picture camera was to show the changing body positions of a cat as it was dropped upside down from a height, turned over, and landed on its feet. The pictures were taken in 1894 by a French physiologist named Marey, to illustrate a lecture for the French Academy of Sciences. Despite his pictorial evidence, many physicists in his audience were skeptical. To turn over when falling freely requires a falling body to acquire angular momentum without pushing against anything, and they said that Marey's cat must have twisted itself on take-off.

The problem continued to intrigue scientists. In 1916, Henry R. Muller and Lewis H. Weed, of Johns Hopkins University, examined the physiology of the falling reflex. They found that normal cats could turn over and land on their feet even if dropped from less than a foot above the ground. So could blindfolded cats and cats in whom the vestibular (balancing) organs in both ears had been destroyed. (When that organ was destroyed in just one ear, the animal's response was sluggish; it could still complete the turn but not from so close to the ground as a normal cat can.) However, when Muller and Weed blindfolded cats in whom one or both of the vestibular organs had been destroyed, the cats dropped like rocks. The same thing happened when the experimenters surgically damaged the sites in the cortex of the brain which govern the functioning of eyes and ears. Conclusion: The brain and either the eyes *or* the balancing mechanism in the ears are essential to the performance of the maneuver.

An occasional investigator came back to the subject, but not until 1960 did the British physiologist Donald McDonald interest himself in the physics of the falling reflex. He duplicated Marey's sequence of films, but his camera was better. It exposed 1,500 frames per second and could therefore provide a clear record of each movement in a series which cats perform in only one-eighth of a second.

McDonald found that a cat, when dropped upside down, gathers its fore legs in close to its head, spreads its hind legs, bends its waist at a right angle, and then rotates the fore part of the body through 180 degrees about its axis. (See Figure 10.) This maneuver brings the head and fore legs into a ground-facing position. The rear part of the body has meanwhile done a tiny counterrotation (five degrees) and the hind limbs have been brought into line with the rest of the body. The cat arches its back as soon as it has made its turn, extending its legs—first the fore legs, then the hind legs—into a vertical position relative to the ground. All in one-eighth of a second! It takes far longer to tell it than to do it.

McDonald initially believed that uncontrolled spin is prevented by the tail functioning as an air brake, but when he tried dropping a Manx cat he discovered that it too could make a perfectly normal landing. "Therefore,"

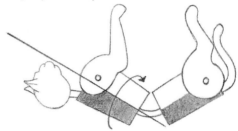

FIGURE 10. *Only one-eighth of a second is required for an upside-down cat to turn over when falling. Safe landings from heights greater than 60 feet are unlikely, although there is one cat of record who survived a fall from 120 feet.*

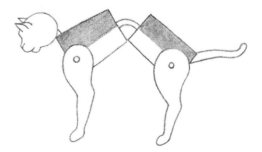

he concludes, "fine adjustments in posture must be made by contracting various body muscles rather as a trained acrobat does."

One requirement for a successful landing, however, is that the cat must be horizontal when it starts its fall. Responding to the doubts of the 1894 French physicists, McDonald avoided the possibility of twist on take-off by throwing some cats about three feet up in the air and then filming their descent. Whenever "they became up-ended through a bad throw no cat managed to correct itself; it fell with the body vertical despite vigorous movements. Once one pair of feet touched the ground, however, it corrected its position immediately." Inertial forces make it virtually impossible to rotate a vertical body at a right angle to its longitudinal axis.

Fundamentally, Muller and Weed's findings still stand. A congenitally deaf cat which McDonald blindfolded was unable to turn over and land on its feet. But of the two systems—the eyes and the vestibular organs in the ears—McDonald found that the eyes are more important. Normal cats landed clumsily when blindfolded, even when dropped from as low as three feet. Sight is essential, he believes, if a cat is to survive a fall from a great height.

McDonald declined to drop cats from ever-increasing heights in order to find out what the limit is. Instead, using a model of the right weight and shape, he calculated that a cat's terminal velocity is about 40 m.p.h., and that this speed is reached in about sixty feet.

> I have heard of cats falling safely from trees of that height [Mc-Donald says], but if this is so it shows remarkable resilience in landing. This speed represents that of a man falling nearly 50 feet, which would usually be fatal. The cat has, of course, much less momentum because of its smaller weight; but it has smaller muscles to absorb the shock, although they may be more efficient. We lack sufficient precise knowledge of what the speed of landing is to put this comparison on a quantitative basis, but it looks as if the only human parallel to a normal cat is a highly-trained circus performer.

Anne Walker's tomcat therefore seems to have been the Great Wallenda of the feline world. *Animal Facts and Feats* says he survived a 120-foot fall from the window of his owner's London apartment. He was sitting on a radiator beside an open window when a rainstorm broke and was startled when Miss Walker jumped out of bed to close the window. He leaped in the wrong direction and fell eleven stories to the ground. He wouldn't eat for several days thereafter, but no bones were broken.

An experiment which required a laboratory setting was Leyhausen's test of the theory (Chapter 2) that each innate action draws energy from its own neural reservoir and that the levels of energy in these reservoirs are different. Do cats kill because they are hungry, or is the urge to eat separate from the urge to kill?

The design of the experiment was simple. Leyhausen provided live mice to both hungry and well-fed cats until none of them would catch and kill any more, meanwhile observing their behavior. At first, *all* the cats went through the whole repertoire of chasing, catching, playing with prey, killing, and eating. The hungry cats initially shortened the play period and killed and ate their catches faster than the cats who weren't hungry. No more than three mice were eaten by the cats who had been fed before the experiment began, but these cats continued to kill. The hungry cats kept killing *and* eating; some of them ate as many as twelve mice. After catching their tenth mouse, though, all the cats slowed down. From the fifteenth mouse onward they lost interest in chasing or catching, and their predatory drives were so weakened that the mice began to intimidate *them*. Leyhausen watched one mouse bite a cat on its paw, after which the cat yowled and retreated. (See Figure 11, p. 180.)

That experiment helped scientists better understand the neurology of feline behavior because it showed that hunger and killing are separately motivated. It had a practical application too, insofar as it convinced people who use cats as mouse or rat traps that the hunger drive is not essential to successful hunting. (That proposition was also tested in the field by people like Elton and Davis, whose experiments were described in Chapter 7.)

Phrases like "hunger drive" weren't even in the scientific vocabulary at the turn of the century, and the neurology of behavior was more guessed at than understood. Psychology, in its nineteenth-century beginnings, concerned itself with measuring sensory and cognitive responses to stimuli and trying to explain how the brain might act as an intermediary. Animal subjects were used in part because all mammalian brains are similar and therefore anything discovered about animals' mental processes might apply to human beings, and in part because the still-new doctrine of evolution had heightened scientists' interest in comparative studies of different species. Dogs and rats were initially the animals of choice, but cats soon joined them.

The British zoologist St. George Mivart is probably responsible. In organizing a textbook published in 1881, he took a novel approach. Instead of discussing animals in general, he decided to describe *one* animal in detail— "an animal easily obtained and of convenient size . . . the common Cat"— and then compare it to other animals. He devoted more than 300 pages to anatomical description of so detailed a nature that the book could still serve as a dissection manual. The British scientist Patricia Scott dates the use of cats for biomedical research from the publication of Mivart's book.

In 1897, only two years after Roentgen discovered X rays, the first visualization of the gastrointestinal tract was achieved by the Harvard physiologist Walter B. Cannon, using the cat as his experimental animal. After being fed bread soaked in milk to which bismuth had been added, a cat was strapped onto a stretcher positioned above the tube which generated what were then called Roentgen rays. Using hand fluoroscopy, Cannon could see the changing shape of the cat's stomach and other organs as the food moved through the digestive tract.*

Inasmuch as earlier investigators had been limited to examining people or animals with surgically damaged stomachs or intestines, or had had to use probes which irritated the GI tract, Cannon was thrilled to be able to observe the behavior of a normally functioning gastric system. It has, he said, "an unsuspected nicety of mechanical action." He made another discovery, too: whenever his feline subjects became anxious or frightened, peristalsis ceased. As soon as they were petted and reassured, their gastric movements began again. Cannon concluded his report by saying, "It has long been common knowledge that violent emotions interfere with the digestive process, but that gastric motor activities should manifest such extreme sensitiveness to nervous conditions is surprising." Visual confirmation was so impressive that Cannon then launched his great research on the physiology of emotion.

---

* Although the possibility of being "burned" by X rays was very early recognized, the danger was underestimated. According to Lloyd E. Hawes, of the University of Massachusetts, an expert on the history of radiology, the tube was protected by a metal diaphragm, to prevent scatter, but the technicians did not wear protective clothing. Hawes says that Cannon learned his X-ray technique from Dr. Francis Williams of the Boston City Hospital, and there are "good photographs of Williams fluoroscoping in a stunning morning suit with striped pants and a tailed coat."

About the same time that Cannon was concentrating on the workings of cats' digestive systems, the psychologist Edward L. Thorndike became interested in the working of their brains. In his book about the cat, Mivart had said that the animal "has memory, imagination, a power of sensible perception," and the ability "to so associate sensations and images of objects in various relations as to draw practical inferences." Thorndike may or may not have been responding to that particular challenge, but at any rate he constructed his famous "puzzle boxes" in 1898 and set cats the tasks that were later to become so common—pulling cords, pressing levers, stepping on platforms in order to get a piece of meat. From then on, cats were widely used for laboratory tests of learning ability; in fact, in 1915 L. W. Cole (himself a raccoon man) complained that "the psychology of mammals is a mere generalization of the psychology of cats."

For a long time, one of the hotly disputed topics in psychological circles was whether animals (including man) could learn anything simply by watching someone else do it. True, they *seemed* to; but to say that one could learn by observation alone was to fly in the face of the prevailing theory that learning requires active participation by the learner, actual physical interaction with some aspect of his or her environment. In the years between 1898 and 1968, dozens of papers appeared in scientific journals on the subject of observational learning, and every range of opinion from positive to doubtful to negative was expressed.

A typical experiment of this sort was done in 1944 by Marvin J. Herbert and Charles M. Harsh, of the University of Nebraska. Cats were set a group of five problems, one of them being to use the apparatus shown in Figure 11. By spinning a turntable, a cat could bring a piece of meat close enough to the edge of the cage to obtain it. Some cats were required to solve this problem all by themselves, during which their "work time and activity paths" were recorded. Other cats were put into boxes from which they could watch the learning process occur. Still others were allowed to watch the working cat only after it had learned the job and was performing it skillfully. Then the "observer" cats were tested on the same jobs. Herbert and Harsh discovered two things: first, that all the observer cats, when their turn came, learned the job faster than cats who had not had an opportunity to watch a performance; and, second, that cats who had watched another cat through the whole course of the learning process were more efficient than cats who had watched only the final skilled performances of their companion felines.

One might think that this experiment would have answered the question, but people continued either to repeat or refine it. There is now so little doubt about the importance of "learning by watching" that some scientists believe it to be more important than "learning by doing." Included is a group of investigators at the New York Medical College's Brain Research Laboratories, among them E. Roy John and Phyllis Chesler. After reviewing the experiments which had been done up to 1968 (including their own), they decided that "observational learning may be the primary method of acquiring language, ideas and social habits in man, and [of ensuring] survival in lower organisms."

Chesler has demonstrated how this "primary method" works among cats. She used eighteen kittens, all between nine and ten weeks old, all of whom lived with their mothers in a home or homelike laboratory setting. The problem was to learn to press a lever within twenty seconds after a flickering light went on. The reward was a tiny dipperful of blended milk and meat. Six kittens were given no help; they were simply put into the test apparatus and were watched to see whether they could solve the problem by trial-and-error methods. Six kittens observed an unknown adult cat learn the job. Six others watched their mothers do it. Results? The kittens in the first group never learned how to get the food. That was true also of two of the kittens who were observing the unknown adult; the other four in that group learned the job but it took them eighteen days on the average. However, it took only four and a half days on the average for the kittens who were watching their own mother to learn to press the lever themselves. (This may explain naturalists' reports that lions in different parts of Africa hunt different types of game—zebras in one place, buffalo in another. Like mother, like daughter.)

It is impossible to review here the great variety of learning experiments in which cats and other animals have been involved; whole books have been written about particular categories of such experiments. It seems to be generally agreed, however, that cats supplement many instinctive actions with learned behavior; that they can unlearn or inhibit or modify whatever they have learned; that they can generalize (apply what they have learned in one situation to another); and that they can learn by insight. (Insight is the process by which one grasps the basic principle which governs the doing of a systematic task. Speed of problem-solving is enormously increased upon realizing, for example, that the "right" choice is the object—whatever its size, shape, or color—which is unlike all the others.) Cats demonstrate these various levels of intellectual ability to a greater degree than rats, chickens, or horses; are at approximately the same level as dogs; and are not so capable as primates or human beings.

Now, why is it important for anyone to find out that cats can learn to combine a complicated series of actions—for example, pulling a string to release a ball, pawing the ball into a chute in order to trip a lever which opens a door to food—but that they can't learn to push three buttons in a 1-2-3-2-3-3 order? A series of such experiments (on cats or other animals) provides information about the learning strategies which are commonly used for different kinds of tasks, the relative difficulty of those tasks, and what kind of motivation stimulates learning. Such research has been widely used to test the validity of particular learning theories and to apply the results to human educational practices. To give only one example, the teaching machines which program instruction in carefully measured increments grew out of animal research.

During the past thirty or so years, many psychologists have been studying the effect of early experience upon developing organisms. A basic investigative technique has been to deprive experimental animals of some normal experience and then compare them to animals who have had the experience. Harry Harlow, for example, has raised several generations of monkeys who were inadequately mothered, in part to find out what kind of mothers they in their turn would become. (Terrible.) Ronald Melzack and others have raised dogs in isolation and with the barest minimum of sensory stimulation to find out how important sociability and early use of the senses are in the development of emotional stability and intelligence. (Very.) Cats have been so used, too, and at two levels: to see how they behave after they have been deprived of a normal experience, and to see how deprivation affects the growth of the brain.

An example of the first kind of inquiry is the work done in the 1960's by Richard Held and Alan A. Hein, now at the Massachusetts Institute of

Technology. Interested in the development of sensorimotor responses, they devised an ingenious apparatus in which they tested ten pairs of kittens aged eight to twelve weeks. Each pair was put into a miniature carousel, one kitten riding in a gondola which did not permit its feet to touch the ground, the other kitten providing the motive power through a tiny neck yoke which was connected by a chain-drive mechanism to the gondola. However it moved, its movements were transmitted through mechanical linkages to the gondola in which the other kitten was riding. Both kittens, then, experienced movement, but only one of them was actively producing it.

The result was that the passive kittens were greatly retarded in their ability, as shown in later tests, to direct their paws to a visual target. Nor could they tell the difference between the shallow side and the deep side of a visual cliff (the apparatus for testing depth perception which was described in Chapter 10). Held and Hein concluded that *self-produced* movement with its concurrent visual feedback is necessary for the normal development of visually guided reaching behavior.

A following experiment emphasized the visual feedback part. This time, six kittens were raised in the dark for the first four weeks of life, then were permitted to move freely for six hours a day in a normal environment. They were fitted with funnel-shaped collars which were so light they did not impede locomotion but were large enough to prevent the kittens' seeing backward or downward. (In other words, they could not see their limbs.) They too had great difficulty in later tests of paw placement. When attempting to hit a ball dangling at the end of a string, for instance, they couldn't get their eyes and paws together. The conclusion this time was that a kitten must be able to see its limbs throughout the period when it is learning to use them if it is to be able to use them well.

A second type of deprivation study examines the visual cortex of the cat brain to see how the cells in a particular part of it are affected by early sensory experience. This work is based on the 1962 discovery by Harvard's David Hubel and Torsten Weisel that certain cells specialize in the detection of lines (bars, slits, edges of things). Other investigators then raised kittens, from the time their eyes opened, in tubular cages whose walls were striped. It took only a few weeks of living in such an environment to create a permanent disability: the kittens raised among vertical stripes could see only vertical lines and those reared among horizontal stripes could see only horizontal lines. Conclusion: Early sensory experience directs postnatal development of brain cells.

That conclusion is now being disputed by still other brain researchers. They say the visual disability of "stripy" kittens may not be due to the failure of brain cells to develop but to the degeneration of cells present at birth which atrophy as a result of inadequate stimulation during a critical development period. The resolution of that controversy should not alter the basic finding that brain structure is abnormal if the young organism is deprived of sensory "inputs." Roger Lewin, who recently summarized the controversy for *New Scientist*, says, "The issue is important because it has to do with environmental influence on brain development, a phenomenon that has implications ranging from the emergence of bird song at one end of the spectrum to achievement of intellectual potential in humans at the other."

As a group, the animal deprivation studies have reinforced observations made on human infants who have been poorly mothered, have had few opportunities to use their senses or to move their bodies. As a result, welfare agencies have closed down as many orphanages as possible and have placed abandoned children in the more personalized environment provided by foster homes. The inception of the Head Start Program also owes something to deprivation research.

Now, what about the role of cats in biomedical research?

They have been used for some long-term studies; for example, in a series of experiments designed to find out under what circumstances a mammal can safely drink sea water. As laboratory animals, however, cats are not as tractable or as emotionally resilient as dogs, and seem to be much more susceptible to infectious disease inside the laboratory than outside it. They cannot be used in the testing of many drugs intended eventually for human consumption, particularly those that include phenol rings in their chemical structure. Aspirin, for instance, is highly toxic to cats. Another of their pharmacological peculiarities is that they lack the enzyme which in humans converts morphine into a sedative. This is true also of horses; in both species, morphine is an excitant.

But in one biomedical specialty, the cat reigns supreme: brain research. Boudreau and Tsuchitani say, "More is known about the anatomy of cat sensory systems than those of any other animal. . . . Most of the neurophysiological work in audition, skin, muscle, joint, and some chemical senses has been performed on cats. No other animal has been studied in such detailed fashion." A tremendous body of knowledge has been assembled and recorded in atlases which show the anatomy of the cat brain as it would appear if sliced into thin crosswise sections. One can tell by reading these maps how deep a given neural structure lies and also where it is with reference to the front, back, or sides of the head. The cat has become the experimental animal of choice because cat heads are so uniform that an atlas of one cat brain is an atlas of all cat brains and the stereotactic apparatus which is used for the insertion of microinstruments can be operated from a series of standard settings.*

Some of those instruments are miniature scalpels, others are suction tubes through which tissue samples can be withdrawn, and still others are electrodes that record the activity of nerve cells which are responding to given stimuli. Cats are always anesthetized when surgery is done (whether visually or by internally performed lesions). If so drastic a procedure is undertaken that the cat could not thereafter survive, it is not allowed to regain consciousness. At the other extreme, electrodes are sometimes left in place after their first use so a later series of recordings can be made. Their presence does not cause discomfort or affect behavior. Sooner or later, though, most cats used in brain research are killed in order to examine the tissues in that part of the brain which has been under study.

The use of "split-brain" cats is one example of such research. First, the main nerve pathways which lead from the eyes to the opposite side of the brain and those that lead from one hemisphere to the other are cut. The result is to isolate the two hemispheres, each of which then functions independently of the other. The cat in effect acquires two brains in one skull. Roger Sperry, of the California Institute of Technology, pioneered this technique in the late 1950's, and many other behavioral biologists are now using it.

Clem, the cat wearing goggles in Figure 11, was used by John Robinson, of Sonoma State Hospital in California, and Theodore J. Voneida, of Case Western Reserve University, for some experiments done in 1964. The object was to learn how information acquired from two half-brains is inte-

---

* The resistance to mutation of feline genes for size and structure is in this instance a pronounced disadvantage to the species.

grated and applied by the animal to the accomplishment of some purposeful action. Clem and four other cats were required to choose the more intense of two lighted panels in order to receive a food reward. Filters in the goggles permitted the light from a given panel to enter only one eye and to be registered on only one hemisphere, yet the cats were still able to compare the two intensities of light and make the correct choice of panel. This and later research by the same two investigators has helped to identify the specific neural mechanisms which process—as distinct from register—the information sent by the eyes to the brain.

Studies of this sort have provided information useful to physicians and therapists who treat brain-damaged human beings. Some of it is directly applicable to people who, because of accident or surgery, also have split brains —and whose left hands quite literally don't know what their right hands are doing.

When an experimenter expects cats to do something that is unnatural for them (like using their paws to push instead of pull) or the experiment requires them to be under restraint (held in a harness, for example), they can be most uncooperative. Two psychologists, reporting the results of a study, said with a sigh that some of their test animals seemed only to have learned *not* to learn. Another scientist noted that three of his six cats merely went to sleep when placed in the cage from which they were supposed to watch a demonstrator cat, and two others spent their time viciously hissing and spitting at the demonstrator "without making any attempt to work."

When cats are not "working," their laboratory experience is similar to that of cats who are at boarding kennels. They don't like being caged (unless that is all they've known), but they learn to tolerate it, usually by sleeping much of the time. In laboratories, cats sleep as much as fourteen hours out of the twenty-four. Bored and elderly house cats probably do the same.

In the vast majority of American research institutions, animals are properly housed, fed, and cared for; are spared pain during or after an experiment; and are humanely killed if an experiment necessitates it. Some of the safeguards are relatively new and came about because of political action by organized groups of animal lovers—most importantly, passage of the federal Animal Welfare Act of 1966 and its subsequent amendments. This act instructs the United States Department of Agriculture to set standards governing the care, treatment, and use of animals and requires research facilities both to register with the USDA and to report annually to it, certifying their compliance with the law.

In 1975, registered research facilities reported to the USDA that they had used 51,439 cats during that year. That figure is incomplete, although nobody knows by how much. Nongovernmental groups have estimated that up to 200,000 cats are used annually for research—a figure that is probably on the high side, for the only institutions which have been exempted from reporting to the USDA are secondary schools and laboratories run by the federal government itself. Interestingly enough, federal agencies are required to comply with the USDA guidelines for treatment of animals but have not been required to make annual reports to their sister agency. Beginning in 1976, however, they too must report.

There is comparable legislation in Great Britain, but the laws are more venerable (1876) and they go further. A British scientist who wishes to use certain experimental procedures must secure permission from the Home Secretary, whereas the American law specifically forbids the Department of Agriculture "to promulgate rules, regulations, or orders with regard to design, outlines, guidelines, or performance of actual research or experimentation by a research facility as determined by such research facility." In the United States, each institution is allowed to determine the character of its own research. Most of them have internal protocol review committees which must approve every research proposal before the experimenter is allowed to proceed. The effectiveness of such self-regulation depends, of course, upon the knowledge, standards, and vigilance of the review committee.

Another reason for treating animals humanely throughout their laboratory stay is that they are very costly to replace. There was a time when such animals as dogs and cats were obtained from municipal pounds or were bought from dealers who caught strays or stole pets for resale to laboratories. These practices have been virtually eliminated now because the federal law which was quoted above also requires that dealers be licensed (and inspected) and that laboratories must buy their animals from licensed dealers. Anonymous cats do not now turn up in laboratory cages; dealers must keep records on their animals and mark them so they can if necessary be traced back to a source. The supervisory and clerical work involved in these procedures, as well as the housing and feeding requirements which have been im-

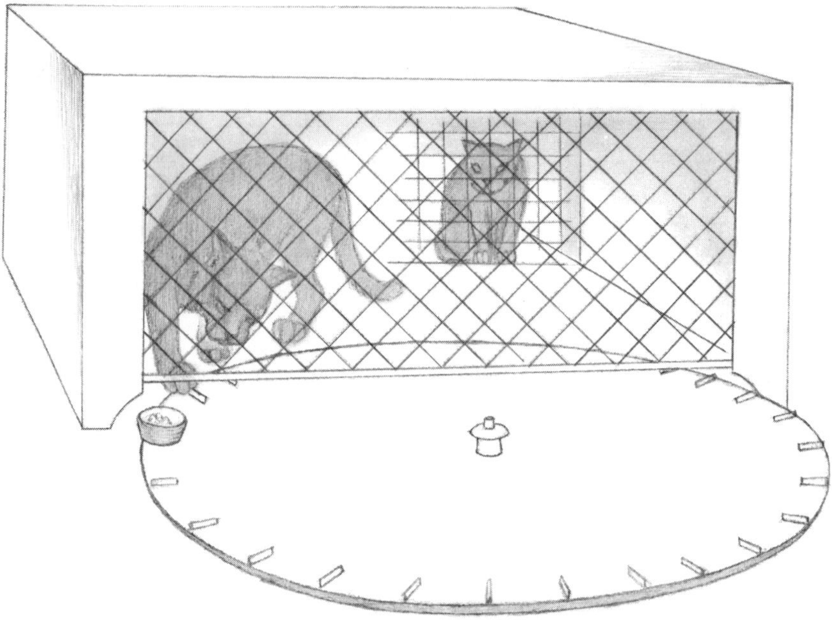

FIGURE 11. *An observer cat watches a demonstrator cat learn to get meat from turntable (top); a mouse bites a cat who is surfeited with killing (center); a split-brain cat compares light of different intensity striking each eye (bottom).*

posed on dealers, have raised the cost of such cats from perhaps $5 each in 1966 to $20 today (and twice that if the animal has already been conditioned to laboratory life).

Municipal pounds are in a special category. Many of them are not "dealers," having themselves decided or having been pressured by animal-welfare groups not to sell animals to laboratories. Those which do sell animals for research purposes have increased their prices (for some of the reasons mentioned in the preceding paragraph) from about $2 in 1966 to $6 or more today. Six dollars is a lot to pay for an animal which is likely to be sick and malnourished and is therefore a poor experimental subject. Many labs therefore prefer to use suppliers who can be relied upon to provide healthy animals. If they want to be really sure, they can buy cats that are bred specifically for research purposes and are certified free of those pathogens which can launch an epidemic in the laboratory. Such cats cost $250 each. The per-animal cost is equally high for institutions which decide to establish their own colonies, as many do in order to be sure of the cat's background or physical condition. Researchers are under great pressure to take good care of animals in whom so much money has been invested, and to use them wisely.

Nevertheless, the perfect world has not yet come, and some of the anti-vivisectionists' charges of cruel treatment or purposeless experimentation can still be substantiated. Over all, however, the use of animals for scientific research continues to be justified by the benefits which accrue from it, and many groups of animal lovers are therefore now concentrating on setting standards and establishing controls over such research instead of attempting to prevent it. For example, the American Humane Association (a federation of animal-welfare agencies) has rigorously evaluated various methods of euthanasia and has satisfied itself that the use of succinyl-choline chloride is not humane but that the introduction of nitrogen into a cabinet and the so-called "high-pressure low-altitude" methods are humane (if used according to the instructions which the AHA makes available to research facilities, municipal pounds, and animal shelters).

Robert L. Hummer, a spokesman for the AHA, recently said,

We believe that experiments utilizing animals should be conducted when they will yield data which cannot be obtained any other way. . . .

We do not accept the anthropomorphic view that an animal in confinement is an unhappy animal. Man and other animal species can be conditioned to restricted environments which meet their physical needs. We recognize the myriad of advances in human and animal medicine and in the quality of life which biomedical research has produced. We feel, however, that the animals which have made this research possible deserve the best possible treatment.

For that reason, the AHA and similar organizations have adopted a watchdog role relative to the observance by research facilities of both the letter and the spirit of the Animal Welfare Act. Hummer himself believes that additional legislation and educational programs are needed. He recommends, for example, that veterinarians be added to university or hospital protocol review committees and that the use of live animals by primary or secondary schools (which are exempted from control by current legislation) should be greatly restricted; also that children who use animals for Science Fair exhibits should be more closely supervised.

He sets the same goal for *all* users of animals: "Those responsible for the design of experiments, the care of animals, and the conduct of experimental procedures should possess what Dr. Albert Schweitzer called 'a reverence for life.' "

CHAPTER 14

The Little Differences

CAT OWNERS CAN LEARN a lot about their pets if they look and listen and take notes as systematically as laboratory observers do. One such home-study project might be the keeping of records on the body language which cats use to express their emotions. When Kitty hisses and spits and lays her ears back, for example, she is obviously in a belligerent mood. But is that belligerence due to anger or fright? If her body is low to the ground, her fur is erected all over her body, and her eyes are dilated, she is frightened, and the threats she is issuing are defensive in purpose. She doesn't want to fight, but she will if she has to. In contrast, an aggressive cat—a male who is challenging another male, for example—stands tall, erects only the hairs along his spine and tail, and constricts the pupils of his eyes.

Paul Leyhausen has thoroughly studied the scores of variations in feline posture and position of limbs and appendages which convey different kinds of messages to the discerning eye. The most impressive fact about the cat's "display" repertoire, he finds, is the extent to which the emotions that motivate feline flight and fight are *concurrently* present. Between the pure forms of defensive and offensive threat, as described just above, there are countless intermediate stages. When one reads the total message conveyed by ear and tail position, facial expression, and posture, it becomes apparent that cats try to keep all options open until the very moment of decision; they are equally prepared to advance, hold fast, or withdraw. Sometimes their posture reflects two emotions at once—for example, in the sideways "crab walk" which results when the front half of the cat is retreating and the rear end is advancing.

In Figure 12, the cat at the top of the page has no reason to be alarmed about anything. It trots along with an alert but placid expression on its face, ears pointed slightly forward, tail up. However, should it hear an unexpected sound or see something unfamiliar, it pauses, turns its ears outward, and drops its hindquarters in preparation for a possible run or jump. There is a critical distance, different for each cat, which determines whether it will run from an enemy, try to scare it away, or attack it.

If the first option is closed, it tries to gain time and space for a retreat by growling, hissing, or hitting out with its paws. (These, incidentally, will probably be wet. Cats have sweat glands only in their footpads, which excrete moisture when the cat is frightened as well as when it is hot.) Such a display of belligerence is intended to frighten off the dangerous animal or person (a veterinarian, say, who is about to examine it). The cat shown at the bottom of Figure 12 has reached the end of that particular row. Its next step will be to put the *enemy* on the defensive by rolling over and slashing at it with claws or teeth.

However, if the enemy is too big to fight or its dominance has already been established, a cat who is on the defensive may make itself as flat as possible but will not hiss or spit. Cats who are introduced into laboratory cages where there is already a resident cat behave in this fashion. Leyhausen believes that this passive crouch indicates only helpless fear, but Michael Fox, the Washington University animal psychologist who also knows a lot about cats, believes that it is a gesture of submission whose purpose (as among dogs and wolves) is to cut off an attack by appeasing an aggressor. Fox also classifies as "submissive" certain feline approaches to people—the erect tail of a cat when greeting its owner, for example, or some cats' custom of rolling onto one side when they are inviting a loved human being to play with them.

One can also argue about the emotion a cat is expressing when it has been punished for stealing food from a kitchen counter. It characteristically runs only a short distance away, often to its home place in the kitchen, and turns its back on the person who swatted it. This may be submission or merely a recognition of defeat. Refusing to look directly at a victor is a standard feline expression of social inferiority. Social superiority, on the other hand, can sometimes be gained by being physically above the other cats or people in a household; hence, cats' fondness for sitting on top of mantels, cabinets, and refrigerators.

Cats are notable for the amount of grooming they do. Their self-licking is not solely hygienic; sometimes it is what psychologists call "displacement activity." Such behavior occurs among both people and animals when it suddenly becomes impossible to complete a course of action already begun or when two mutually incompatible urges are aroused at the same time. A junior executive who is being reprimanded by a superior may break a pencil in half instead of punching the boss in the nose. A cat who would like to go somewhere but does not dare pass a higher-ranking animal standing in its path will lick itself. According to Lorenz and Leyhausen, the cat's position at the time influences how the movement is performed. "If it is standing or sitting," Leyhausen says, "it usually licks down over its shoulder; if it is walking, it can stop and likewise wash down one side but more often brings the forepaw it has just raised as far as its mouth and licks it, or it swings the hind leg which was just moving forward farther forward and up, sitting down abruptly as it does so, and starts to wash the hind leg."

Tails are eloquent barometers of feelings, too. Claire Necker quotes a charming bit of verse from Katherine van der Veer, describing a cat who

> . . . *sits like any gossip at the casement,*
> *Her agile tail reporting what she sees.*

Cats flick their tails in situations where humans would thumb their noses, Necker says; and indeed a cat who is refusing a disliked food usually combines a contemptuous jerk of its tail with the hind-leg scratching motions normally used to cover over excrement. "A wide-awake contented cat waves its tail slowly and gently to and fro," Necker continues. "A sleepy cat languorously moves its tail tip. . . . An angry cat lashes its tail violently from side to side. The tail tip of an excited cat quivers. When preparing to leap on prey, real or imagined, the entire cat is poised and motionless except for the tail tip which twitches in anticipation." During attack, the tail streams straight behind its owner, usually with a downward crook in it.

Cats vary as much within their species as people do within theirs. Some cats are so dull-witted from birth that never in their lives do they learn that a door which is ajar can be nudged farther open. Other cats can open shut doors and get the lids off garbage cans as easily as if they had two hands with opposable thumbs. Some cats are born with unshakably equable dispositions and others are so high-strung they go all to pieces when a doorbell rings. The kind of household a cat lives in also affects its temperament. Like human infants, cats do better in orderly and predictable environments. Disorganized and excitable families can produce cats with ulcers.

There is also a genetic basis for differences of temperament. This is made obvious by the fact that such differences are enhanced by inbreeding. The number of genes involved is unknown, but the inheritance of temperament is probably comparable to the inheritance of intelligence, in which many genes combine to produce the trait. Geneticists have bred very aggressive and very docile strains of mice, and dog fanciers have created animals as different as the even-tempered beagles and the scrappy little terriers. Similar differences occur among breeds of cats (although they are not so pronounced as breeders like to think they are).

In general, the Siamese are more extroverted and more active than the sedate and slow-moving Persians. People who are fond of Siamese say they are especially loving and devoted to their people. They are certainly more talkative than any other breed of cat, and they are more likely than Persians to climb up the draperies and stroll about among the traverse rods. Breeds which have some Siamese in their ancestry—the Himalayans, Balinese, and Burmese, for example—are not quite so active, not quite so vocal, and take to discipline a little better, but the Siamese influence is still present. Abyssinians are said to be volatile in mood and insistently affectionate (but choosy). Like Burmese, they enjoy water play. Manx are quiet, gentle cats, as are Russian Blues and other shorthairs. But no experienced cat owner is surprised to discover that a particular Persian is a rowdy or that a particular Siamese is a brooder.

In 1944, Mildred Moelk did the only systematic survey of feline vocalization which appears in the scientific literature. She reported that cats' repertory of sounds includes nine consonants (*f* as in "fun," *g* as in "go," *h* as in "halt," *m* and *n* as in "men," another *n* sound, as in "rung," *r* and *t* as in "rat," and *w* as in "we"); five vowel sounds (*a* as in "father," in "hat," and in "comma," *e* as in "let," and *i* as in "machine"); two dipthongs (as in the French *auf* and *eux*); and an umlaut (as in the German *über*). To these an *a:ou* sound is added. It begins as *a* while the mouth is open but ends as *ou* as the mouth is gradually closed.

A basic form of feline vocalization is the murmur, which is produced with a closed mouth. Murmurs are composed of an initial *m*, the main rush of breath *(h)*, which is usually given a roll-like flip or trill *(r)*, and a dying away of breath *(n)*. The whole sequence can be represented as *mhrn*. The quality of this sound, Moelk notes, can vary according to the highness of the *hr*, the presence or absence of trill, and whether the intonation is level or falling. Cats make their *mhrn*'s serve many purposes. They can greet a friend, call a kitten either coaxingly or commandingly, ask a favor, and (by changing the final *n* to an *ng* and letting the intonation drop) say "thank you."

When making the *a:ou* sound, the cat's impulse to voice the breath usually begins before the mouth is opened, therefore the sound comes out as *ma:ou*. If the cat opens its mouth quickly and the air rushes in, an *i* sound may be added to give a full-fledged meow *(mi-a:ou)*. The *a* is the most important and variable element, for it receives the full force of the breath impulse, while the *o* and *u* are merely the inevitable products of the gradually closing mouth.

Moelk says, "The initial vowel can be low and relaxed (the *a* in 'father') or high and tense (the *a* in 'hat'). The voice of one cat can be distinguished from that of another chiefly because of the differences in their normal initial vowel sounds. One can then judge its mood or wish by whether there is an increase or decrease of tension in its vowel sounds." If Tiger heavily stresses that initial *a*, he is confident he'll get whatever he wants. If things don't seem to be working out, the *ou* sound will lengthen and rise in pitch. If the *a* is high and tense and the *ou* continues to rise, Tige is more than bewildered; he's worried.

Moelk also mentions a series of sounds which are made with the open mouth in a rigid position, while breath is forced through it. These include hisses, spits, growls, and yowls, "but they defy any rendition using sounds of the English alphabet." She can only partially describe the tomcat's mating cry, for example, which contains "two *eux* sounds, then an *a* as in 'comma.'" Fox, incidentally, reports that some cats have a combination growl-bark, which they use when alarmed.

This repertoire of vocalization develops slowly. Kittens rely heavily on meows, marked initially by great shrillness and intensity. Only as they mature do they become as capable as their mothers of turning *mhrn* into any of a thousand words. As is true of all solitary species of animals, the feline vocabulary is limited, but it is adequate. Edward Topsell speaks with wonder about how the cat "whurleth with her voyce, having as many tunes as turnes, for she hath one voice to beg and complain, another to testifie her delight and pleasure, another among her own kind . . . insomuch as some have thought that [cats] have a peculiar intelligible language among themselves."

Speaking of "whurling" brings to mind a charming old tale which explains purring. The damsel in distress was a princess who was set an impossible task in order to save her own true love from death. She had to spin 10,000 skeins of linen thread within thirty days. Realizing that she couldn't do it alone, she asked her three cats to help. All of them worked night and day and finished the job within the specified time. The cats' reward was the ability to purr, a memorial to the whirring sound of the spinning wheel.

Modern explanations of the purr are less poetic and not much more informative. The vocal cords are fibrous elastic bands whose vibration produces the voice. Behind them in the larynx are two membranous folds which are called the false vocal cords, and these are the source of the purr. But how can a cat make a continuous noise while inhaling and exhaling? According to Moelk, the character of the purr changes; the inhaled stroke is the louder and rougher and the exhaled stroke is smoother and gives continuity. One can feel the vibration more strongly during inhalation, she says.

Claire Necker quotes the author of an old book, *Wood Notes*, as saying, "Made close observations this morning on Tim's purring. I find he varies the intervals. Have now heard him in a perfect fifth. He ranges, then, from one to five of the scale. The rhythm is also varied; there is a crescendo and retardando as well, and the dynamics are good. So far the higher tone is always given with the inhaling."

Some cats are more enthusiastic purrers than others.

Cats like regularity. When they are free-roaming, they visit their various favorite spots in set order, hunting at particular times and sleeping at others. As house cats, they accept the schedules imposed by their owners, but they want those schedules maintained. No cat owner needs an alarm clock. If Puss is used to being fed at seven, he will be scratching at the bedroom door at six-thirty. Cats can also keep track of a time period longer than twenty-four hours. If the members of a family normally "sleep in" on weekends, Puss will learn that routine and wait a couple of hours for breakfast.

FIGURE 12. *Cats express emotion with their entire bodies. Top: an alert and happy cat; center: one who has become slightly apprehensive; bottom: a frightened cat who can't escape an enemy and is threatening to launch an attack against it.*

On Monday morning, however, he'll be back at the bedroom door at six-thirty.

Gustav Eckstein, whose own research interest was in canaries and finches, wrote charming essays in which he used anecdotes about animals to illustrate fundamental life processes. His essay on the time sense featured an orange tomcat named Willy who lived near him in Cincinnati. Willy left his home promptly at 7:30 on Monday evenings, crossed a number of streets to a nurses' residence where Monday Bingo games were regularly held, and sat on a window sill from 7:45 to 9.30 P.M., "apparently to see and hear the human species gamble and scream." Willy did this only on Mondays; his schedule on the other days of the week was quite different.

Willy's owners left home to go to work at 8:10 A.M., and the cat (who liked to sleep in the house during the day) knew he had to get there by 8:10 or he would be shut out. One of his owners told Eckstein, "If Willy is somewhat early—say five minutes after eight—we can see him amble slowly up over the hill, perhaps stop to stretch a moment in a patch of sun. But if he is late—say eight minutes after eight—he comes prancing."

Many human beings also have built-in clocks and see nothing odd about cats' possessing a good sense of time. Some human beings are also sensitive to atmospheric changes and can thus "predict" a change in weather, but legend credits cats with that ability to a much higher degree. Cats have been weather prophets for as long as men have been observing them. Edward Topsell told his readers that if a cat who is grooming herself should "put her feete beyond the crowne of her head, it is a presage of rain." Jonathan Swift, in the eighteenth century, changed the signal but confirmed the fact:

> *While rain depends, the pensive cat gives o'er*
> *Her frolics, and pursues her tail no more.*

As, once again, did Arthur Guiterman, in the twentieth century:

> *The Cat on your hearthstone to this day presages,*
> *By solemn sneezing, the coming of rain!*

There are many accounts, both ancient and modern, of peculiar animal behavior in advance of earthquakes. In 1971, for example, two Los Angeles police units reported seeing hordes of rats scurrying in gutters—in the best leaving-the-sinking-ship tradition—on the night before a major quake hit the area. In February of 1976, two days before the Guatemalan earthquake that killed 23,000 people, a certain species of ant simply vanished from sight, the chirping of crickets took on a curiously sporadic character, chickens began to race around frenziedly, and pigeons kept flying into the air as if panicked. These and older examples have in common the fact that they were significant only by hindsight.

The People's Republic of China, however, is making a systematic effort to use animal behavior as one element in a massive effort to *predict* earthquakes. Since 1970, there has been organized in China a network of modern seismographic centers, staffed by 10,000 professionals, and a corps of 100,000 amateurs who report odd subterranean sounds, changing water levels in wells, and abnormal behavior by animals.

Chinese officials told visiting American seismologists in 1975 that the combined information from both the scientific and the amateur observers had enabled them to predict three major earthquakes and thus evacuate towns in affected areas in good time. Before one of them, the earthquake that struck Liaoning Province in February of 1975, it was reported by the amateurs that wells had become roiled and muddy, pigs were refusing to enter their sties, horses and sheep were running about wildly, and hibernating snakes were slithering out of their holes.

But neither animals nor people were able to sense the imminence of the catastrophic earthquake that leveled Tangshan in August of 1976. Although the scientists had predicted a major quake in that northeastern area of China "sometime before 1980," the actual event occurred without foreshocks or other warning.

And what about that kind of clairvoyance which enables an animal to sense impending danger even though there are no visible manifestations of it? Cats are said to be especially blessed with this kind of psychic power. It is, Claire Necker says, "documented by the experience of British cat owners during World War II. Long before air raid sirens sounded, British cats were somehow alerted to danger, and the families with whom they lived soon learned to heed their warning. Usually the cats asked to be let into a well-protected part of the house and their unerring choice of a secure niche is as incomprehensible as their forewarning of a raid."

Fact or legend? For purposes of this book, recollections were sought from Mrs. F. X. de Clifford, chairman of the Cats Protective League. "It was a queer time," she says. "People were all short of sleep, full of anxieties, and, of course, terrified. Nearly everyone was a bit extra-superstitious." Then she relates a series of anecdotes, taken from her wartime London diaries, which either support a theory of precognition or leave the question open:

Dogs undoubtedly did give warning. With their much keener hearing they knew when planes were coming but still far away, and they knew planes meant moving to shelters, so they often went into the shelters well ahead of the sirens. Some dogs, I believe, were able to tell enemy engines from Allied ones.

Cats were different. I don't think any seemed to hear the planes. But some did seem to know something. I have a note about one lady, Miss Lucy Pettigrew, who lived in the East End where the bombing was bad. She used to come down to the shelters at intervals, not regularly. She arrived before the alarms were sounded and it was always a very bad raid when she came. She said that her cat always warned her quite early in the evening. He would ask for his supper early, only eat about half of it and then lead the way to the door.

I had a friend living in a convent in the suburbs; she used to telephone me and say, "The convent cat is down in the shelter and that means a big raid"—and it always did.

There were many other stories. Several people declared their animals insisted on going out just before their houses received direct hits, but I never could confirm this myself.

My own cats were Russian Blues. I lived in a large old house in Kensington, which had a deep basement with a storeroom below it. I used to go out several nights a week, firewatching, and always left my cats and their kittens in the storeroom, which was the safest part. On two occasions, when I was not going out, the mother cats dragged their kittens by their necks to the storeroom and settled down for the night, and on both occasions there were bad raids—so bad indeed that I joined the cats. But that might have been co-incidence. . . .

To me it was one of the few consolations of that unhappy time, people in London did take care of their pets. I often saw the Heavy Rescue men carefully carrying out a dog or cat which had been buried in ruins, even on occasion canary-birds. I never heard anyone suggest that the animals should not have the same attention as human beings. We all felt that they deserved it, since they shared our lives.

Another unsolved mystery has to do with the ability of some cats (and some dogs) to find their way over terrain they have never traveled before to owners from whom they have become separated. Sheila Burnford's *The Incredible Journey*—that marvelous tale of a 250-mile odyssey through the Canadian wilderness by a Labrador retriever, a bull terrier, and a Siamese cat—is predicated upon such an ability.* There are also enough non-fictional examples of truly prodigious feats of travel to convince doubters that a few unusual animals *do* have extraordinary homing powers.

With respect to cats, the examples fall into two groups: those having to do with their ability to get back to a home *place*, and those having to do with the ability to find their own *people*.

As one would expect of the Count de Buffon, that eighteenth-century ailurophobe ascribes the former ability to laziness. "When carried to a distance of a league or two," he says, "cats return of their own accord, probably because they are acquainted with all the retreats of the mice, and all the passages and outlets of the house, and because the labor of returning is less than that which would be necessary to acquire the same knowledge of a new habitation."

Later cat watchers, of a more scientific bent, ascribed cats' homing ability to instinct. J. Henri Fabre, in his 1914 book about mason bees, tells also of a young tomcat who was given to friends who lived in another part of Avignon. The cat escaped and promptly returned home.

> And it was no easy matter [Fabre says]. He had to cross the town almost from end to end; he had to make his way through a long labyrinth of crowded streets, amid a thousand dangers, including first boys and next dogs; lastly—and this was perhaps an even more serious obstacle—he had to pass over the Sorgue, a river running through Avignon. There were bridges at hand, many, in fact; but the animal, taking the shortest cut, had used none of them, bravely jumping into the water, as its streaming fur showed.

That cat was one of a line sired by the same male, and a later descendant found *his* way home from the town of Serignan to the town of Orange, traveling more than four miles and also swimming a river in order to reach

---

* Anyone who knows the story only from the Walt Disney film is urged to get the book. This is a case of words being better than a thousand pictures.

his objective. Fabre concluded that full-grown cats "have, in their own fashion, the instinct of my Mason-bees."

He also checked the accuracy of the legend which holds that swinging a cat in a bag will disorient it so it can't find its way home. "Intelligent and trustworthy people, not given to jumping to conclusions, have told me that they have tried the trick [but] none of them succeeded," he says. "Though carried to a great distance, into another house, and subjected to a conscientious series of revolutions, the Cat always came back."

A series of rigorous experiments (at least for the cats involved) was undertaken by F. H. Herrick in 1922. Here are some highlights:

1. A tomcat was taken out on a Wisconsin lake in a rowboat. He positioned himself at the end of the boat closest to home and mewed. Herrick and his companions turned the boat in circles and even wrapped the cat in a blanket to eliminate visual cues, "but whether right side, left side, bow, or stern, Tom was always on the part of the boat nearest home, and straining as far as he could in that direction."

2. An adult female was put in a sack, carried over an irregular course (mainly by car) to a city 4.6 miles away, where she was left in a room in which the window was open at the top. Forty hours later she was home, "having made her way through city and suburban streets, crossed a railroad gully, and ascended a series of terraces to a height of 400 feet."

3. A cat with kittens at home was put in a sack and six times carried by car to distances varying from one to three miles. She was put in a box which could be opened by remote control from a tent seventy-five feet away. "The cat's behavior on release was an immediate orientation toward home," the observer reported. "There was no pausing and sniffing, no running around in circles, no peering one way and then another, no effort to locate the trail of the car that had brought her there—she simply turned in the direction of home and started."

It took the cat eight hours to get home from a mile away, ten hours to make it from two miles, and seventy-eight hours from three miles away. The investigators even anesthetized the poor animal on one of the outward trips; this slowed her down but didn't defeat her. The account of her tribulations ends with this sentence: "Finally, her owner had her taken to a distance of 16-½ miles, from which she never returned." What a reward for a plucky cat!

In 1954 the German neurophysiologists H. Precht and E. Lindenlaub tested the homing orientation of cats by putting them in sacks, transporting them varying distances from home, then turning them loose in the center of a maze. Its honeycomb design provided a series of virtually identical paths to a runway which circumscribed the apparatus and in which there were six equally spaced exits. The cats were fitted with collars from which a cord led to a spool in the center of the maze. As the cats prowled their way out of confinement, the cord unwound and remained along the course as a record of their route. The object of the experiment was to see how many would choose an exit which pointed in the direction of home, and how they would go about finding it.

The tested cats included house pets and laboratory animals, males, females, females with litters from which they had been separated, and half-grown cats. Hardly any of them wandered around in the maze; they went as directly as possible to the outer rim and to an exit. But their homing sense was only fair and was directly related to how far they were from home. About 60 percent of their choices were correct when home was less than five kilometers away. At greater distances, a right choice was purely a matter of chance.

Cats who were returned to their homes after each maze trial did a better job of orienting than cats who were kept in the lab between tests. Young cats who had been raised in laboratory cages had no sense of "home" at all, even if they were very close to it when put into the maze. There was one exception, a big tomcat who chose correctly time after time. Precht and Lindenlaub hauled him and the maze for miles in varying directions from his home, tested him a dozen times—and the cat never made a mistake.

The current physiological explanation for animals' homing ability— those that have it—is that they may possess an unusual sensitivity to the geomagnetic field of the earth which enables them to keep a compass fix on their home region regardless of distance and direction of travel. But this theory does not explain the capability of some few animals to find absent owners or mates in distant places where the animal has never been.

Consider, for example, the achievement of Pooh, a two-year-old tomcat who walked 200 miles over a four-month period in order to rejoin the people who had given him away when they moved from Newnan, Georgia, to Wellford, South Carolina. Chat Beau, a four-year-old male, found *his* family in Texarkana, Texas, after their move from Lafayette, Louisiana. The distance he covered was almost 300 miles and it took him four months to get there. A three-year-old Persian named Smoky did the 417 miles between Tulsa, Oklahoma, and Memphis, Tennessee, in twelve months. And Sugar was a supercat who followed her family from Anderson, California, to Gage, Oklahoma, a 1,500-mile journey which she completed in fourteen months. These cats were not seeking familiar places but beloved people.

With the exception of Pooh (who did his traveling in 1974), the feline exploits described above are reported in a 1962 paper by J. B. Rhine and Sara Feather, of Duke University's Parapsychology Laboratory. The two scientists appraised more than 500 accounts of animals who were alleged to have exhibited "psi" phenomena (precognition, extrasensory perception, or psychokinesis); their special interest was the ability of animals to find companions despite separation by miles of unfamiliar territory. Rhine and Feather call that ability "psi-trailing."

They asked themselves four questions: Is the report honest, not a hoax? Is the arriving animal accurately identified by some physical or behavioral trait? Is there evidence of travel? Are there supporting witnesses? When all the screening was done, they found themselves with cases involving twenty-eight dogs, twenty-two cats, and four birds who had successfully trailed either a mate or a human companion.

The Chat Beau who arrived in Texarkana, for example, had a scar on one eye, an old smudge of Louisiana tar on his tail, and could growl like a dog (a trick the Louisiana Chat Beau had learned in the course of being reared with puppies). The Smoky who turned up in Memphis had a tuft of red hair under his chin and liked to "play" the piano along with the daughter of the house, just as the Smoky in Tulsa had done. Sugar was identified by a deformed left hip joint. As for Pooh, the cat who arrived in Wellford, like the cat who had been left in Newnan, had a scar on his side, a black spot on one foot, and a preference for a certain sleeping rug.

Skeptics say that people who very much want to believe a found animal is the one they lost may exaggerate points of similarity. Perhaps that happened in these and other cases. But perhaps there really *is* an occasional Sugar who has a gift denied to most cats and most people. Rhine himself, now long in retirement, looks back on the period of concentration on the animal cases with a renewed sense of emotional involvement. In a recent letter, he says,

"How deeply moving these performances are; what they tell us of the bonds of affection that so controlled the animals' lives through hardship and long periods of wandering in the wilds. Not food, not sex, not fear—just plain love, isn't it? I told [Pitirim] Sorokin, who gave much of his life to the study of altruism, that he had better study animals, too."

CHAPTER 15

The Health Record

CATS' HEARTS BEAT at the rate of 110 to 130 times per minute, a third again as fast as the human heart. Cats are less likely than dogs and people to have atherosclerosis and are most unlikely to have cerebral hemorrhages. They have excellent resistance to infections, except for those caused by a nasty little protozoan called *Toxoplasma gondii* and those resulting from bacterial contamination of wounds. Because the outer layer of feline skin heals with astonishing rapidity, infective organisms become encapsulated and abscesses may develop.

Cats can also suffer from allergies, arthritis, asthma, cancer, cataracts, diabetes, diarrhea, eczema, epilepsy, parasitic infestations, toothache, urinary-tract disorders, and diseases caused by viruses. These last are the worst, the most dreaded by owners. Topping the list is the one which used to be called cat distemper, then feline enteritis, and is now called feline panleukopenia. It is an acute gastrointestinal illness from which at least half the cats who get it die. Kittens are especially at risk. In the United States, it shows up every year at the first approach of cold weather, peaks in December, falls off in February, and appears sporadically throughout the rest of the year. A vaccine will prevent it.

Cats' lungs expand and contract twenty to thirty times per minute, a respiratory rate that is a shade faster than that of humans. Cats are just as susceptible as we are to upper respiratory infections caused by viruses, and at least three kinds have been identified in the laboratory—feline pneumonitis, rhinotracheitis, and picornovirus infection. They are hard to diagnose because all have the same clinical signs and they are hard to treat because vaccines do not exist or are ineffective.

It must have been a cat with one of these ailments who inspired the phrase "sick as a cat." A cat with a cold is absolutely miserable. Inasmuch as the narrow oval openings from the frontal sinuses into the nasal cavity are only about one millimeter wide and four millimeters long, they can be quickly blocked. Add watery eyes and sneezes and one gets a thoroughly wretched animal.

"Cats are tidy creatures and easily discouraged by messy illnesses," says Jean Holzworth of the Angell Memorial Animal Hospital in Boston. If they can't smell their food, they will stop eating and drinking; Holzworth believes that most deaths from these respiratory infections are due to lack of nourishment rather than to fatal changes in the respiratory tract itself.

The cat flus are especially dreaded by breeders, pet-shop owners, the animal husbandry staffs in scientific laboratories, and anyone else who houses a number of cats in the same quarters. Because cats do not normally live in groups, they do not routinely develop antibodies for these diseases and can be as vulnerable to them as the American Indians were to the smallpox that European explorers imported to the Western Hemisphere in the sixteenth century. Quarters are hard to disinfect, and those animals that recover from the disease may become carriers that infect new animals born into or added to the colony. Thus there is an endless cycle of disease and possible death.

Leukemia, a cancer of the blood in which the red cells are destroyed, is two and a half times more common among cats than among people. That feline leukemia can be (and usually is) caused by a type C virus was discovered in 1964, thus adding cats to the list of animals (chickens, frogs, rabbits, mice) in whom certain kinds of cancers are linked to viral infection. There is a rare disease called Birkett's lymphoma which affects children living in Africa and is thought to be of viral origin, but there is no evidence that viruses are causative agents in other human cancers. However, all mammalian systems are much alike and it is reasonable to suppose that such linkages will be discovered. Therefore, a great deal of research attention is currently being directed toward the type C viruses.

One of the curious facts about these particular microorganisms is that many of them have been discovered in animals who have not been infected through contact with carriers. Inasmuch as the theory of spontaneous generation has long been discredited, the puzzling question was: Where do such viruses come from? In the course of the past fifteen years, biologists have found the answer, and an elegant bit of sleuthing it was.

A unique property of viruses provided the clue. Unlike bacteria, viruses can propagate themselves only in the cells of living organisms. They inject their nucleic acid (the same kind of nucleic acid that in other living things is the basis of reproduction) into the cells of a host, where it subverts the metabolic machinery of the host cells and uses it to make more viruses. Sometimes the host organism dies as a by-product of this takeover of its cellular processes. Sometimes, though, the viral nucleic acid simply combines with the nucleic acid in the chromosomes (including the sex chromosomes) of the host. If the infected animal recovers from the infection, the virogenes in its chromosomes will be copied as faithfully as the original genes whenever the nucleic acid in those chromosomes replicates itself. The virogenes normally remain in a latent state. Like ungerminated seed, however, they carry the potential for regeneration. Given the right triggering circumstances, they can "order" the body to make the viruses for which they are the blueprint—and *voila!* the host species has spontaneously created the viruses that attack it.

If *that* seems eerie, what follows will seem even more so.

Scientists can compare virogene sequences in the chromosomes of various animals and thus reconstruct their evolutionary history. George J. Todaro, Raoul E. Beneviste, Charles J. Sherr, and others at the National Cancer Institute have been doing this for the past six or so years, and have made some startling discoveries. There is, for example, a type C virus whose genes appear in the chromosomes of baboons and other Old World monkeys but not in the chromosomes of the apes (chimpanzees, gorillas, gibbons, orangutans) or man. The initial infection of a baboon must therefore have occurred more than 40,000,000 years ago because that is roughly the point at which the apes began to become differentiated from the monkeys.

There is also a partially related sequence of the same virogenes in the domestic cat and in three small wild cats which are native to Africa or Europe (*F. margarita, F. chaus, F. silvestris*). Unfortunately, the domestic cat's closest wild relative, *F. libyca*, has not been tested, but Todaro says there is every reason to believe it too carries the virogenes found in its cousins. Those genes do not appear in the chromosomes of the larger African cats (serval and caracal), in those of the small cats of Southeast Asia, or in the New World cats. Again, therefore, it is possible to date the period when some ancient cat was infected with a baboon virus: 5,000,000 to 10,000,000 years ago, after the small wild cats of Africa and Europe and the other cats had established themselves on different branches of their family tree.

Now, what about the virus that causes feline leukemia? Gene sequences partially related to it have been found in the chromosomes of laboratory cats who had been certified pathogen-free, in ordinary house cats, in the three wild cat species mentioned above, *and* in the chromosomes of rodents, especially rats. According to Raoul Beneviste, immunologic studies support the belief that cats were infected by viruses of rodent origin at "a point in recent evolutionary history." He concludes his 1975 report (written with Sherr and Todaro) by proposing that feline leukemia has resulted from the activation of genetically transmitted, rodent-derived virogenes which are rarely expressed in the feral population because wild cats don't associate with one another. However, in the urban-living domestic cat and in multi-cat households where contact among animals is extensive, the cat whose virogenes suddenly begin to produce active leukemia viruses infects both itself and others.

The preceding paragraphs have been a necessary oversimplification of a large and complicated topic, and one possible misconception could result. No reader should assume that the virogenes carried by his or her individual cat will inevitably become active. Type C virogenes are normally suppressed. There is even some evidence that in their latent state they provide immunological benefits to the organism which carries them. They must be useful as well as potentially dangerous, Todaro believes, or they would not have been carried along in the chromosomes of so many kinds of animals for so many millions of years. He and his associates have just begun a project in which they are crossing the leopard cat of Southeast Asia, which does not carry the feline leukemia virogenes in its chromosomes, with the domestic cat, which does. The scientists hope they will eventually be able to "breed out" the virogenes from domestic cats and ascertain whether the risk of their developing cancer is then diminished or eliminated.

After the viral diseases, parasitic infestations are the next worst scourge of cats. Many of them affect other animals too. There is a mange, for instance, which is caused by a mite called *Sarcoptes scabiei;* it has a *canis* and a *cati* form. Dog fleas, cat fleas, and human fleas occasionally exchange hosts, but given a choice will stay with the species for which they are specialized. Lice, incidentally, are rarely found on cats; they prefer dogs and people.

Many different kinds of worms parasitize cats, using their blood or tissue or the shelter of their internal organs for the parasite's own reproductive benefit. There are several varieties of tapeworms (helminths), some of which live in the intestines of their feline hosts; others lodge in the bile ducts or the lungs. The hookworms (nematodes) may invade the kidneys, the peritoneal cavity, or the skin. The roundworms (ascarids) prefer the intestines. There is also a fluke called *Opisthorchis felineus* which makes its home in the liver.

The skin infection known as ringworm is not caused by a worm but by a fungus. A cat who is host to this growth has roundish scaly lesions, usually on its head or face, from which the hair has fallen out. There are several other fungi which affect the internal organs, among them one that invades the upper respiratory tract and another which establishes itself in the lungs.

All of these parasitic diseases are debilitating or disfiguring, but are not normally fatal. They are more widespread in tropical climates than in temperate zones.

As long as people and cats have been associated, cats have been perceived in a dual role relative to human health. Folk medicine abounds in recipes which include some part of the feline anatomy among their ingredients. The frequent preference is for black cats, whose therapeutic powers are especially great when applied to diseases of the eye. "Take the head of a blacke Cat, which hath not a spot of another colour in it," Edward Topsell advised in 1607, "and burne it to powder in an earthen pot leaded or glazed within, then take this powder and through a quill blow it thrice a day into thy eie . . . and so shall all paine fly away."

Almost 200 years later, the magic still worked. The passage below, quoted by Sillar and Meyler in *Cats Ancient and Modern,* is a 1791 entry in the diary of one Reverend James Woodforde.

The Stiony [an archaic contraction of sty-on-eye] on my right Eye-lid still swelled and inflamed very much. As it is commonly said that the Eye-lid being rubbed by the tail of a black Cat would do it much good if not entirely cure it, and having a black Cat, a little before dinner I made a trial of it, and very soon after dinner I found my Eye-lid much abated of the swelling and almost free from Pain . . . Any other Cat's Tail may have the above effect in all probability—but I did my Eye-lid with my own black Tom Cat's Tail.

Black cats' tails, when detached from their owners and buried under a doorstep, are also alleged to ward off illness in the house. Their skin, if applied to rheumatic joints, relieves pain. Their blood cures hives. It is entirely possible that some believers in folk remedies are still willing to give these nostrums a try.

However, among the science-oriented populations of the industrialized nations, there is more interest today in the causative than in the curative relationship of cats to human disease. Fernand Méry ascribes the renewed popularity of cats in the mid-nineteenth century to Pasteur's discovery of germs, after which "no one dared to stroke a dog or horse without wearing gloves for protection . . . But the cat? It was known to be the only domestic animal that spent entire days licking and cleaning itself with praiseworthy scrupulousness. If there was one animal that one could accept into one's home and caress without fear, it was this innocent. . . ." Unfortunately, such trust was misplaced: cats *do* transmit diseases to human beings.

In *Diseases of Man Acquired from His Pets*, B. Bisseru, of the London School of Hygiene and Tropical Medicine, lists 303 diseases for which animals are vectors; 165 of these occur in the United States. They include diseases borne by worms, insects, fungi, bacteria, and viruses. Dogs top the list; they are susceptible to 116 diseases which they can transmit to people. Rodents are next (103), then wild primates such as monkeys (87), then cats (76). After cattle (67), the numbers dwindle—from birds (56) to horses (48) to rabbits (30).

Rabies is one of the most serious of those diseases. A virus, it is transmitted via the saliva of an infected animal. People are much more likely to be bitten by rabid dogs than by rabid cats. The number of recorded bites is small, but *any* incidence is too high because without treatment rabies is fatal. Furthermore, it can be prevented by pet inoculation. What concerns public health officials most about rabies is that its frequency is now very high in wildlife species, especially skunks. Free-roaming exurban cats and dogs or strays who have been abandoned and are eking out a precarious existence in rural areas are very much at risk and can be expected to carry the disease to human contacts. In Illinois, in 1974, 125 rabid animals were reported—seven dogs, thirteen cats, the rest skunks, bats, or foxes.

Cancer researchers are equally concerned about the possible role of feline leukemia virus in human leukemias. If cats can catch leukemia from one another, might not people catch leukemia from cats? That question has been much in the minds of scientists for the past decade. Up to the end of 1972, twelve studies had been reported, some of them comparing cases of animal cancer to the incidence of the disease among human beings in the same households, others reversing the base and checking the presence of dogs, cats, or other pets in the households of people who had cancerous diseases. The cancer rate among veterinarians has been studied, too.

C. Richard Dorn and Robert Schneider, in summarizing this work, say the results "generally do not support the hypothesis of interspecies transmission of malignant neoplasms." One study, however, by I. D. J. Bross, R. Bertell, and Robert Gibson, of the Roswell Park Memorial Institute in Buffalo, has indicated that there may be a connection between childhood leukemia and the presence of *sick* cats in the same household. They found that 7.3 percent of 300 childhood leukemia victims had had a contact with sick cats, whereas among a group of 831 well children only 4.6 percent had been so exposed.

And then there's cat-scratch disease, an inaccurately named ailment because people can get it even if a cat hasn't scratched or bitten them; simple association can do the trick. The cause is unknown but is believed to be a virus. Cats are nothing more than mechanical carriers, for they never show the symptoms of the disease themselves and nobody has been able to induce it in them. The agent, whatever it is, infects human lymph nodes. They sometimes enlarge and develop abscesses. Mild fever and general malaise accompany the disease, which can last for several weeks. It is often mistaken for infectious mononucleosis.

In 1967, under the title of "The Cat Menace," William D. Coe, of the University of Florida, described a number of cases of cat-scratch disease which had come to his attention as a student-health-service physician. One lad, who kept a cat in his dormitory and studied with it draped around his neck or in his lap, was miserably ill for three months. Another pair of sufferers was a married couple who allowed their cat to sleep on their bed. Coe was astonished by the "defensiveness of pet-fanciers who consider pets an extension of themselves" and especially by the fact that "the fellow who was ill for three months saw no point in giving up his contaminated cat." Coe himself came to a different conclusion. The final sentence in his article proposes that household cats be abolished.

"The females live not above five or seven yeares, the males live longer especially if they be gelt." So said Edward Topsell more than 300 years ago, a statement that is still partially correct.

James B. Hamilton, Ruth S. Hamilton, and Gordon E. Mestler reported in 1969 on the causes and age at death of 629 cats who had been seen over an eight-year period at the clinic of the University of Pennsylvania School of Veterinary Medicine. They found that castrated males outlive intact males at all stages of life; they are less likely to die during their first five years, have greater resistance to infection, and live longer. Of those who made it to the age of five, the average age of death was 10.8 years, whereas that of intact males was 8.6 years. Of living tomcats over ten years old who were seen in the clinic, only 7 percent had not been castrated.

Females, like their counterparts in human society during the course of the past two centuries, now outlive males. Intact females live, on the average, two and a half years longer than intact males. Spayed females follow a life course similar to that of castrated males; they are less likely than intact animals to die in youth, are more resistant to infectious diseases, and live to an average age of 10.5 years. For both neutered males and females, life span is lengthened if the gonadectomy is performed before the cat is six months old.

However, before any reader rushes out to have a cat surgically altered in order to prolong its life, he or she should note that neutered animals are twice as likely as intact animals to develop leukemic cancers. The Hamiltons and Mestler found that 12 percent of spayed females and 10 percent of castrated males but only 5 percent of intact females and 4 percent of intact males died of leukemias. Gonadectomy somehow confers greater resistance to infections but increases susceptibility to cancer.

Purebred cats, incidentally, do not live as long on the average as cats conceived in the course of random matings. The University of Pennsylvania researchers note that this is true also of purebred dogs and say that "the most plausible explanation of this phenomenon seems to be a lack of hybrid vigor which is known to shorten the life of inbred strains of flies and mice."

It should be mentioned that the cats whose histories were recorded by the Hamiltons were probably not typical of the general feline population. A life expectancy of possibly one more year is estimated for young house-cats who are dumped along roadsides or are left behind at summer homes when their fair-weather families return to the city in the fall. Only the super-cats among urban strays manage to feed themselves adequately and avoid being killed by cars or dogs. In general, long life results from watchful care at home and medical attention as needed. Dog owners are more likely than cat owners to give their pets that kind of attention; most veterinarians find that 75 percent of their patients are canine. But those cats who are well looked after can live far beyond the eleven years the University of Pennsylvania study sets as the average age of death.

Doting owners are often so proud of having an exceptionally old cat that they add on a few years to make a good story better. Hence the tales of thirty-seven-year-old felines are suspect. The closest thing to a scientific study of potential maximum ages in cats was done in 1956 by the British zoologist Alex Comfort. He located a number of cats who were alleged to be approaching or over age twenty and satisfied himself that ten of them were nineteen to twenty-seven years old. Four had been neutered, six were intact.

> In regard to persistence of teeth, activity, grooming, and hunting, the condition of these senile cats is strikingly better preserved than in dogs, very old specimens of which are usually in a pitiable state [he says]. Mating continued throughout life in some of our oldest entire males. . . . The cat would appear to be quite the longest-lived of the smaller domestic animals, its maximum age of just under 30 years comparing with 18–20 in terriers [if raised] under household conditions.

Owners of elderly pussies sometimes dramatize their longevity by pointing out to friends that "one year in a cat's life equals seven human years." But that's not quite true, Adolph Suehsdorf says. "A ten year old cat and a seventy year old person might be said to have travelled a similar distance down life's road, but at no other milestone does the ratio have much relevance. Eight month old cats bear young far more frequently than five year old people, and truly ancient cats—more than twenty years—are certainly more common than senior citizens of 140."

For cats as for people, proper nutrition is essential to health. Because cats are carnivores, literal-minded owners sometimes limit them to an all-meat diet, and wonder why they don't thrive. There is a lot of difference between a dish of chopped raw beef and a mouse; eating the latter provides bones and some vegetable matter as well. To eat nothing but meat upsets the body's calcium-phosphorus balance and causes a host of disorders.

Muscle meat, such as beef heart, provides virtually no Vitamin A, which cats cannot synthesize for themselves and must obtain from external sources such as eggs, milk, or liver. Without Vitamin A, cats lose weight, develop night blindness, are more susceptible to infections, and may become infertile. A pure liver diet, however, is just as harmful as pure beef heart; skeletal deformities may result. Nor should a cat be fed excessive amounts of fish—tuna, for instance—which contain highly unsaturated fats. They deplete the animal's store of Vitamin E and give rise to a disease called steatitis. (A 1972 article in *Consumer Reports* advises buyers of fish-based commercial cat food to check the label for the presence of Vitamin E supplement.)

Cats require high-protein, high-fat diets—four times as much as dogs, which is a major reason for not feeding dog food to cats. Patricia Scott, writing in a widely used manual on the care and management of laboratory animals, says,

> Kittens should have at least 32 percent of the dry constituents of an average mixed diet as protein, and an adult cat not less than 21 percent. In a diet containing about 70 percent water [as in canned commercial cat foods] these minimal figures would be equivalent to 10 percent of protein for growth and 6 percent for maintenance, but good diets for cats usually contain 12 to 14 percent of protein on a wet basis.

Scott says that fat should form 15 to 40 percent of a dry diet (the cat chows sold in sacks or boxes are dry diets), but she does not give equivalent figures for a wet diet. Michael Fox, in a 1975 pet-advice column in *McCall's*, says that a wet diet should be 10 percent fat. He advises a carbohydrate content of 5 percent; Scott says that carbohydrates (cereals or potatoes) are not essential but are "a cheap source of calories." Everyone seems to agree that an average-sized adult cat (about nine pounds) needs approximately 400 calories per day. That amount is provided by a quarter of a pound of dry or semi-moist cat food. The same amount of canned (wet) food contains about 125 calories.

Of the fat-soluble vitamins, A and E have already been mentioned. Vitamin D seems to be less important to cats' welfare than to that of human beings, although rickets has been reported in kittens raised in the dark. Of the water-soluble vitamins, cats require Vitamin B_1 (thiamine), Vitamin B_2 (riboflavin), Vitamin B_6 (pyridoxine), and niacin. There is no evidence that folic acid, biotin, Vitamin B_{12}, and Vitamin C (ascorbic acid) are essential to cats. Nor is it necessary to add iron to their diets; unlike dogs, cats can readily absorb this mineral from meat.

There is an unresolved argument about the ash content of feline diets. (Ash is the mineral residue which remains after oxidation.) In summarizing the few nutritional studies which have concerned themselves with ash, the National Research Council's Committee on Animal Nutrition said in 1972 that some scientists have linked high-mineral diets to the development of kidney or bladder stones but others have found no connection, even when the ash content of a diet was as high as 30 percent. Scott advises adding a pinch of salt to meat, especially if the cat is old. The salt encourages the cat to drink more water, which reduces the concentration of urea in the bladder and helps to prevent the precipitation of minerals into the urinary tract.

It is a great convenience to feed one's cat the commercially prepared foods available in cans or boxes. Let the conscientious owner be warned, however: these products are not equally nutritious. Although the labels appear at first glance to offer a wealth of information, many do not in fact tell the purchaser whether the food will maintain the cat in good health. For example, "Crude protein, 11%" sounds fine, but if it happens to be protein from a vegetable source it may lack some of the amino acids that are necessary to cats.

The Federal Trade Commission requires manufacturers of pet foods to label their products in such a way that the purchaser can "determine the nature and composition of the product and the purposes for which it is suitable." Much cat food is labeled only as to nature and composition. Wise owners should therefore look for unequivocal statements such as "This food contains all the vital nutrients your cat needs for normal growth and maintenance," or "This product is not a complete food." Packages labeled as specially formulated for kittens should be checked to be sure they are extra-high in protein content. If a label says the product is "a delicious addition to the diet" or is "guaranteed to have taste appeal," it is probably not a balanced food on which the cat would thrive if it were to be fed that product exclusively.

Many veterinarians recommend that some portion of the diet be in the form of dry chows, because the hard pellets help to keep feline teeth free of tartar. A varied diet should be offered at the time kittens are weaned, otherwise the cat when grown may be finicky and stubborn about food. Probably the best rule of thumb is to use commercial cat food about 80 percent of the time, supplementing it with extra fat, fresh meat, egg yolks beaten into a little milk, cottage cheese, or whatever special treats a cat is fond of.

For anyone who has the time to cook for a pet, Joan Harper's *The Healthy Cat and Dog Cook Book* is full of recipes for economical and nutritious dishes like Fishhead Stew, Kitty and Doggy Pot au Feu, Vitamin Crisps, and Chicken Loaf. By permission, here's the recipe for the latter: Obtain 2 pounds of necks; ask your butcher to grind them, or partially freeze them and put them through a home grinder, or boil them until the bones are soft enough to crush. Add 1 cup of fresh greens (broccoli, celery, collards, spinach, etc.) which have been chopped in a blender with some water or stock and 1 clove of garlic. Add 2 tablespoons of bacon fat, 2 slices of grated whole-wheat bread, and 1 egg. Mix all together in a bowl, then place in used dog or cat food commercial food cans. Bake 30 to 45 minutes or until firm and slightly brown.

A healthy Siamese can weigh as little as five pounds, but the majority of cats tip the scales somewhere between seven and twelve pounds. A few jumbo felines have been reported; *Animal Facts and Feats* names as the champion a female tabby who, at the age of eleven, had a girth of thirty-seven inches and weighed forty-two pounds. (Whether she was unhealthfully obese or simply outlandishly big is not recorded.) Considering their usually small size, however, cats have an astonishing ability to survive long periods without food or water. *Animal Facts and Feats* awards the endurance record to a London cat who was trapped in an elevator shaft for fifty-two days in 1964. According to Georgina Gates (writing in 1928), a cat who was subsequently christened Tom Cadillac was accidentally shipped in a Cadillac chassis from the United States to Australia—a seven-week trip—and was still alive on arrival. He had eaten the engine grease and the car's instruction manual while in transit. How truly spoke Pilpay, the Indian Aesop, when he said, "It has been the providence of nature to give this creature nine lives instead of one."

In their ability to withstand emotional stress, cats tend to be less hardy than dogs, but there are many exceptions. In 1975, for example, two Siamese cats, Bubble and Squeak, were flown from London to Chicago to rejoin their owner, Mary Wilkinson, but only Bubble disembarked. Squeak had escaped from his carrier en route and was hiding somewhere in the cargo hold. Mrs. Wilkinson was allowed into it on the chance that she could lure him out. (Reporting the story in the Chicago *Sun-Times*, Bob Greene told how she "lay down on her stomach and began to coo, 'Here, Squeak. Here, Squeak. Come to Mama, Squeak.' Squeak did not appear. Mrs. Wilkinson continued to coo. The airlines men began to laugh. Mrs. Wilkinson began to cry. The airlines men stopped laughing.") Her efforts were unavailing, and the plane eventually returned to England with Squeak still aboard.

On the following two days, the stowaway made two more transatlantic crossings—London–Montreal, Montreal–London—before airlines cargo personnel found him. They whisked him off to the R.S.P.C.A. for food, water, and a physical examination, then popped him onto another Chicago-bound plane. That time he made it and was happily reunited with his family. He suffered no ill effects from his 19,790-mile marathon, but Mrs. Wilkinson reported that Bubble was a nervous wreck as a result of his own single flight and because he missed Squeak.

The feline blood-producing and blood-circulating system is greatly affected by stress, whether of emotional origin or due to physical trauma. Blood transfusions are therefore sometimes needed to help cats recover from diseases that a dog or a human being could conquer without such help. There are two feline blood types, A and B (not the same as human type A or type B blood). The majority of cats are type A. Blood banks exist in a few places, but most veterinarians must follow the practice of human physicians before 1937 and transfuse from a live donor. In a pinch, dog blood can be used for a cat; however, the red cells perish within twenty-four hours.

Cats' red blood count is higher than that of human beings. According to the University of Minnesota's U. S. Seal, that's because the individual cells are smaller but must carry the same amount of hemoglobin. White cell counts are very much higher than ours—12,500 in cats versus 7,000 in humans. Some thousands of those cells result from cats' tendency to respond to stress (as when in a clinic for a blood test) by producing abnormal numbers of leukocytes. When a cat is sick, veterinarians have to guess at what percentage of the white cell count represents a genuine immunological response to disease and what percentage has been evoked by fright.

Some human beings react to stress by taking to drink. So do some cats. At least, that's what happened to the animals used by the University of Chicago's J. H. Masserman and K. S. Yum in a 1946 experiment. Their cats were first trained to respond to a light-and-sound system and to depress a switch mechanism in order to get food. After they had learned how to do this, half of them were subjected to unexpected blasts of air or mild electric shocks just as they were about to claim their reward. Not surprisingly, they developed great aversion to the food box, refused to try to get food regardless of how hungry they were, and became thoroughly neurotic in behavior.

All of the cats—the normal ones as well as those who had become neurotic—were then given doses of alcohol (1 to 2 cc per kilogram of body weight). All got drunk. Like human beings under the influence, they became more animated initially but rapidly lost their ability to coordinate eye and paw. At the height of their inebriation they couldn't respond to signals or operate the mechanism that delivered food; they simply sniffed and poked at the sides of the food box as if hoping for a miracle. That was significant behavior, however, on the part of the neurotic cats: while intoxicated, they were willing to get into the food box and tried like the normal cats to obtain food from it.

When the experiments with the box resumed (with disturbances of the kind which had caused the original neuroses eliminated), a supplement was added to the cats' regular diet. Saucers of milk were provided, one containing fresh whole milk; the other, milk laced with alcohol (5 percent). The normal cats spurned the adulterated milk, but the neurotic cats drank it preferentially—for about two weeks. During that period, most of them completely lost their fear of the food box. As soon as they did, they stopped drinking the milk to which alcohol had been added. Since two weeks is too short a time for a physiological addiction to develop, Masserman's neurotic cats must simply have discovered that alcohol provides relief from an intolerably stressful situation, and drank it until their psyches were whole again.*

There are occasional references in literature to cats with a taste for liquor. According to Carl Van Vechten, W. Lauder Lindsay (1880) mentions a cat who was fond of porter and Jerome K. Jerome (1893) writes of another who drank from a leaking beer tap until she was intoxicated. Van Vechten also quotes a note (1879) from Miss Savage to Samuel Butler in which she reports her cat's liking for mulled port and rum punch. More recently, Doreen Tovey (1960) speaks of "two sleek young Seal Points from Chelsea who drank sherry." Dell Shannon's popular mystery stories featuring Lieutenant Luis Mendoza of the Los Angeles Police Department include a cat named El Señor who is addicted to rye whiskey.

To find out whether these anecdotal and fictional tipplers have present-day company, a telephone poll of fourteen Chicago-area veterinarians was undertaken. None of the fourteen had ever had a feline patient who needed drying out, and ten of them had never heard of cats with a taste for alcoholic beverages. Four knew, or knew of, such cats. One took beer by licking it from its owner's finger, another drank it from a saucer, and a third liked martinis. All the polled veterinarians, however, have had to minister to tipsy dogs.

These animals may drink to relieve tension, to be sociable, or perhaps because they have genes for it. No heritability studies of cats or dogs have been made, but David Rodgers and Gerald E. McClearn have found a strain of mice which possess and transmit to offspring a taste for ethyl alcohol. Maybe the nineteenth-century temperance workers were right when they claimed that drinking fathers beget drinking sons.

* Incidentally, dominant and subordinate cats in Masserman's laboratory colony reversed roles during this experiment—either when a dominant cat became neurotic or when it became inebriated.

CHAPTER 16

Cats and the Law

THE FLORIDA PHYSICIAN quoted in the last chapter was quite right: many cat owners *do* consider their pets to be extensions of themselves. Childless individuals, especially those who are estranged from the human members of their family, find in feline company a quality of comfort they can't get from electronic people on the television screen or the sporadic attention of acquaintances. Their gratitude occasionally takes a sufficiently munificent form to be reported in the press. *Animal Facts and Feats* says the richest heirs of record were Hellcat and Brownie, both fifteen years old when they inherited $415,000 from Dr. William Grier of San Diego in the early 1960's. But thirteen-year-old Blackie, who in 1975 was bequeathed £22,000 by Mrs. Ivy Blackhurst of Sheffield, will also live in comfort for the five or so years remaining to him.

The report in London's *Daily Telegraph* of Blackie's bequest said that the first record of an English cat inheriting a fortune was during the reign of Charles II; the money was left by the Duchess of Richmond. Cardinal Richelieu provided a pension for the fourteen cats he left behind him, and the Marquise du Deffand built an elegant tomb for hers. Agnes Repplier speaks of a nineteenth-century lady named Mlle. Dupuy whose "music-loving cat listened with critical attention when his mistress played upon the harp, manifesting his pleasure if she played well, and his annoyance if she blundered." Mlle. Dupuy therefore "attributed her skill as a harpist mainly to this cat's taste and judgment; and to mark her gratitude for so great a service, she bequeathed him at her death a town house, a country house, and an income sufficient to maintain both establishments."

Although Mlle. Dupuy's family contested and broke her will, bequests favoring animals are not often challenged today, according to Murray Loring in *The Risks and Rights of Animal Ownership*, especially if the testator has left something also to his human heirs or has specified, as did Dr. Grier and Mrs. Blackhurst, that the residue of the estate should go to a charitable institution after the cats' death.

Felines have appeared so infrequently in court records that R. Vashon Rogers was quite right when he said in 1891, "Cats are not of any very great importance in the eyes of the law." There was a time, for example, when their legal status as domestic animals was arguable. In 1914, in Maine, Alonzo Carter killed Carl Thurston's fox hound while it was attempting to kill Carter's cat on Carter's land. Thurston sued, asking damages of $50 for the loss of his dog. He lost the case because the common law holds that "any person may lawfully kill a dog which is found worrying, wounding, or killing any domestic animal, when said dog is outside of the inclosure or immediate care of its owner or keeper." Thurston appealed the decision to the state's Superior Court, arguing that cats are not domestic animals. He lost there, too. The court ruled not only that cats *are* domestic animals but also that they may be "properly considered things of value."

Stating the obvious? Not at all. One cannot seek damages for the loss of something unless it has value in the eyes of the law. There is an old distinction between domestic animals who are "beasts of burden or have a real and intrinsic value for food" (horses, sheep, cattle) and those which "are kept to satisfy the mere whim or pleasure of the owner" (cats, most dogs, other small mammals). Animals in the latter group have historically been considered to be "qualified property." These second-class citizens of the owned animal world may or may not be "subject of larceny"; that is, of sufficient value to enable an owner to claim compensation for their loss. Maine law obviously did not specifically list cats as among the domestic animals or Thurston would not have tried to prove the contrary. Whether his dog was "subject of larceny" never came up because Carter was considered to have been justified in killing it.

In a 1924 Oklahoma case, a man named Helsel decided that his chickens—"Plymouth Rocks of a very ancient and illustrious strain, who trace their ancestry back to the landing of the Mayflower"—were being killed by a white Persian cat owned by a man named Fletcher. Helsel shot Fletcher's cat, and Fletcher successfully brought suit for damages of $150. In this case, the cat *was* adjudged "subject of larceny." Note that the cat's having trespassed on Helsel's property did not justify the killing. Most jurisdictions hold that owners are not normally liable for the acts of their trespassing dogs or cats, for the reasons stated in the following decision:

One Teresa Bischoff sued G. Leroy Cheney in the Connecticut courts in 1914 because Cheney's Angora cat had trespassed on her property and there bit her. She lost her suit for damages because

> the practical impossibility of preventing a cat trespassing, the infrequency of damage from its wandering, and the freedom to roam permitted it by all makes especially reasonable the rule that no negligence can be attributed to the mere trespass of a cat which has neither mischievous nor vicious propensities, and consequently no liability attaches for such trespasses, since an owner cannot be compelled to anticipate and guard against the unknown and the unusual.

There is one exceptionally important phrase in that statement: "a cat which has neither mischievous nor vicious propensities." People who seek damages for being bitten or scratched by other people's pets have generally been required to prove that the pet was not only mischievous or vicious, but also that its owner was aware of the fact. In 1933, for example, another Connecticut lady—by name, Ruth C. Pallman—lost a suit against the A&P in which she alleged that the store's cat had "attacked" her. The A&P's lawyers convinced the court that the cat had never before "displayed a vicious or mischievous disposition." And in an earlier (1921) Massachusetts case, a Mrs. Goodwin lost her suit against the E. B. Nelson Grocery Store in part because she could not produce sufficiently persuasive evidence that the cat who bit her was known by store employees to be vicious. The other circumstance which affected the outcome of the action was that Mrs. Goodwin had brought her dog into the grocery store, thus provoking a fight between the dog and the resident cat, *after* which she grabbed the cat. No wonder it bit her! The court ruled that her own negligence had been a contributing factor to the incident.

In other words, people have responsibilities too. In an 1887 case in Scotland, a man named Webb asked £1 in damages from his neighbor McFeat because McFeat's cat had killed Webb's carrier pigeon. Neither owner was found to have been adequately watchful of his pet and had thus enabled "both the quadruped and the winged animal to be in trespass on neutral territory." Webb therefore lost his suit. But the judge did not require him to pay the court costs. The reason (substituting everyday English for some of the legal terminology) was that McFeat "had not at first sympathized with Webb's loss, but rather put him at defiance, and forced him to prove that it was McFeat's cat who slew his bird." Therefore McFeat was not allowed to profit by Webb's loss.

As is apparent from the foregoing examples, people who "go to law" over cats are often motivated primarily by righteous indignation. There is no better example of this than an 1898 English case which is being included here for the enjoyment of readers who regularly exhibit their cats at shows. Two ladies became partners in a Persian cat named Roy, one of them providing the purchase money; the other, the cat's board and lodging. In due course, Roy was entered in a National Cat Club show at London's Crystal Palace and won several prizes, including a championship medal. Despite the fact that his entry blank had borne the names of both owners, one of them later asserted that Roy was all hers, including his prizes. She then spirited him off to a cat show in Brighton, entered him as *her* cat, and took some more prizes. Whereupon, her partner initiated a suit—which she won—to establish legally her right to a share of Roy and his prizes. The record is silent, unfortunately, as to the length of time the ladies' partnership thereafter endured.*

In its May 1968 issue *Cats Magazine* reported a bizarre British cat case. Its central figure was a television personality known as Arthur, whose ownership and treatment were in dispute. The man who owned Arthur, asserting that he had only rented the animal to the pet food company which used the

---

* Because of inability to find citations, two offbeat suits involving cats have been omitted. In one of them, a man is said to have charged his next-door neighbor with alienating his cat's affections. In the other, a man tried to get a court order restraining a neighbor's cat from terrorizing *his* cat. The citations for the cases summarized above are as follows: Thurston v. Carter, 92 Atl. Rep. 295; Helsel v. Fletcher, 225 Pac. Rep. 514; Bischoff v. Cheney, 89 Conn. 1; Pallman v. A&P, 167 Atl. Rep. 733; Goodwin v. E. B. Nelson Grocery Store, 239 Mass. 232; Webb v. McFeat, 22 Jour. of Juris. 669. The tribulations of the ladies who owned Roy were reported in 42 Sol. Jour. 711; the case was Harris v. Slater.

cat in its commercials, had denied them Arthur's services. He had done this, he said, because they had extracted the cat's teeth in order to force him to eat cat food by dipping his paws into the can. The pet food company's claim that it owned Arthur was substantiated, and the cat was ordered into court so the presence or absence of teeth could be checked. It then transpired that Arthur's defender had removed him from the jurisdiction of the British courts by depositing him for safekeeping in the Russian embassy. Furthermore, he went to jail rather than produce the cat.

It is generally agreed that animals deserve humane treatment, and to this end all states in the Union have anti-cruelty laws. However, as Emily Stewart Leavitt of the Animal Welfare Institute points out, they vary greatly in their provisions. Six states protect only "owned" animals. Sixteen states qualify their laws by prohibiting only "unnecessary" or "willful" cruelty. Seven states do not require that animals be fed and watered, and nineteen do not require that they be sheltered from the weather. Twenty-three do not forbid their abandonment. Some laws are directed toward particular species, prohibiting cockfighting or dog baiting, for instance, or the use of live birds for target practice by gun clubs. Others pertain to the working conditions and care of draft animals or the transportation and slaughter of food animals.

In sum, a given animal's right to redress for such cruelty as it may suffer depends on the state it lives in. Furthermore, the likelihood of its getting such redress depends on the vigor with which such cases are prosecuted. Penalties for violation of the various anti-cruelty laws range from $5 to $1,000 and imprisonment from ten days to "up to a year."

There is also a body of law, most of it honored only in the breach, which seeks to compel animals to behave in ways acceptable to people. At one time or another, American municipalities have set curfews for cats and dogs or have forbidden them to howl at night. Such ordinances have been no more successful than the tenth-century Welsh law which said that "whoever shall sell a cat is to answer for its not going caterwauling every moon." Dog lovers have managed to pass laws forbidding cats to disturb dogs "in any fashion." Bird lovers have required cats to be belled, have forbidden pet owners to keep birds and cats in the same household, and have even written into state law (Idaho's) a provision that schoolchildren shall be informed "of the destructiveness of the common house cat to bird life and to the necessity of protecting the same against . . . said common house cat."

Probably the most famous of the attempts to regulate feline behavior was Senate Bill No. 93, passed in 1949 by the Illinois Legislature at the urging of a Chicago group called The Friends of Birds. Some of the legislators may have been genuine bird lovers, but the majority who voted passage were Republicans who saw in the bill a chance to embarrass their new Democratic governor, Adlai E. Stevenson. Whatever he did about it, they thought, he was bound to anger either bird lovers or cat lovers. Stevenson's wit and gift for phrasing were not then appreciated beyond his home state, but he became a national figure when he vetoed the "Cat Bill," and many newspapers printed his veto message. Slightly cut, here it is:

TO THE HONORABLE, THE MEMBERS OF THE SENATE
OF THE SIXTY-SIXTH GENERAL ASSEMBLY

April 23, 1949

I herewith return, without my approval, Senate Bill No. 93 entitled, "An Act to Provide Protection to Insectivorous Birds by Restraining Cats." . . . I veto and withhold my approval from this Bill for the following reasons:

It would impose fines on owners or keepers who permitted their cats to run at large off their premises. It would permit any person to capture, or call upon the police to pick up and imprison, cats at large. It would permit the use of traps. The bill would have statewide application—on farms, in villages, and in metropolitan centers.

. . . I cannot agree that it should be the declared public policy of Illinois that a cat visiting a neighbor's yard or crossing the highways is a public nuisance. It is in the nature of cats to do a certain amount of unescorted roaming. Many live with their owners in apartments or other restricted premises, and I doubt if we want to make their every brief foray an opportunity for a small game hunt by zealous citizens—with traps or otherwise. I am afraid this Bill could only create discord, recrimination and enmity. Also consider the owner's dilemma: To escort a cat abroad on a leash is against the nature of the cat, and to permit it to venture forth for exercise unattended into a night of new dangers is against the nature of the owner. Moreover, cats perform useful service, particularly in rural areas, in combatting rodents—work they necessarily perform alone and without regard for property lines.

We are all interested in protecting certain varieties of birds. That cats destroy some birds, I well know, but I believe this legislation would further but little the worthy cause to which its proponents give such unselfish effort. The problem of cat versus bird is as old as time. If we attempt to resolve it by legislation who knows but what we may be called upon to take sides as well in the age old problems of dog versus cat, bird versus bird, or even bird versus worm. In my opinion, the State of Illinois and its local governing bodies already have enough to do without trying to control feline delinquency.

For these reasons, and not because I love birds the less or cats the more, I veto and withhold my approval for Senate Bill No. 93.

Respectfully,

Adlai E. Stevenson

Today, however, there is widening doubt about the right of cats to "do a certain amount of unescorted roaming," however natural it may be. Little by little, it is beginning to penetrate the public consciousness that there is a huge homeless population of cats who are frequently diseased, whose care or disposal is a drain on public funds, and whose surplus presence is largely due to people who already own cats. One way to finance municipal pounds and to guard against the most dreadful of the animal-borne diseases, rabies, is to require that cats as well as dogs be licensed and vaccinated. Many cities and towns have passed such laws. Some have even gone so far as to require pet owners either to keep their pets indoors or walk them on a leash. Such laws can also promote civil harmony, by preventing the rancor that is sure to develop between neighbors when the Smiths' cat leaves muddy footprints all over the Millers' newly washed car or the Johnsons' cat regularly messes up the Brown children's sandbox.

There's only one thing wrong with such legislation: it is almost impossible to enforce. Cat owners are not yet prepared to treat their pets like dogs. The Chicago suburb of Matteson, for instance, has a human population of 6,100 and an owned feline population of (probably) 1,300, yet it sells only twenty cat licenses a year. Unless one employs a huge corps of cat catchers or neighborhood canvassers, one must depend on voluntary compliance. Leash laws are equally resisted. Kittens can be trained to a leash but not cats who come late to the discipline. They either sit down and have to be dragged along, or they weave erratically back and forth in front of their owners, with many pauses for reflection, requiring multiple changes of leash-hand and frequent braking. The progress of a human being and a cat unwillingly yoked together by a leash is disorderly in the extreme. People who lobby on behalf of cats' freedom to roam do so at least in part to preserve their own dignity.

One freedom that many people would like to deny cats (and dogs) is the freedom to procreate—and with good reason. Dogs are fifteen times and cats are more than thirty times as prolific as human beings. In the United States, the two species are currently reproducing at the rate of 2,000 to 3,500 offspring *per hour* (versus 415 human babies during the same time period). That estimate, incidentally, is on the conservative side; it is the one used by Carl Djerassi, Andrew Israel, and Wolfgang Jochle, in a well-researched 1973 report on the pet population explosion, instead of the much higher birth-rate estimates frequently used by animal-welfare groups. The lower figure is shocking enough, for it adds up to as many as 30,660,000 puppies and kittens per year. According to the Pet Food Institute, there were 35,000,000 to 40,000,000 owned dogs and 22,000,000 to 30,000,000 owned cats in the United States in 1974. At least half again as many households would have to acquire puppies or kittens *each year* in order to absorb the annual increase in the canine and feline population.

Nobody knows how many people enjoy having a houseful of kittens but refuse to accept responsibility for a houseful of cats. (Or dogs.) What *is* known is that 18,000,000 unwanted animals pass through the nation's municipal pounds and animal shelters each year, the majority of them healthy pets relinquished or abandoned by their owners. *Of these, more than 13,000,000 are destroyed.* The handling cost is about $7 per animal,* or $125,000,000 per year, 75 percent of it spent on killing and disposing of pets for whom no homes can be found. According to Djerassi and his colleagues, "Tons of dead animals are buried in city dumps, incinerated, or sent to rendering plants to be cooked, ground, and used in fertilizer or cattle feed." Clark Whelton, writing in *Esquire* in 1973, gives a particular example: "Animals destroyed by the New York A.S.P.C.A. go to a renderer where they are converted into tallow or meat and bone meal. From this and other sources, 25,000 lbs. of animals are converted by this one factory per week."

Estimates of the *total* American dog and cat population range from 70,000,000 to 110,000,000 animals. Djerassi, Israel, and Jochle say that this relatively wide range is due to

---

* An average figure. Los Angeles estimates its cost at $20; New York, $25.

the decentralized and even disorganized nature of our animal control practices (facilities run directly by city, county, or state governments; private humane organizations contracted to a municipality; private humane organizations operating independently), so that statistics are often not available on a county, let alone state, level. Registrations are a poor source for estimating total animal populations since less than half of all dog owners register their animals and most areas have no compulsory cat registration.

The figures above were arrived at by adding to the number of owned cats and dogs the approximately 1,000,000 military dogs, the 18,000,000 pound animals, the dogs and cats in research laboratories—a 3,000,000 estimate was used, which is probably too high—plus an indeterminate number in pet shops and an equally indeterminate number of strays.

Suppose we take an intermediate figure of 90,000,000 dogs and cats in the United States and arbitrarily decide that half of them are cats. Subtract from that 45,000,000 the owned cats, the ones who are annually destroyed (perhaps 6,500,000), and the laboratory cats (perhaps 100,000). Subtract further, a possible 100,000 cats in pet shops, and one is left with 8,000,000 to 16,000,000 cats who are strays. These are the alley cats of the cities, the feral cats of rural areas. The life span of individuals among them is short, especially if they were raised as house cats and then abandoned by inhumane owners, but there are enough of them in any given year to create serious environmental problems.

There is nothing new about overproduction of cats or human destruction of them. Between 1905 and 1914, for example, Boston's Animal Rescue League destroyed an average of 21,000 cats per year, a number equivalent to 3 percent of the human population (interestingly enough, a rate that Colin Matheson found was still being duplicated in the 1930's in the United States and Great Britain). Awareness of the huge feline surplus was much in Edward H. Forbush's mind when he published his 1916 anti-cat booklet. He knew that domestic animals gone feral are more likely to approach human habitations than truly wild species and are therefore "more destructive to wild life about the dwellings of man than any . . . wild creature." He also knew that most people don't like to shoot or trap domestic cats (or dogs), even if they have become feral. Nevertheless, that is what he advocated. The cat "will become an influence for good or ill according as we mould it, restrain it, and limit its activities," he said. It is "our duty" to check an undue increase in the feline population overall "and to eliminate the vagrant or feral cat as we would a wolf."

From time to time, employees of municipal animal control agencies round up as many stray cats as they can catch and cart them off to the pound. They almost inevitably bag some owned cats who happened to be out for a stroll when the posse rode by. The wrath of owners whose pets have been "abducted" shakes to the foundations their respective City Halls and thereafter deters such operations. There is one drive on record, however, which indicates how large a feral cat population can become. Earl Hubbs, in his 1951 California survey of the food habits of feral cats (Chapter 1), reported that a Colusa rancher considered them such a menace he hunted them throughout one calendar year, using dogs and guns. He killed 650, "a removal of one cat per twenty-one acres."

How much destruction of wildlife are such animals responsible for? Oliver Pearson's article on carnivore-mouse predation (Chapter 7) provides one answer. That too was a California study. However, the area surveyed was not a ranch out in the country but unpopulated grassy land only a half mile east of Berkeley. In June of 1961, the thirty-five-acre tract harbored about 12,600 mice (of three different species). The mice were preyed on by a variety of carnivores, mostly cats. Mice were already in short supply by September, but five or six cats continued regularly to hunt the area until January of 1962, and two were still there in March. By then, 88 percent of all the mice had been eaten—the meadow mice first, then the harvest mice, then the house mice. ("The cats had not merely skimmed the cream off the meadow mice population," Pearson says, "they had taken almost every one.") If feral cats can so nearly destroy a wild rodent population, they can do a great deal of harm to other species too.

Roger Caras, the wildlife expert whose reports are widely heard on radio, believes that feral dogs and cats exist in such numbers that they are now wildlife's Public Enemy No. 2 (man being No. 1). Some of these animals, he says, "can live on the edge of a city or town by raiding garbage pails. Automobiles . . . kill about a million wild animals of all kinds every day and this is another source of food for the scavengers. But road kills and garbage supply only a small part of the food needed by the . . . millions of feral cats and dogs that wander around America." Although they will always attack a target of opportunity, they tend to specialize. Cats "play havoc with ground-nesting young and inexperienced birds and small mammals." Dogs, too, "learn how to detect nests of baby cottontails or how to jump a pheasant at dawn or dusk." Caras also joins public health officials in warning that these domestic animals who have gone wild "represent a highly mobile reservoir for rabies."

In 1974, Berton Roueché wrote a chilling little story called *Feral* in which cats who had been abandoned by the summer people in a New York village learn to hunt in packs and kill people. That's the fictional part; so far, the small cats—whether of wild or domestic species—hunt alone. (Feral dogs are a worse scourge than cats, because they *do* hunt in packs and can bring down cattle, sheep, goats, and deer. The Colorado Wool Growers Association, for example, reported in 1971 that sheep and lambs worth $117,300 had been lost that year to feral dogs.) But Roueché's tale quite accurately pictures the horror of people who discover for themselves that their suburban woods and meadows harbor a giant population of cats who are tough, fierce, and dangerous—because human beings have given them no alternative.

There are two ways to control population: by high death rates or low birth rates. The American people have opted (the majority without even realizing that they *have* opted) for the former course. According to Djerassi, Israel, and Jochle, "It is unlikely that much of the . . . public is aware of the magnitude of the annual pet destruction in the United States, and the fact that this has been the principal method of keeping the burgeoning dog and cat population from becoming uncontrollable." *The animal control agencies destroy more than 12 percent of the country's dog and cat population each year.* The unestimated millions of others who are abandoned by their owners take a little longer to die, and do it more painfully. Djerassi and his colleagues put the cost of these practices at more than $180,000,000 annually—the cost of maintaining municipal pounds and public health programs related to dog- and cat-borne diseases, of handling sanitation problems created by vagrant animals foraging in garbage cans and defecating in public places, and of livestock or poultry losses by farmers.

Much of that money could be saved, and the lot of pet animals vastly improved, if more people had their dogs and cats neutered. The state of California now requires everyone who adopts a pet from a municipal pound to pay a fee for neutering, essentially a deposit which is forwarded to the

FIGURE 13. *The luck of the draw places some cats in the happy position of sharing both bed and board with indulgent owners. However, perhaps a third of America's 45,000,000 cats are strays who barely scrape out a living and tend to die young.*

veterinarian who does the operation. Humane associations everywhere are urging sterilization for pets. The New York A.S.P.C.A. now franks its outgoing mail with the legend ADOPT AN A.S.P.C.A. PET; HAVE IT NEUTERED, and the Pet Pride people ask those who adopt cats to sign what they call The Promise. Zero Pet Population Growth, a Los Angeles organization, publishes a pamphlet in which it lists, among other "facts of life," this one: "Letting your pet have a litter is *not* the way to explain the 'miracle of birth' to children. The 'miracle of birth' is lost in the cruel destruction of life. The lesson that children learn from it sooner or later is: Life is cheap, easy to destroy and forget."

Other psychological reasons for human reluctance to neuter their pets have already been mentioned (Chapter 9), but cost is also a factor. Many pet owners refuse to spend $50 to $80 for spaying. Therefore the animal-welfare groups are also urging nationwide establishment of low-cost spay and neuter clinics like those pioneered by the city of Los Angeles. The first one was opened in 1971; now there are two more. They have neutered 28,739 animals (mostly dogs) so far. They charge $17.50 for spaying and $11.50 for castration, prices that are below true cost by about $3 per animal. However, the Los Angeles City Council cheerfully provides the necessary subsidy, knowing that (1) it costs about $20 to handle each animal in the city pound and (2) that impoundment has dropped by 18.9 percent, and 21.7 percent fewer animals have had to be destroyed since 1971.

Robert I. Rush, general manager of the Los Angeles City Department of Animal Regulation, says the clinics are a major factor but not the only one in the reduction of unwanted animals. Southern California humane associations continue to engage in vigorous programs of public education; the leash laws (for dogs) are being more strictly enforced; and dog owners are increasingly buying the half-price dog license—$3.50 if the pet has been neutered, $7 if it is intact.

When the chemical sterilants are available, and if their price can be brought down to $10 or less per year, it may be possible to halt the pet population explosion. Djerassi and his colleagues note that there is almost no federal support for research aimed at the production of canine and feline contraceptives. A tax of only one cent on the pet food sold annually in the United States would, they say, produce $14,000,000 per year for animal control purposes.

Zero Pet Population Growth lists another "fact of life" in its pamphlet. "The joys of motherhood are not part of your pet's goals in life," the organization says. Don Marquis's mehitabel would agree. "what in hell," she said, "have i done to deserve all these kittens."

CHAPTER 17

Man and Beast Together

IN ADDITION TO being an environmental problem themselves, cats share with other creatures the perils of living in a polluted world. The mysterious ailment that struck down two leopards in the Staten Island Zoo in 1970 was eventually diagnosed as lead poisoning. Its source was atmospheric fallout, the metallic deposits on the animals' fur being ingested in the course of grooming themselves. If the big cats can be thus affected, so can the small cats. Those in our urban ghettos are also as likely as slum children to eat materials contaminated with lead-based paints.

Country and suburban cats can be poisoned by absorbing residues from pesticides such as Paris Green, insecticides incorporating organophosphates or chlorinated hydrocarbons, and various farm and garden products containing arsenic. Arsenic persists in soil for many years and lingers around livestock dipping vats and in straw stacks. Cats are also sometimes killed by poisons (strychnine, warfarin, thallium) meant for rats. What an ironic twist of fate!

Nor is the sheltered house cat necessarily assured a long and healthy life. Drain openers and grease dissolvers which contain alkali and household disinfectants which contain carbolic acid are dangerous, especially when used in spray form. Fortunately, cats hate the hissing sound of pressurized spray, and make themselves scarce. Those at risk are the ones who can't run into another room.

Indoor cats may be exposed only to sunlight that is filtered through window glass and may therefore develop Vitamin D deficiencies. Cats with a taste for grass will, if denied it, nibble the leaves of household potted plants. Philodendron, dieffenbachia, English ivy, and caladium are all poisonous to cats. Holly berries fallen from Christmas wreaths or table centerpieces have also claimed their victims.

City and suburban cats who are allowed outdoors face many of the same dangers city people do, and have less protection against them. Nobody takes a young cat by the hand and teaches it how to get safely across the street. Animals learn by trial and error, and many do not survive the training period. When Ronald J. Kolata of the University of Pennsylvania's School of Veterinary Medicine recently analyzed the case histories of 7,803 animals that had been admitted to the school's Trauma Emergency Center in the course of one year, he found that motor-vehicle accidents caused the highest mortality rates in both cats and dogs. Males were seen more frequently than females, which supports the assumption that males wander more. The average age of hurt dogs was 1.9 years; of cats, 1.3 years. It is the youngsters who are at greater risk of injury, Kolata says, because pets "learn to cope with the hazards of their environment through experience."

Injured animals that year represented 12.8 percent of the hospital's case load, but Kolata believes that figure "probably does not reflect the true incidence of trauma in urban dogs and cats. It is likely that many injured animals are not [given] medical attention because the owner believes the injury is not serious, the animal dies before the owner is aware that it is injured or before medical attention can be sought." Only 18 percent of the Trauma Emergency Center's patients were cats, which can mean that (1) cat owners are less likely than dog owners to seek medical attention for injured pets, or (2) cats are not injured as frequently as dogs. Both possibilities could be true. In 1970, when C. Richard Dorn compared the use of veterinary services in different parts of the country, he found that from 6.4 to 48.9 percent of dog owners and 13.2 to 73 percent of cat owners had never used veterinary services.

And then there is the problem of crowding. Nobody really knows how harmful excessive population density may be to people or the higher animals, but a great deal is known about its effect on rodents. Much of this work has been reviewed by D. D. Thiessen and David A. Rodgers. In both wild and laboratory populations of mice, they say, increased population density is associated with *hyper*activity of the pituitary glands and the adrenals and *hypo*activity of the gonads. Puberty occurs later in life, reproductive organs of adult males are smaller, fewer sperm are produced. There is more fighting for females but fewer offspring; litters are smaller and fewer young survive. There is also evidence suggesting that the general level of resistance to disease declines.

As for cats, Paul Leyhausen has observed that a cage hierarchy becomes more absolute in proportion to the crowding of the animals. Relative dominance (Chapter 8) is the usual pattern when several cats live together but still have elbow room. As that space diminishes, however, a despotic "boss" cat and several "pariahs" appear. The latter are continually attacked by the other cats in the colony; as Leyhausen says, "the community turns into a spiteful mob." Play stops altogether, moving about is reduced to a minimum, there is a continuous hissing and growling. The cats are never relaxed; normal alertness is replaced by chronic wariness.

In lesser degree, many free-roaming city (and perhaps even country) cats are having similar problems. Neil Todd says that crowding has reached the point where the tomcats in many populations cannot establish territories of the required size. He estimates their need as one-tenth of a square mile each. But in Boston alone there are 150,000 cats within the city's 1,500-square-mile area. Forgetting altogether the territorial requirements of females and castrated males (who defend only the territory immediately adjacent to home) and considering only the approximately 30,000 intact males in that particular city, each commands a territory only one-twentieth of a square mile in size.

The result of such crowding, Todd says, is a vast increase in fights between males, an excessive amount of spraying, failure to bury feces, incontinence of nervous origin, and skin ailments resulting from continuous grooming which is emotionally motivated (displacement activity). Unfortunately, evolutionary change proceeds at a snail's pace compared to the rate of change that civilization has brought about, and cats are still governed by nature's scheme for controlling overbreeding—the establishment of territories, clearly defined by scent marks and frequent patrolling of boundaries.

Cats were also evolved to function best in a bisexual system. "Vast numbers of neuter animals are now being injected into the environment to add a new unstructured situation with which the cat must cope," Todd says. "The occurrence of neuters can therefore only add to the confusion."

He believes that psychosocial pressure on the feline population will eventually change the species so that domestic cats will become more sociable than they now are, will acquire more tolerance for territorial restriction, and will develop absolute dominance hierarchies like those of group-living animals. They will, in other words, become more doglike than catlike in behavior. That seems a gloomy prospect for an animal whose behavioral hallmark is self-reliance and independence of spirit.

But that day is still far distant. Cats are now at a mid-point in their evolutionary history. As Elizabeth Coatsworth said in "Calling the Cat":

> *Now, from the dark, a deeper dark,*
> *The cat slides,*
> *Furtive and aware,*
> *His eyes still shine with meteor spark*
> *The cold dew weights his hair.*
> *Suspicious,*
> *Hesitant, he comes*
> *Stepping morosely from the night,*
> *Held but repelled,*
> *Repelled but held,*
> *By lamp and firelight.*
>
> *Now call your blandest,*
> *Offer up*
> *The sacrifice of meat,*
> *And snare the wandering soul with greeds,*
> *Give him to drink and eat,*
> *And he shall walk fastidiously*
> *Into the trap of old*
> *On feet that still smell delicately*
> *Of withered ferns and mould.*

In sum, cats have adapted so well to the ecological niche their ancestors discovered in ancient Egypt that fundamental biological and behavioral changes have occurred, and the species can no longer survive as well in the wild as in the company of men. Yet the domestic cat is not reconciled to the cages, the fences, and the leashes of civilization, nor to the obligations of dependency that men would like to place upon it.

In the course of sharing our houses and our history with cats, *our* feelings have been ambivalent too. In our myths and legends, cats appear in both heavenly and hellish guise. They animate our superstitions, bringing luck or misfortune according to the folklore of a given culture. Varied in form and personality, they grace the art museums of the world: meek little Renaissance cats, imperious Egyptian cats, feline courtesans and demons from Japan, dutiful Victorian mothers, complacent French ones; witch cats, lap cats, alley cats. Everyone can find a pictured cat to match his own perception of the feline personality. Memorialized in prose and verse, they inhabit our libraries and classrooms: scary cats like Poe's, silly cats like Lear's and Eliot's, symbolic cats like Carroll's. If not all fogs come on little cat feet, at least those in the United States do.

Without cats, our language would be the poorer. If we were bereft of "catnap," would "doze" do as well? Could "moving warily" or "being equivocal" replace "pussyfooting"? Would it rain as hard if it rained only dogs? Nervous people have catfits. Angry people have catfights. It takes but one word—"catty"—to describe a spiteful person; a choice between two —"kitten" and "pussycat"—to praise or possibly slander a girl of dating age; and a single phrase—"cat-and-dog life"—to sum up the status of a troubled marriage. Although ardent cat lovers consider the interpretation pejorative, it is nevertheless the dictionary consensus that "catlike" is a synonym for stealthy. Catcalls are as derisive today as they were in the eighteenth century, when they were little whistles which made sounds like a cat. Curiosity still kills the cat. (And satisfaction brings it back.) Cats all look gray at night. We let them out of the bag. They get our tongues. They still need belling.

Feline anatomy has inspired a multiple of shorthand phrases and descriptive terms which add color and texture to our speech. A cat's-paw is a dupe (thanks to La Fontaine), but cat's-paws are riffles which stir the surface of calm water under a freshening breeze. Cat's eyes are gems or marbles or the reflectors along highways which guide motorists driving in the dark. Cat's whiskers are fine wires in electronic circuits, and catfish have appendages that look like whiskers. Pussytoes are low-growing plants whose flowers are arranged in the shape of a cat's paw. Cat's-claw is a shrubby climber with tendrils that look like claws. Cat-chop is a carpetweed with pointed teeth along the leaf margins. Cat snakes stalk lizards in the manner of cats. Cat-birds make a mewing call. And caterpillars are cat-haired worms (from Old French *catepelose* out of Latin *catus* and *pilosus*). The kittens saved from drowning by the trees along the riverbank—those that dipped their supple branches into the river for the kittens to cling to—are annually reborn as silky catkins on the pussy willows. A double dose of feline etymology, that: catkins are densely packed clusters of tiny flowers, some of which hang like pendants from the branches of deciduous trees. Whoever named them thought they looked like kittens' tails.

Cats are firmly established now within the human family circle. They aren't everyone's favorite pet; perhaps one household in five has one. But those people who don't mind getting up to let the cat out or staying up to let the cat in are a force to be reckoned with. Their attitudes toward their animals have social and political consequences, and their expenditures have considerable impact on the economy. Consider these facts:

The purebred cats who are sold each year represent a gross value of some $25,000,000. The 1,500,000,000 pounds of commercial cat food which are annually sold in the United States cost their buyers about $780,000,000. Add the cost of milk and home-prepared cat food. We spend about $80,000,000 annually for the filler we put in cat boxes. The 17,800 veterinarians in small-animal practice don't break down their income figures according to kind of animal treated, but if as few as 10 percent of cat owners were to take Kitty to the vet each year and spend as little as $10 on the visit, they would together pay about $30,000,000. Vaccinations, however, cost $35 and surgery twice that. To board a cat costs at least $5 per day.

As for the little extras, how they can add up! There is a Louisiana mail-order house which says it sells "everything for pampered pets," and indeed it seems to. One can get jeweled collars, leashes with built-in folding umbrellas, car seats, a tote bag for carrying the cat to visit friends, a life jacket for boating types, automatic feeders and placemats, a host of grooming aids, electric sleeping pads, privacy screens to hide the litter box, scratching posts, and carpet-covered climbing trees. It is doubtful that cat owners could entice their pets into the high chair ($22.95) or persuade them to wear the snow-suits and vinyl boots.

For their own use, cat lovers can obtain from stores or other mail-order firms such things as aprons and T-shirts imprinted with cat pictures, similarly decorated stationery and calendars, cat sculptures or jewelry picturing cats, and pet portraits hand-painted from photographs supplied by the owner. They can also collect cat stamps; there are now about 100, collector Merry Anne Dooley says. The United States has never memorialized cats on its stamps, but there are some beauties from other countries. A 1967 Turkish stamp, for example, features (as it should) a big white Angora. Poland pictured Puss in Boots on a 1968 stamp, and Luxembourg did one in 1966 which recreated the witch's cat of the Middle Ages. One of the most interesting is from a series issued by Spain in 1930 to commemorate famous aviators. It includes a portrait of Charles Lindbergh in the upper left-hand corner and a black cat in the lower right-hand corner looking up at the *Spirit of St. Louis* overhead. The cat represents the one that Lindy left behind because he didn't want to risk its life along with his own.

One can also inter a cat in any of 415 pet cemeteries in the United States and Canada. In the Chicago area, a cat burial costs about $85. In a Tokyo pet cemetery, an animal's owner can buy a tomb (for $3,350) to hold his pet's ashes and in which his own ashes can also be deposited when his turn comes.

Bizarre? Silly? Extravagant? Not to people whose cats are truly loved companions. It is pleasant to feel the sinuous windings of a cat around one's legs, to hear its purr, to feel its warmth against the hollow of one's back. A cat is beautiful to look at. It is sometimes comic. When everyone else in the house is out, the cat is there, waiting on the porch or watching from the window, to welcome the homecomer. Cats are small and clean and not very demanding of attention. It is no wonder some cat owners prefer their feline friends to their human acquaintances.

Edward Topsell, warning in 1607 of "the hurt that commeth by the familiarity of a cat," said that people who love cats are "requited with the loss of their health, and sometime of their life . . . and worthily, because they which love any beasts in high measure have so much the lesse charity unto man." But this is the twentieth century. And cats *do* fit beautifully into the human lap.

Notes and Bibliography

Not listed below is material from sources earlier than the nineteenth century, from modern newspapers, or from personal correspondence. References to general-interest magazines are included only in the case of substantial quotation from an article. When a given author is represented more than once, the chapter in this book in which each work is mentioned is supplied.

Animal Facts and Feats. See Wood, Gerald.

Baron, Alan; Stewart, C. N.; and Warren, J. M. (1957) "Patterns of Social Interaction in Cats." *Behaviour* 11:56.

Bartoshuk, L. M. (1971) "Taste of Water in the Cat: Effects on Sucrose Preference." *Science* 171:699.

Beneviste, Raoul E., Sherr, Charles J.; and Todaro, George J. (1975) "Evolution of Type C Viral Genes: Origin of Feline Leukemia Virus." *Science* 190:886.

Bergsma, Donald R., and Brown, Kenneth S. (1971) "White Fur, Blue Eyes, and Deafness in the Domestic Cat." *Journal of Heredity* 62:171.

Bisseru, B. *Diseases of Man Acquired from His Pets.* London: William Heinemann Medical Books, Ltd., 1967.

Boudreau, James C., and Tsuchitani, Chiyeko. *Sensory Neurophysiology with Special Reference to the Cat.* New York: Van Nostrand-Reinhold, 1973.

Brearley, Elizabeth, and Kenshalo, Dan R. (1970) "Behavioral Measurements of the Sensitivity of the Cat's Upper Lip to Warm and Cool Stimuli." *Journal of Comparative and Physiological Psychology* 70:1.

Bross, I. D. J.; Bertell, R.; and Gibson, R. (1972) "Pets and Adult Leukemia." *American Journal of Public Health* 62:1520.

Burnford, Sheila. *The Incredible Journey.* Boston and Toronto: Little, Brown and Co., 1960. (Ch. 14.)

—— (1967) "Simon at Seventeen." *Ladies' Home Journal* 84:40. (Ch. 10.)

Cannon, Walter B. (1898) "The Movements of the Stomach Studied by Means of the Röntgen Rays." *American Journal of Physiology* 1:359.

Caras, Roger. (1973) "Meet Wildlife Enemy No. 2." *National Wildlife* 11:30.

Centerwall, Willard R., and Benirschke, Kurt. (1973) "Male Tortoiseshell and Calico (TC) Cats." *Journal of Heredity* 64:272.

Chapman, V. A., and Zeiner, Fred N. (1961) "The Anatomy of Polydactylism in Cats with Observations on Genetic Control." *Anatomical Record* 141:205.

Chesler, Phyllis. (1968) "Maternal Influence in Learning by Observation in Kittens." *Science* 166:901.

Clark, J. M. (1975) "The Effects of Selection and Human Preference in Coat Colour Gene Frequencies in Urban Cats." *Heredity* 35:195.

Cole, J. (1955) "Paw Preference in Cats Related to Hand Preference in Animals and Men." *Journal of Comparative and Physiological Psychology* 48:137.

Comfort, Alex. (1956) "Maximum Ages Reached by Domestic Cats." *Journal of Mammology* 37:118.

Committee on Animal Nutrition, National Research Council. *Nutrient Requirements of Laboratory Animals* (2nd ed.). Washington, D.C.: National Academy of Sciences, 1972.

Conway, William Martin. *Dawn of Art in the Ancient World.* London: Percivalt and Co., 1891.

Cooper, K. K. *The Significance of Past Sexual Experience in the Reappearance of Sexual Behavior in Castrated Male Cats Treated with Testosterone Propionate.* Master's Thesis, New York Univ., 1960.

Dagg, Anne Innis. (1973) "Gaits in Mammals." *Mammal Review* 3:135.

Dale-Green, Patricia. *The Cult of the Cat.* London: William Heinemann Co., 1963.

Davis, David E. (1957) "The Use of Food as a Buffer in a Predator-Prey System." *Journal of Mammology* 38:466.

DeVoss, J. C., and Ganson, Rose. (1915) "Color Blindness of Cats." *Journal of Animal Behavior* 5:115.

Dewsbury, Donald A., and Rethlingshafer, Dorothy A. *Comparative Psychology.* New York: McGraw-Hill, 1973.

Djerassi, Carl; Israel, Andrew; and Jochle, Wolfgang. (1973) "Planned Parenthood for Pets?" *Bulletin of the Atomic Scientists* 29:10.

Dooley, Merry Anne. (1969) "P. O. Pussy Cats." *Cats Magazine* 26:1.

Dorn, C. Richard. (1970) "Veterinary Medical Services: Utilization by Dog and Cat Owners." *Journal of the American Veterinary Medical Assn.* 156:321.

Dorn, C. Richard, and Schneider, Robert. (1972) "Public Health Aspects of Cancer in Pet Dogs and Cats." *American Journal of Public Health* 62:1460.

Dreux, Philip. (1974) "The Cat Population of Peninsule Courbet, Iles Kerguelen." *Polar Record* 17:53.

Eckstein, Gustav. *Everyday Miracle.* New York: Harper and Row, 1948.

Elton, C. S. (1953) "The Use of Cats in Farm Rat Control." *British Journal of Animal Behaviour* 1:151.

Ewer, R. F. (1960) "Suckling Behaviour in Kittens." *Behaviour* 15:146. (Ch. 10.)
—— *Ethology of Mammals*. New York: Plenum Press, 1968. (Second reference in Ch. 2; first reference in Ch. 8; second reference in Ch. 9; reference in Ch. 10).
—— *The Carnivores*. Ithaca, N.Y.: Cornell University Press, 1973. (First reference in Ch. 2; reference in Ch. 3; second reference in Ch. 8; first reference in Ch. 9; both references in Ch. 11).

Fabre, J. Henri. *The Mason-Bees*. New York: Dodd, Mead and Co., 1914.

Forbush, Edward H. *The Domestic Cat*. Economic Biology Bulletin 2, Massachusetts State Board of Agriculture, 1916.

Fox, Michael. "The Behaviour of Cats." In *Behaviour of Domestic Animals*; ed., E. S. E. Hafez. London: Bailliere, Tindall and Cassell, 1975.

Franti, C. E., and Kraus, J. F. (1974) "Aspects of Pet Ownership in Yolo County, California." *Journal of the American Veterinary Medical Assn.* 164:166.

Gates, Georgina S. *The Modern Cat: Her Mind and Manners*. New York: Macmillan Co., 1928.

Gay, Margaret Cooper. *How to Live with a Cat*. New York: Simon and Schuster, 1948. (Rev. ed., 1969.)

Gibson, E. J., and Walk, R. D. (1960) "The Visual Cliff." *Scientific American* 202:64.

Guillery, R. W. (1974) "Visual Pathways in Albinos." *Scientific American* 230:44.

Gunter, Ralph. (1951) "The Absolute Threshold for Vision in the Cat." *Journal of Physiology* 114:8.

Halstead, Bruce W. (1958) "Poisonous Fishes." *Public Health Reports* 73:302.

Hamilton, James B.; Hamilton, Ruth S.; and Mestler, Gordon E. (1969) "Duration of Life and Causes of Death in Domestic Cats." *Journal of Gerontology* 24:427.

Harper, Joan. *The Healthy Cat and Dog Cook Book*. For information, write author at Box 332, Rt. 3, Richland Center, Wis. 53581.

Hatch, R. C. (1972) "Effects of Drugs on Catnip-Induced Pleasure Behavior in Cats." *American Journal of Veterinary Research* 33:143.

Hearn, Lafcadio. "The Little Red Kitten" in *Fantastics and Other Fancies*. Boston: Houghton Mifflin Co., 1914.

Hein, Alan, and Held, Richard. (1967) "Dissociation of the Visual Placing Response into Elicited and Guided Components." *Science* 158:390. (The experiment using a neck collar.)

Held, Richard, and Hein, Alan. (1963) "Movement-Produced Stimulation in the Development of Visually Guided Behavior." *Journal of Comparative and Physiological Psychology* 56:872. (The experiment using a gondola.)

Herbert, Marvin J., and Harsh, Charles M. (1944) "Observational Learning in Cats." *Journal of Comparative and Physiological Psychology* 45:450.

Herrick, F. H. (1922) "Homing Powers of the Cat." *Scientific Monthly* 14:525.

Hess, Eckhard H. *The Tell-Tale Eye.* New York: Van Nostrand-Reinhold, 1975.

Hildebrand, Milton. *Analysis of Vertebrate Structure.* New York: John Wiley and Sons, 1974.

Holzworth, Jean. (1971) In "Proceedings of a Colloquium on Selected Feline Infectious Diseases, Sept. 15–17, 1970 at Cornell University." *Journal of the American Veterinary Medical Assn.* 158:830.

Howell, A. Brazier. *Speed in Animals.* Chicago: University of Chicago Press, 1944.

Hubbs, Earl L. (1951) "Food Habits of Feral House Cats in the Sacramento Valley." *California Fish and Game* 37:177.

Hummer, Robert L. (1976) "Research Animals: the AHA Viewpoint." *Lab Animal* 5:37.

Iljin, N. A., and Iljin, V. N. (1930) "Temperature Effects on the Color of the Siamese Cat." *Journal of Heredity* 21:309.

Jackson, Basil, and Reed, Alan. (1969) "Catnip and the Alteration of Consciousness." *Journal of the American Medical Assn.* 207:1349.

John, E. Roy, et al. (1968) "Observation Learning in Cats." *Science* 159:1489.

Kipling, Rudyard. *Just So Stories.* London: The Macmillan Co., 1902.

Kolata, Ronald J., et al. (1974) "Patterns of Trauma in Urban Dogs and Cats." *Journal of the American Veterinary Medical Assn.* 164:499.

Kovach, J. K., and Kling, A. (1967) "Mechanisms of Neonate Sucking Behavior in the Kitten." *Animal Behaviour* 15:91.

Kuo, Z. Y. (1930) "The Genesis of the Cat's Response to the Rat." *Journal of Comparative and Physiological Psychology* 11:1.

Laut, Agnes C. *The Fur Trade in America.* New York: The Macmillan Co., 1921.

Leavitt, Emily Stewart. *Animals and Their Legal Rights.* New York: Animal Welfare Institute, 1968.

Lewin, Roger. (1975) "Cat's Brains Are Controversial." *New Scientist* 68:457.

Leyhausen, Paul. *Verhaltensstudien an Katzen* (4th ed.). Berlin and Hamburg: Paul Parey, 1975. This book, Leyhausen's major work, has not been translated into English. Part of the material, especially his observations on cats' predatory behavior, appears in the Lorenz and Leyhausen book cited below. His observations of cats as social animals appears as a chapter, "The Communal Organization of Solitary Mammals," in *Symposia of the Zoological Society of London,* No. 14, 1965. The two references listed directly below contain material that does not appear elsewhere.

―――― (1963) "Über sudamerikanische Pardelkatzen." *Z. Tierpsychologie* 20:627. (Ch. 2.)

———— "Addictive Behavior in Free Ranging Animals" in *Psychic Dependence,* Bayer-Symposium IV. New York: Springer-Verlag, 1973. (Ch. 4.)

Lorenz, Konrad. *Man Meets Dog.* Boston and New York: Houghton Mifflin Co., 1955.

Lorenz, Konrad, and Leyhausen, Paul. *Motivation of Human and Animal Behavior.* New York: Van Nostrand-Reinhold, 1973. (Ch. 2; especially with reference to reservoirs of neural energy.)

Loring, Murray. *The Risks and Rights of Animal Ownership.* New York: Arco, 1973.

Masserman, J. H., and Yum, K. S. (1946) "An Analysis of the Influence of Alcohol on Experimental Neuroses in Cats." *Psychosomatic Medicine* 8:36.

Matheson, Colin. (1944) "The Domestic Cat as a Factor in Urban Ecology." *Journal of Animal Ecology* 13:130.

McDonald, Donald. (1960) "How Does a Cat Fall on Its Feet?" *New Scientist* 7:1647.

McMurry, Frank B. (1945) "Three Shrews Eaten by a Feral House Cat." *Journal of Mammology* 26:94.

McMurry, Frank B., and Sperry, Charles G. (1941) "Food of Feral House Cats in Oklahoma." *Journal of Mammology* 22:185.

Méry, Fernand. *The Life, History and Magic of the Cat.* New York: Madison Square Press, Grosset and Dunlap, 1968.

Mivart, St. George. *The Cat.* London: John Murray, 1881.

Moelk, Mildred. (1944) "Vocalizing in the House Cat." *American Journal of Psychology* 57:184.

Muller, H. R., and Weed, L. H. (1916) "Notes on the Falling Reflex of Cats." *American Journal of Physiology* 40:373.

Necker, Claire. *The Natural History of Cats.* South Brunswick and New York: A. S. Barnes and Co., 1970.

Nelson, Neal S.; Berman, Ezra; and Stara, Jerry F. (1969) "Litter Size and Sex Distribution in an Outdoor Feline Colony." *Carnivore Genetics Newsletter,* December 1969, p. 181.

Palen, Gary F., and Goddard, Graham V. (1966) "Catnip and Oestrous Behavior in the Cat." *Animal Behaviour* 14:372.

Pearson, Oliver P. (1964) "Carnivore-Mouse Predation: An Example of Its Intensity and Bioenergetics." *Journal of Mammology* 45:177.

Pennycuick, C. J., and Rudnai, J. (1970) "A Method of Identifying Individual Lions with an Analysis of the Reliability of Identification." *Journal of Zoology* 160:497.

Pirie, Antoinette. "The Chemistry and Structure of the Tapetum Lucidum in Animals." In *Aspects of Comparative Ophthalmology;* ed., Oliver Graham-Jones. London: Pergamon Press, 1965.

Pitt, Frances. *Wild Animals in Britain* (2nd ed.). London: Batsford, 1944.

Poe, William D. (1967) "The Cat Menace." *Journal of the American College Health Assn.* 16:207.

Powers, J. Bradley, and Winans, Sarah H. (1975) "Vomeronasal Organ: Critical Role in Mediating Sexual Behavior of the Male Hamster." *Science* 187:961.

Precht, H., and Lindenlaub, E. (1954) "Über das Heimfindevermögen von Säugetieren. I. Versuche an Katzen." Z. *Tierpsychologie* 11:485.

Repplier, Agnes. *The Fireside Sphinx*. Boston and New York: Houghton Mifflin Co., 1901. (All references except for the one cited below.)

—— *Americans and Others*. Boston and New York: Houghton Mifflin Co., 1912. (Ch. 8.)

Rhine, J. B., and Feather, Sara R. (1962) "The Study of Cases of 'Psi-Trailing' in Animals." *Journal of Parapsychology* 26:1.

Roberts, Warren P., and Kiess, Harold D. (1964) "Motivational Properties of Hypothalamic Aggression in Cats." *Journal of Comparative and Physiological Psychology* 58:187.

Robinson, John S., and Voneida, Theodore J. (1964) "Central Cross-Integration of Visual Inputs Presented Simultaneously to the Separate Eyes." *Journal of Comparative and Physiological Psychology* 57:22.

Rodgers, David A., and McClearn, Gerald E. "Alcohol Preference of Mice." In *Roots of Behavior;* ed., E. L. Bliss. New York and Evanston: Harper and Row, 1962.

Rogers, R. Vashon. (1891) "Cats." *The Green Bag* 3:350.

Rosenblatt, Jay S. "The Behavior of Cats." In *Behavior of Domestic Animals;* ed., E. S. E. Hafez. Baltimore: Williams and Wilkins Co., 1962. (Ch. 9.)

—— (1972) "Learning in Newborn Kittens." *Scientific American* 227:18. (Ch. 10.)

Rosenblatt, Jay S., and Aronson, Lester R. (1958) "The Decline of Sexual Behavior in Male Cats after Castration." *Behaviour* 12:285.

Rosenfeld, Sherman B. *The Role of Pheromones in the Sexual Behavior of the Cat*. Master's Thesis, San Diego State Univ., 1975.

Roueché, Berton. *Feral*. New York and Evanston: Harper and Row, 1974.

Rudnai, Judith. See Pennycuick, C. J.

Scott, Patricia. "The Cat." In *UFAW Handbook on the Care and Management of Laboratory Animals* (3rd ed.). Baltimore: Williams and Wilkins Co., 1967.

Seal, Ulysses S. (1969) "Carnivora Systematics: A Study of Hemoglobins." *Comparative Biochemical Physiology* 31:799.

Searle, A. G. (1949) "Gene Frequencies in London's Cats." *Journal of Genetics* 49:214. (Ch. 5.)

—— (1959) "A Study of Variation in Singapore Cats." *Journal of Genetics* 56:111. (Ch. 5.)

—— *Comparative Genetics of Coat Colour in Mammals.* London: Logos; New York: Academic Press, 1968. (Ch. 12.)

Seitz, Philip F. D. (1959) "Infantile Experience and Adult Behavior in Animal Subjects." *Psychosomatic Medicine* 21:353.

Shaler, N. S. *Domesticated Animals.* New York: Charles Scribner's Sons, 1895.

Sillar, Frederick Cameron, and Meyler, Ruth Mary. *Cats Ancient and Modern.* New York: Viking Press, 1966.

Smithers, R. H. N. (1968) "Cat of the Pharaohs." *Animal Kingdom* 61:16.

Stevenson, Adlai E. *The Papers of Adlai E. Stevenson* (Vol. 3); ed., Walter Johnson. Boston: Little, Brown and Co., 1973.

Suehsdorf, Adolph. (1964) "Cats in Our Lives." *National Geographic* 125:508.

Thiessen, D. D., and Rodgers, David A. (1961) "Population Density and Endocrine Function." *Psychological Bulletin* 58:441.

Thompson, Joseph C., et al. (1943) "Genetics of the Burmese Cat." *Journal of Heredity* 34:119.

Todaro, George J., et al. (1974) "Endogenous Primate and Feline Type C Viruses." In *Cold Spring Harbor Symposium on Quantitative Biology,* Vol. 39. Cold Spring Harbor Laboratory.

Todd, Neil B. *The Catnip Response.* Ph.D. Thesis, Harvard Univ., 1963. (Ch. 4.)

—— (1962) "Behavior and Genetics of the Domestic Cat." *Cornell Veterinarian* 53:99. (Ch. 17.)

—— "Domestic Cat Populations: Ownership Patterns." Working paper; sent as personal communication. (Ch. 7.)

Todd, Neil B.; Robinson, Roy; and Clark, Julian M. (1974) "Gene Frequencies in Domestic Cats of Greece." *Journal of Heredity* 65:227. This paper includes a summary of many of the other cat censuses.

Tovey, Doreen. *Cats in the Belfry.* London: Elek Books, 1957.

Van Vechten, Carl. *The Tiger in the House.* New York: Alfred A. Knopf, 1924.

Warren, J. M.; Abplanalp, Judith B.; and Warren, Helen B. "The Development of Handedness in Cats and Rhesus Monkeys." In *Early Behavior, Comparative and Developmental Approaches;* eds., Harold Stevenson, Eckhard Hess, Harriet Rheingold. New York: John Wiley and Sons, 1967.

Wegener, Jonathon C. (1964) "Auditory Discrimination Behavior of Normal Monkeys." *Journal of Auditory Research* 4:81.

West, Meredith. (1974) "Social Play in the Domestic Cat." *American Zoologist* 14:427.

Whelton, Clark. (1973) "What Can You Do About 50,000,000 Stray Cats and Dogs?" *Esquire* 79:140.

White, Suzanne. *Suzanne White's Book of Chinese Chance.* New York: M. Evans and Co., 1976.

Widdowson, E. M. "Food, Growth, and Development in the Suckling Period."

In *Canine and Feline Nutritional Requirements;* ed., Oliver Graham-Jones. Oxford and London: Pergamon Press, 1964.

Wilkinson, J. Gardner. *Manners and Customs of the Ancient Egyptians* (Vol. 2). London: John Murray, 1841.

Wood, Gerald. *Animal Facts and Feats.* Garden City, N.Y.: Doubleday and Co., Inc., 1972.

Zeuner, F. E. *A History of Domesticated Animals.* London: Hutchinson, 1963.

Index